# BORN IN A TIME OF HOPE

To Bryan and
Stephanie
in commemoration of
our past.
Hazel.

# BORN IN A TIME OF HOPE

*Confessions of a baby boomer*
*1946–1978*

HAZEL ROY

*To my mother who died too soon*
*and to who I owe so much*

*To my family who become more precious*
*to me with every passing year.*

*To my comrades and friends who are still*
*fighting the good fight to make a better world*



First published in 2017 by Hazel Roy

Typeset by Carnegie Book Production



British Library Cataloguing-in-Publication data
A catalogue record for this book is available from the British Library

Paperback ISBN 978-0-9559451-1-3

Printed and bound in the UK by Jellyfish Solutions

# FOREWORD

For years I have been vowing I would write up some of the stories from my life encouraged by others who have said I have a gift for writing or who enjoyed my first book on Nepal. It is one of those things we all defer. But this year has seen a giant wave of friends and acquaintances contracting cancer or other terminal illnesses and already the roll call of cherished old friends who have departed forever suggest this cannot be endlessly deferred. Reaching 70 in July seemed a deadline I ought to work towards.

This is not just a personal memoir though. I am conscious of having lived through some momentous times politically and I wanted to record some of those experiences before they are lost forever. I am aware of how the work of campaigners is all too often hidden from history distorted or ignored by the media and I wanted to record what it was like to be involved in those movements because it is a legacy we need to pass on to those younger than us who are inheriting a world fraught with risks and challenges. If they can learn anything from our experiences – all to the good. At the onset I thought I would be writing one book, but realised as the work progressed that it would have to be split into two parts. My story divides fairly neatly into the years of my childhood and early adulthood in London and Birmingham, and my subsequent life in Manchester, which I plan to tackle in Part Two.

Revisiting my past has involved me in plenty of research, not just as a memory prompt but in the realisation that there were events I lived through which at the time I imperfectly understood. Hindsight, coupled with the lifting in some cases, of political and security moratoriums has enabled me to put a lot of my experiences in context and it has been an interesting and fulfilling experience. All memoirs are unreliable given the events depicted are seen solely through the eyes of the writer. I am sure others whose lives interconnected with mine would not always see things the same way, but I defend the right to tell it my way. Any mistakes and omissions are mine and mine only.



July 12 2016

# 1946–1957
# A POST-WAR CHILDHOOD

I am a 'baby boomer', born in 1946, on the outskirts of London and brought up by a generation still traumatised by the Second World War. I remember it as an era of scarcity, of cramped living space, of malodorous homes, of bomb sites and gloomy bomb-shaken houses full of dust and damp, of green smog and freezing winters and make do and mend.

The only childhood home I remember was my grandmother's small house in Addiscombe, Croydon where I was to live the first 16 years of my life. At the age of three months I was deposited at her front door in a pram piled high with possessions by my angry mother, who used the need to care for her newly widowed mother as the pretext to separate from my moody quarrelsome father.

Doris and Fred – chronically mismatched – had met when my mother was training as a nurse and my father still drifting from one unsatisfactory job to another. Fred, named after his postman father, was one of a generation forced into work at 14 to supplement the meagre income of a working class London family.

The resentment of being cut off from an education he craved, and blaming his mother's meanness for his loss of the few opportunities open to boys of his class, my father found his salvation in politics and obtained an eclectic education through the New Left Book Club and the Communist Party, while a second hand bicycle fed his thirst for travel and a sixpenny seat in the 'gods' fed his love of theatre. He was 19 when he saw his first production in 1926, *The Constant Nymph* at the New Theatre in St Martin's Lane, which included a Mr John Gielgud in the cast. He always unerringly picked the most significant plays or players.

My maternal grandfather is almost unknown to me. The census of 1911, the year before my mother's birth reveals him living in Poplar London and describes his occupation as a 'Dining Rooms keeper'. Sometime in my childhood I understood that my grandparents had run a café for dockers on the East India Dock Road, which could explain my grandmother's greasy spoon approach to the culinary arts.

As lower middle class business people the Halladay's had by the 1930's acquired a small semi-detached on the outskirts of Croydon, and keen for social mobility, must have been pleased when their two sons secured places at the prestigious Alleyns Grammar School and their daughter a scholarship to Lady Edridge Grammar School, all offering the promise of respectable middle class careers. A respectability my mother threatened to disrupt, when having enjoyed a season or two with the local am-drams "The Croydon Stagers", she revealed an interest in going on the stage. Her father, fearing the worst, informed her that no daughter of his was going to appear on a stage showing off her legs in front of strange men. Dutifully, my mother turned to nursing only to be told she would never stick to it.

Showing the same stubborn determination I was to inherit, she submitted to the draconian rigours of pre-war nurse training, obtaining eventually not only her SRN but the Nurse of the Year award.

Her real rebellion was to introduce my father into her family, her parents being a crucial rung above his more humble origins. Politically they were poles apart. Yet despite my mother's educational advantages it was my father who thirsted after books and delighted in the written word, who spent evenings combing the dictionary to extend his vocabulary and who remembered fondly a father who read him Tolstoy as a boy. He was a dedicated autodidactic.

The war saw Fred and his brother Harold in the ARP (Air raid precautions). Harold was a conscientious objector but my father had applied and been rejected by the army due to a minor heart defect and varicose veins like the Nile delta. His compatriots found this amusing and unfair as he could out walk the lot of them and had a physique many athletes would envy. My mother was by then qualified as a State Registered Nurse and working at Dulwich Hospital. My dad used to say he dug out those buried under buildings and sent them to my mother to patch up. The ARP was not a soft option. The experience of the London blitz and seeing his first dead body had a profound impact on him and revealed a talent for writing that deserved a career as a journalist. I later found this hastily scrawled account entitled 'First brush with death:

> *Jack comes tearing across the yard from the depot. He is breathless. "First party out! Number six out!" It is my squad. "Alright" I say crossly getting up. Goodbye sleep.*

*Outside the livid sky is rent with the thunder of guns. The air throbs and shakes. I race for the car. Dave and Murray are there before me, already clambering in. "Where's the splints? There's no damn splints here". "Blast the splints! Get in. Where's Bert? Where the hell is that bastard? Always last".*

*A dark figure dives through falling shrapnel to us. The splints are on my seat. I hurl them into the dark well behind and am cursed by someone whose shins they clout.*

*The engine pounds. We move off. "Longworth Drive, Sydenham!" yells someone from the dark outside. We leap toward the open gate, toward the hill. Each is tense, pre-occupied, ears strained to catch the whistle of a bomb. The journey is in silence. A mile on we see the glow of flames. To the right and left. Again. Not this one. The next. At the end of the road flames roar up from a shattered gas main. On either side buildings are reduced to ashen heaps of bricks and rubble, ghost lit by the flames. Firemen pound the mains with water, immobile red-lit figures behind their gleaming hose.*

*The barrage is at its height. Shrapnel and shell fragments burst and fall in all directions. But no thunder of God or man can drown the inflexible relentless drone of hostile aircraft overhead. We fling ourselves flat as a whistle that we know too well cuts the mad cacophony above. Orders are needless. Each man knows his job. The car is left a hundred yards away and Stott and I clump as rapidly as possible over clay and debris of trees and copings to reach our casualties. I stumble and bend down. At my feet is huddled all that remains of a human being. No legs, no arms, no pulse. We pass on. Another. On his back. One leg gone, the other nearly. Face green and bloody, spattered with clay. I kneel to take his pulse. No arm. Stott is on the other side and luckier. "Still there" he says quietly. "Just".*

*I call for a blanket. It is there. We cover him and I pull out a rubber tourniquet. Stott wipes his face. Dave takes the pulse again. Not twenty seconds have passed by but it seems an age. I see in Dave's face that we are too late. The final test, a mirror before the mouth. It remains unclouded. The driver brings up the jute shroud. Two remain to lift the enwrapped body into a side garden. It is the first time I have gazed on death. I am reminded dully of the dummies that we practised with many months ago.*

My father said he was surprised they survived the Blitz given they were in the thick of it. My mother recalled cycling hell for leather over Dulwich Common on her way to work with bombs falling close behind her. Croydon was not only a prime target because of its airport and munitions factories, but blocked by hills, many of the bombs intended for Central London were falling short.

The little house in Northway Road was subjected to so much pummelling from the bombing that, years later, when the house was redecorated, none of the doors would shut properly and there wasn't a right angle left in the whole house.

Sometime during the war my parents married – with some considerable reluctance on my father's part – since he vastly preferred a bachelor life. On the night before the marriage, one of the veins in his legs burst and blood fountained up to the ceiling. My mother rather grimly applying a tourniquet is reported to have said, 'you'd try anything to get out of this marriage wouldn't you?' Why did she try so hard? It seems she took her men very seriously and my father was a handsome chap, rather reminiscent of the film star Robert Colman, and more reckless and challenging than anyone she had ever known. There was an attraction seemingly in that – and sex appeal without doubt. Many years later I was to find many passionate love letters from my father's previous girl friends exiled to a case in the bicycle shed.

Children were also not on my father's agenda, but a pregnancy happened anyway, cut short by a late miscarriage in an Anderson shelter of what would have been my brother. Then after the war and taking medication to correct what was diagnosed as a 'weak cervix', my mother gave birth to me – two years before the advent of the National Health Service. Overnight my father's attitude to parenthood changed. In his memoirs I found the following description of his first sight of me *'Placed in a row of other tagged babies I recognised her at once. So sublimely perfect. Tiny hands and feet. Serenely sleeping. Something I had never felt before suddenly surged up, and I wanted to hold and embrace her.'* The miracle of bonding is a close second to the miracle of birth and my dad was smitten. Ever alert to financial need, made more urgent by my birth, was a carefully preserved letter later found among his belongings addressed to the Surrey Reformed Benefit Society requesting the cash benefit he was entitled to on the birth of *'one small daughter, weight 6lb 10ozs, eyes blue, hair dark, disposition typically female'*.

I am told I was a good baby – a strong and deep sleeper. At three months I slept through a bus trip to Canterbury, a visit to a noisy teashop and did not wake till hours later in my parents flat in Woodside, a flat my mother was shortly to vacate. So despite being enamoured by my birth my father's temper had clearly not improved, and the extra responsibility of parenthood combined with living on a restricted income would have been at odds with a spirit that yearned for independence and non-commitment, a yearning that must have angered and distressed my loyal and serious minded mother.

Their separation did not last for long. After a few months my father gave up the flat (the source of endless later rows) and moved in with us at my grandmother's house. This was clearly not to the liking of my grandmother who swiftly set down rigid demarcations in the already compact house. We were allocated the small back living room approx. 12 x 12 with a door leading out to the back garden.

My grandmother moved into the 'best' front room replete with a piano, ornate mantelpiece and gate-leg table where she ate all her meals. Oppressively fusty dusty and smelly it nonetheless attracted the sun which is more than could be said for our living space. Grandma ate with us only on Christmas Day. This was mutually agreeable as the strong bodily odour she emitted was almost overpowering. I remember as a small child holding my breath when I was asked to take in her dinner.

More than anything, this is the reason I never felt close to my grandmother, that, and her moribund moaning and tendency to live in the past. It was clear that she felt life with us was, at best, to be endured and that the best of her life was already over. Often heard to mutter under her breath 'Daily Worker-more like Daily shirker if you ask me', she greeted remarks with which she disagreed with the emphatic expression 'fish hooks' – I never understood why.

Later I was to learn that my grandmother born and brought up in the Victorian era had absorbed the same prurient attitudes to anything to do with physical and sexual functions. On her wedding night her new husband had to leave her with a book, which described the 'fate worse than death' that was about to be visited on her person. Anything to do with bodily functions distressed her and when after 5 pregnancies (two babies dying in infancy) she developed a cervical prolapse, she was fitted with an internal truss. This was supposed to be changed at periodic intervals but my grandmother had no intention of submitting to such an indignity a second time, hence the source of the odour, made worse by her refusal to bath.

On the one occasion my mother did manage to coax her into the bathtub as a 'special' for Christmas, my father begged her not to repeat the experiment, as the smell got recycled around the rest of her instead of being localised in one spot. Her prurience extended to keeping her daughter ignorant of puberty and my mother often re-lived the horror of discovering blood on her underwear at grammar school and believing she had injured herself internally.

The kitchen and bathroom at 64 Northway Road were cheerless and primitive even by the standards of the day. The bathroom was chilly and contained a claw-foot bath situated under a badly fitting window where the wind whistled through, a sink with a cold-water tap (the hot tap was seized up and never used) and a lavatory with a flush on a long metal chain connected to a rusty overhead cistern. The one towel was changed weekly and being damp and smelly, face washes with a flannel were pretty cursory – no one bothered much about the other bits.

Looming over the bath was a huge geyser that heated the water on weekly bath nights. It terrified me. Sunday night was bath night. It was quite a ritual. Bed sheets were changed on Sundays, along with vests and pyjamas and a clean towel was produced for the bathroom. To light the geyser involved turning a metal handle anti clockwise and watching till you saw the water pouring through a tube at the top and starting to run out of the long tap at the front into the bath. It was like something Emmett would have constructed. You then had to lift a valve at the bottom releasing the gas and strike a match and light the small blue flame. The valve then had to be twisted sideways into the base of the boiler. At which point the flame often went out and the process had to be repeated. If the flame stayed alight there was a huge whooshing sound followed by a loud roaring bang and the geyser would start shaking. It was like a primitive rocket about to set off to the moon. I was convinced it was going to blow up – it seemed very alien and dangerous.

Eventually the bath filled with water so hot it was hardly bearable and everyone (except Grandma) took it in turns for a long hot scrub. Emerging the colour of a lobster we enjoyed the luxury of a rub down with a clean towel and the pleasant sensation of clean clothes and clean bed sheets – even if the sheets were often as cold as ice, which meant you clung onto your hot water bottle as if your life depended on it.

Waking on a chilly morning in a warm bed I would often pull my clothes into bed with me, and dress under the covers, as it was cold enough in the winter for your breath to be visible in clouds. Like all girls of my generation I wore an item called a liberty bodice over my woolly vest, which was a fleece lined cotton bodice with big rubber buttons down the front. You knew spring had arrived when your mother told you to leave it off.

Hardly surprisingly chest colds were endemic, treated with Vick rubs and Friars Balsam added to steamy inhalations. Far worse were the conditions outdoors. London had been notorious for many years for its pea-soup fog created by a combination of industrial and domestic pollution. Then in December 1952 came the Great Smog, which killed 4,000 in the aftermath, and 8,000 over the subsequent weeks and months. All transport ground to a halt and schools were closed. We were only sent outside in extremis with a scarf wound tightly round our nose and mouth. One effect of the Clean Air Act of 1953 passed as a result was that many families shifted from coal fires to electric fires and my family acquired one of these complete with a coal effect and flickering light. It was one of our only modernisations.

While our neighbours had by the 50s installed in their kitchens innovations like a serving hatch through to their living room, formica surfaces, fitted cupboards a refrigerator and a twin tub washing machine or spin dryer, my grandmother refused to allow electrical plugs in the kitchen as they were 'too dangerous'. We made largely futile attempts to keep milk and butter cool during the summer months by floating them in a metal bowl of cold water in the larder. The kitchen contained only an ancient and greasy gas cooker on legs, a Belfast sink with a gas hot water cylinder (providing the only regular source of hot water in the house), a slimy wooden draining board, a mangle for all the hand-washed clothes (towels and sheets were sent to the laundry) and a kitchen cabinet with a pull down work surface on which we cut bread.

Next to the cooker my father had constructed a small wooden work surface with a capacious shelf, which housed the galvanised tin bath in which my sister and I were bathed as babies. It later contained an over-spilling eruption of laundry waiting to be ironed-the bottom of the bath never being reached on my mother's 'ironing nights'. On rainy days clothes were hung on an airer over the stove, and picked up the odour of frying food.

There were other smells aplenty in the kitchen. The sink contained a metal 'tidy' where tea leaves and eggshells accumulated. They came close to my nose as my mother battled with washing my increasingly long hair over the kitchen sink. In the subterranean area under the sink various dark grey rags known inappropriately as 'cleaning clothes' contributed their own brand of pungent odours. The cat bowl – never to my knowledge washed between servings added the fishy pong of Kit-e-Kat to the small space, for we were never without a cat, my mother devoting much love and attention to each succeeding moggy.

Eventually my father did decorate our living room and the yellow distempered walls disappeared under washable grey wallpaper replete with Chianti bottles and the treacle brown wood veneer under grey gloss paint. My father thought it was very artistic. Later in my childhood he purchased a Goblin vacuum cleaner that I detested as it always triggered rows. Before this we simply swept up with a dustpan and brush, my mother often sweeping the dust from the lino under the carpet. Using the vacuum cleaner would get my father so worked up about the dirt in the house it always signalled a fight with my mother, especially when he compared her with 'other women'. He would then spoil his own arguments by spitting on stains and rubbing them off with his rather murky handkerchief.

With no adequate storage and with a mother who detested housework, our meals were plain and unimaginative. Fish or meat was fried daily in lard or beef dripping, potatoes and cabbage boiled (the latter mercifully not boiled to death as it was in many households) Roast meat (usually beef, chicken was too expensive) was the only change on Sunday together with Yorkshire pudding and we had cooked breakfast on Sunday too. The only condiments were salt pepper, ketchup, malt vinegar and HP sauce. Herbs and spices were unknown apart for bottled mint sauce for lamb. A treat for me as a child was toast spread with beef dripping and topped with marmite or soft roes on toast. I was dosed daily with Virol and cod-liver oil and my mother would buy me the

National Health orange juice which was now available at the mother and baby clinics. Lack of refrigeration meant my mother shopped daily often returning from her night shift with today's meal in her wicker bicycle basket. Tinned salmon, celery and tomatoes with jelly, tinned peaches and tinned cream for 'afters' were the stuff of high tea on a Sunday when we often entertained.

But the entertaining came later. Before then were the challenging years which began with my sister's birth in 1950 when I was three and a half. Until the arrival of Shirley I was the apple of my father's eye and showed an early precocious interest in the theatre. I remember sitting in the front row of a theatre balcony (turns out it was The Theatre Royal Drury Lane) and hearing a man sing 'The sun is as high as an elephant's sty' which made me wonder how big that would have to be – I had seen a pig sty already and clearly one for an elephant had to be much, much bigger. It was the opening of *Oklahoma* in London – I still have the programme with the date – 1949, so my father was clearly fostering my interest at an early age.

Encouraged by my obvious enthusiasm to tread the boards, I was sent to the baby class at the local dancing school at the top of the road and appeared in my first show standing on a soapbox to sing *'On the good ship lollipop'*. The review of the show was far from flattering, but gave me my first favourable review. The writer wrote that if this was the best the school could do, they should close – with the exception of the three-year-old who sang 'On the good ship lollipop' who 'clearly has a promising future'. Did my rendition of this sugary nonsense explain why I repeatedly pestered my parents to call my unborn sister Shirley? I do not know, but they concurred and in

February 1950 Shirley Jean my sister was born and my life in the spotlight was over.

We now know that the risk of conceiving a Down's Syndrome child increases with age. My father was 43 when my sister was born and my mother 38. Like many others of their generation they had only begun a family after the war and there must have been many who were conceiving children later in life. Shirley was born a 'mongol' as they termed her in the progressive world of 1950. In addition she had a hole in the heart – they called her a Blue baby because her heart did not pump properly so her lips were often blue. She also had residual spasticity and as she grew and tried to stand, one of her legs had to be encased in metal callipers. The shock of her birth caused my mother's hair to fall out in handfuls and she developed a nervous rash on the back of her hands, which lasted the rest of her life.

Consider their situation. My father was by then a clerical assistant in the Inland Revenue and studying for exams to become a clerical officer. In addition he was working overtime in the Telephone exchange in the evening – perhaps he was still hoping to escape the confines of Northway Road. My mother's income as a night nurse was also critical. They lived in a space so cramped it was impossible to open a cupboard door without moving furniture. The lack of space became more of a trial as Shirley grew. I remember her sitting in her pram wedged up against the table and suddenly giving the tablecloth an almighty yank and depositing the entire contents including a pot of hot tea into the pram with her.

Another time she was found eating the cat's food. There was hardly space to turn round, no heating other than a coal fire in the living room and bedrooms so cold that ice readily built up on the inside of the windows in the winter. They had a lively 3-year-old and now a disabled baby who cried distractedly night and day, money problems and my grandmother living in gloomy enmity in the front room – oh and the cat as well.

At six weeks, desperate for more information about my sister's condition they took her to Great Ormond Street Hospital where the consultant told them she could die quite suddenly and would probably not survive a serious illness. There was some hope, if she survived long enough that future heart surgery might be able to close the cavity in her heart. But until then, she was not to be excited or allowed to cry, as she would have difficulty catching her breath.

This had repercussions on me. I was not allowed to 'upset' my sister or get too close to her. I was suddenly 'old enough to help my parents'. My father, whom I adored, now shouted at me frequently. More and more I found myself spending long evenings in the smelly but less stressful front room with grandma. I sat listlessly watching her newly washed damp lisle stockings steaming on the fireguard in front of the gas fire and picking out short tunes on the piano which was in desperate need of tuning. For a three-year-old who had been the centre of attention until recently, it was a sorrowful and confusing time for me.

I remember feeling a great flood of gratitude to our family doctor. When, accompanying my mother and sister on one of our many trips to the surgery, he gave me a long look and then said to my mother 'You know you will have to be very careful not to neglect this other child'. My mother was fiercely indignant but I remember being so grateful that someone had noticed my dilemma.

One solution my mother attempted to ease their load was to send me to a succession of fairly grim post war nurseries. At one I was force fed bread and jam and cocoa – two things I hated – till I was sick. I was told this was my breakfast and they would not tolerate me wasting food. My protests that I had already had breakfast at home (cornflakes and a cup of tea) fell on deaf ears. Eventually news of the repeated vomiting caused my mother to change my nursery school. In the next one I came home with a black eye on the first day after an accident on a seesaw. I think after that they gave up and returned me to the indifferent care of my grandma who now introduced me to her bagatelle board – the only other source of amusement in the front room.

I had considered my plight long and hard and decided that I needed to run away to make my parents sorry and invoke their sympathy. For a week I hid sandwiches in the top drawer of my chest of drawers so I would have adequate food, on what I envisaged would be a long journey. Then one morning I rose at 6am, dressed, packed a small suitcase with sandwiches and then getting a chair to unlatch the front door I crept out, leaving it slightly ajar, so my parents would not be wakened by the door slamming. I made my way through early morning mist to the main road, crossed and waited by the bus stop. Waiting patiently for the bus it gradually occurred to me that I had no money for bus fare and didn't actually know where I was going. Returning home rather shaken by this realisation, I went back to my box-room, undressed and put myself back to bed. My parents never found out about my early attempt to run away.

Thwarted in my escape attempt and prevented from taking out my sibling rivalry on my sister, though I made some sneaky attempts to 'excite' her and once tipped her over in her high chair, I took out my rage on a succession of china dolls who when they proved difficult to dress were told they were 'bloody bloody dolls' and had their faces smashed on the fender. I think I was more than a little disturbed.

There was a wider family who offered some temporary respite. Uncle Charles, my mother's oldest brother, a sallow and serious man who worked in the same bank all his life and lived in a rather upmarket semi in nearby Bromley, occasionally took us in his small car on trips to the seaside. He came for a duty visit to 'mother' every fortnight along with his wife Aunt Elsie, a vast woman with 3 chins who called me 'ducky'. She was dedicated to the Baptist church. She carefully avoided contact with my heathen father. The occasional interchange with Fred would usually end in him telling her she was talking 'bloody nonsense' at which point she would insist on leaving, threatening to never return.

Luckily this threat was never realised as she was our sole source of excellent home baked cakes and scones. When I was a little older I was occasionally sent over to Bromley on the bus to spend the day with my aunt, a rather solitary affair, as she didn't have much to talk to me about, having never had children of her own. But she was well meaning and kept me in bibles and hymnbooks and the occasional present of a 10-shilling note throughout my childhood. And her steak and kidney pies were legendary.

When I later read *Cold Comfort Farm* there were characters that seemed to resemble people in my own family circle. Grandma Halladay could do a pretty good impersonation of Aunt Ada Doom and Elsie's father turned out to have something of Amos Starkadder about him. He preached at the tin chapel at the top of our road and is reputed to have been bound over for breaching the peace when he fixed loud speakers to lampposts outside the chapel the better to denounce the residents of Northway Road and inform them they were all damned.

Elsie, a chip of the old block also took a censorious view of the world. Outside a religious context the word 'damn' was taboo for her and having once heard the 'd' word on a BBC radio play she refused to allow the radio to be turned on for anything other than *The Archers, The News* and *Gardeners Question Time*. She likewise censored their reading material down to *The Church Times, Woman's Own* and *The Gardeners Weekly*. She told me she didn't want the filth of the world intruding into her home. How she would have coped with the 'f' word I cannot imagine. She would probably have had a seizure.

It was a very special and rare day for me when my other maternal uncle visited us. Uncle Eddie was a tall, distinguished man with white hair and a handle bar moustache who worked as a steward on the original Queen Elizabeth liner. He represented the exotic in our lives arriving unannounced with presents from all over the world, a musical box from Japan for me, a marcasite brooch and tartan travelling rug for my grandmother (I still have both the brooch and the rug - now 65 years old) plus loads of presents for my mother too. Married to a Spanish woman called Renee, who I never met (she was killed in a road accident while I was still young), he had three children much older than me, David Gloria and Royston the eldest, who became a BBC cameraman. They occasionally visited with him. Embracing me in a bear hug he would sing me songs like *'cigarees and whiskey and wild, wild women, They'll drive you crazy, they'll drive you insane'*. The embodiment of a free enterprise culture Eddie was a showman who had brashly and successfully talked his way into all kinds of jobs – he exuded bonhomie. He and my father did not hit it off. I do not recall him visiting when my sister was young. I do not think he liked facing up to problems-and for many that was all my sister represented.

I was desperate to start school. I had a photographic memory and could repeat word for word any story that was read to me. Twice, once when I was just four and then later at 4 and a half, my mother attempted to get me into the local primary school nursery class, but was only successful on her second attempt such was the pressure of numbers in the local school. Unfortunately my memory did me no favours for having picked up the book and repeated word for word the story read to me in the nursery class my teachers were convinced I could read fluently and decided to jump me up a year, so I began my first primary year in an A stream class with 6-year-olds. There were 59 children in my class. I was nearly 7 before they discovered I could not read and demoted me immediately to the B stream.

Teaching then was a grim affair. Children were to be seen and not heard and any noise in the classes was discouraged. Children who whispered were stood on chairs with their hands over their head for the whole of the lesson. On one occasion a girl had sticky tape stuck over her mouth. The cane was used regularly and naughty children stood in the corner. I was terrified of the teachers. The outside lavatories were an ordeal because this was where the bullies lurked and toilet paper was kept under lock and key and issued with the terse enquiry 'one sheet or two' – not very encouraging for any child with the squits. School dinners were vile – on one occasion I found rusty wire in my cabbage, on another occasion a live caterpillar in my salad – the only consolation being that it meant the vegetables were pesticide free.

Given the situation at home I was a solitary child at school and had few friends. I envied the children who had mothers waiting at the school gate because I walked home alone from the age of 4 and a half, a journey of half a mile, which involved crossing a main road and several minor ones. My mother after a few practice runs and the strictest instructions that I always had to cross the road at the zebra crossing left me to my own devices. She had no choice – her life was busy enough as it was and unlike most of her contemporaries she was a working woman, nursing three nights a week at the local geriatric hospital and trying to catch up on some sleep during the day – not easy when my sister was around.

Growing up in a post war environment of trust and belief in community, children had the freedom to roam that would seem like child neglect today. Everyone in the road knew each other and they were confidant children were safe in their local territory. Parents assumed children would come home when they were hungry and rarely monitored their movements between meals. The Moors murders of 63/65 jolted that belief in child safety forever, and the generation that followed ours was, as a consequence, never to have the same freedom of movement. Brady and Hindley, the sadistic murderers of five children instilled in a stunned nation that this freedom could come at a terrible price. But by then we were in our late teens and some of us on the way to producing children of our own.

I remember only having two friends at primary school, Gillian Lansdowne who was my special friend and Margaret Dyer. Margaret was the only fat girl in the school (obesity was a rarity in the 50s) and consequently ostracised. As a loner myself, who was often subject to bullying, I chose to play with Margaret though I never regarded her as much of a friend as she was entirely lacking in animation. I do remember her grateful mother inviting me to tea on a couple of occasions to try and cement the friendship. As a 'friend of Margaret Dyer' I was by association marked out for special attention by the bullies.

One vindictive act I connect to the Queens Coronation in June 1953. Every child in the country was given a Coronation Mug and a Blue book entitled 'Elizabeth our Queen' as a commemoration. These were distributed through the schools and given out by school monitors. We were enjoined to keep these volumes in pristine condition and were warned they would be inspected before we took them home to ensure they were still in that state. When the monitor reached my desk, she opened the front cover of my book folded back the first page and licking her thumb deposited a large dirty thumbprint in the middle of the page. When the mark was discovered, it led to a public scolding in front of the whole class. I think I decided at that point that far too much fuss was made of the Queen, the incident undoubtedly triggering a nascent republicanism in me.

One boy, whose name eludes me, persecuted me continuously. Crayons were in short supply so one day I brought in my green crayon from home and he stole it and refused to give it back. I had developed a number of nervous habits due to all the tensions at home and at school and I had started chewing the sleeve of my blazer until I had made a ragged hole on the cuff. My mother was furious with me as it was a new blazer and demanded to know how this had happened. I was too scared to tell her I had done it so I blurted out a lie. I told her that my persecutor had cut it with a penknife when it was hanging in the cloakroom. I did not anticipate what she would do next. 'I shall complain to the Head' she said. I hoped against hope she would not fulfil her threat. Unfortunately I must have been a little too convincing as the next thing I remember is seeing my mother outside the Heads office and then the boy being summoned out of the classroom and sent to the Head. When he returned I dared not look at him and waited for my summons. It never came. I never found out what passed between my mother and the Head but I must have humiliated her that day. I was always too ashamed to mention it and it was never raised again at home. One thing though, that boy never bullied me again.

Gaining an education or specialist help for Shirley proved even more daunting. Little support came to my mother from her family – none at all from Fred's side of the family. My parents joined The Society for Mentally Handicapped Children and went to some social events, but health and social services offered little help. The nearest specialist centre was in Bury St Edmunds many miles from Croydon, and my mother was increasingly haunted by the prospect of my sister gaining no education and declining into a vegetative life-long dependency on them with only an institution to look forward to if she outlived them.

They explored options and had my sister assessed, as she grew into a hyperactive and out of control four-year-old. They were told that Shirley had the capability to be educated but there was only one place she could receive this education. This was Redhill Hospital School where she would need to go as a weekly boarder. Being parted from her youngest child at such a tender age was a terrible dilemma for my mother. She had cocooned Shirley in love against a hostile and indifferent world who saw my sister's birth as nothing short of a calamity, yet she was aware my sister needed specialist help her parents could not supply. Eventually they agreed and Shirley at the age of five was sent to Redhill as a weekly boarder.

This certainly made my life a bit easier but at a considerable cost to my mother's mental health. Each Sunday night we would take the train to Redhill with my sister and walk down a long avenue lined with Poplar trees to the hospital, which was surrounded with extensive grounds. We would leave Shirley in a panelled entrance lobby with a squeaky polished floor and listen to her shrieks as one of the staff, wheeled her pushchair down a long echoing corridor and out of our sight. The return train journey was conducted in total silence. I was too worried by the look on my mother's face to break the silence. She looked as if she would break apart.

Anxious to ensure Shirley was not dressed in institutional clothes, my mother brought her a new tweed coat and had dresses made for her. My father built several large sturdy toys that all the children in the unit could play with. On weekends home, my parents were heartened by the fact that my sister seemed to be making progress. She had learned to eat with a knife and fork and mealtimes were no longer disruptive.

She had also learned to defend herself. Rowing her on a boating lake during one weekend home, she picked up a stick of rock a relative had brought us back from the seaside and whacked me so smartly round the head I saw stars. Gazing out to my mother on the bank expecting sympathy I saw instead a stricken look on her face – "Do not touch that child" she said threateningly. Shirley then flung her arms around me and said "Agggh Pet" – her favourite expression and my mother's face softened. "Oh look" she said "Isn't she sweet?" I felt a welter of emotions. I loved my sister. I understood she was different and had to be looked after differently from other children but I also felt a great sense of injustice and upset.

My paternal grandparents and my dad's sister lived near Peckham and we visited them infrequently. I remember my grandparents' small Victorian terrace – 84 Landells Road with its chilly front room replete with ornamental aspidistra and a tiny back scullery where my grandparents spent all their time. The room, like ours, was packed with furniture with two small arm chairs jammed up near the fire. They had a 'clippy rug', which fascinated me as it was made with scraps of old clothes. The kitchen was damp and cave-like and contained a bath. The lavatory was in the back garden and had strips of newspaper stuck to a nail and wind whistled over the rickety door, which didn't close properly.

My grandfather was a man of few words. He rolled

ciggies sporadically, his jacket and waistcoat peppered with flakes of tobacco and his fingers and moustache stained brown with nicotine. When not smoking he chewed continuously. Small and shrunk in on himself he seemed to inhabit a parallel universe. He would punctuate long periods of silence with sudden statements. I used to stare at him willing him to speak and once to my shock he looked down and addressed me personally – the only time I remember him doing so. "I have a box camera in the attic – it's yours when I die" he told me. Needless to say when he did die there was no mention of the box camera – my cousin later told me he had offered it to him too.

Edie Roy his wife was a mean spirited woman who rejoiced in making life as dour and miserable as possible. She would greet our arrival with the words "I've got nothing in for you" and she clearly disliked my mother who she disdainfully referred to as 'Lady Muck'. This enmity was inflamed when one day my mother arrived to find the old man, barely able to manage the stairs taking up tea to Edie who was having one of her 'turns'. Marching into the bedroom and flinging off the bedclothes she told my astonished grandmother that she was a malingerer and that it was the old man who should be in bed. My grandmother bore her a grudge for life as a result. I did not make myself popular either because on one of these rare visits and oppressed by the atmosphere I went and sat on the front mat in the hall and howled to be taken home.

My father had little time for his mother either, and resented the fact that Edie cared only for her daughter Elsie, who she had scrimped and saved to train as a piano teacher, whereas she had sent my father out to work at the age of 14 and demanded his entire weekly salary in return – offering back only 6d as 'pocket money'. My father was still living under their roof when he started work and she was still feeding him, but the truth of the matter was that the family were seriously malnourished as my father's pigeon chest, a bone malformation from birth attested to.

It is not surprising that with that background my father valued fresh air, fruit and vegetables and, once independent, hoarded his own income with a miserliness Scrooge would have envied. Much later when Elsie's son Bill was diagnosed with TB and the whole Roy family were tested, it was found they had all contracted and survived TB, just as my father had survived the Spanish flu in infancy, which had wiped out more people than WW1. Tough old buggers – they went through life without holidays or decent food. Smoked too much, drank too much yet still survived into their 80s and 90s. Tough, but not especially likeable.

A trip to Landells Road was always followed with a visit to my other Aunt Elsie and Uncle Bill who lived in a commodious first floor flat they rented in nearby Uplands Road. My aunt was a tall gaunt woman with dark suspicious eyes, a colourful vocabulary of expletives and an abiding love of costume jewellery. She wore a ring on every finger, earrings, brooches and necklaces galore, which jingled when she moved. She was the total opposite to my other Aunt Elsie. Her husband Bill was an electrician (not a very good one by all accounts) with a jaw like Desperate Dan and an abiding love of the dogs and the 'gee gees'. When he wasn't in the pub he was making shifty bets with the 'runners' (betting shops weren't finally made legal till 1961), and though he earned a good living, he dissipated the lot on booze, fags and betting.

Elsie taught piano in the front room though the only thing I ever heard her play was *The Blue Danube*. She cooked chips with everything. My cousin Pam, who was the same age as me, sometimes referred to in moments of stress as 'the bleedin' little cow', lived on an unvaried diet of chips, sweets and coca cola. My diet was predictable but it did contain a great deal of fruit and vegetables, living as we did near Surrey Street, one of the best and oldest of outer London markets. I remember when I was quite young spending a miserable week in Peckham with my cousin. Nursing a raging toothache I was terribly homesick. The visit followed one to my home by Pam, which I think she disliked almost as much.

At the end of the miserable week my uncle proposed a trip to Brighton, which cheered me no end. My parents were in the habit of nipping down to Brighton quite regularly during the summer months and I really looked forward to it. Imagine my dismay when having boarded an open top bus at the station we did not get off at the seafront but continued on to the races. All I can remember of that day is the thundering of horses' hooves and having half a crown pressed into my hand – a fortune to me then – with the injunction to 'get lost' for a few hours. Later back in Peckham waiting at the pub door till closing time with a coke bottle in one hand and a packet of crisps in the other, I remember being fervently grateful I was not Pam.

The only other sibling on the Roy side was my Uncle Harold, Fred's younger brother. Of the three children he was most like his father. Quiet and easily put upon, he worked in the print, and was father of the chapel for some time. A talented amateur painter, a number of his still life canvases graced the walls of Northway Road and he was the first to encourage my interest in the visual arts and explain perspective to me. His first marriage was to a small rotund woman called Winnie who had a squint and heavy glasses and I was to learn many years later rather improbably 'played the field'.

When I was young they shared a flat in Sydenham High School for girls where they were the resident caretakers and I enjoyed visiting them at the weekend, and touring the empty schoolrooms, occasionally writing cheeky messages on the blackboards. Later they moved to a flat in Mitcham where the marriage came to a sudden and unexpected end. Unbeknown to Harold he had been living in a ménage a trois, and when the wife of the man in the downstairs flat died, Winnie immediately left him for the widower, a blind boxer.

Attracted to disastrous relationships, Harold went out for a time with a woman called Grace who had serious mental health problems and had tried to hang herself several times. Then he met Doris, 30 years his junior with a bad speech impediment and the mental age and personality of a rather sulky 10-year-old. She had two older brothers who had, between them, been providing a fair bit of support for Doris and they were clearly anxious to pass on the responsibility. Within two months my rather bewildered uncle was seeking advice from Fred as to whether he should marry Doris, as this was what she seemed to expect.

Fred urged caution but Doris clearly had other ideas. A swift marriage was followed by a pregnancy and my uncle became a dad for the first time at 55 and then again at 58. I remember visiting as a rather snooty 15-year-old and being repelled by the squalor and Doris's obvious inability to produce food even fractionally edible let alone cope well with a small baby. At two months she was trying to force-feed Lesley two jars of solids per meal. He vomited it up repeatedly and the whole flat stank of regurgitated milk. It was almost child abuse through ignorance.

I saw little of Lesley and his brother Dennis as they grew up. Harold ended his life trapped inside a council slum on the notorious Phipps Bridge Estate in Tooting – on a good day no-one craps in the lift. Terrified of the gangs that roamed the estate, his care depended on an increasingly vindictive wife and a younger son who had inherited his mother's learning difficulties. According to Leslie, Dennis beat his father regularly. Doris began barring the door to visitors and refused point blank to let Harold attend my father's 80th birthday party.

She is still alive and after my uncle's death used a legacy from her brothers to buy two flats one of which, until recently, she lived in with Dennis. Lesley lives in the other but is unlikely to inherit the flat when she dies as Dennis is due to receive a half share as well as ownership of the flat he currently lives in. Solicitors, who have had to deal with her, frequently phone her eldest son wondering if she is mentally capable. She never has been. Why she didn't use her inheritance to move Harold to a calmer home before he died can only be explained by infantile spite.

Leslie took after his father, and is now a school caretaker. He has also survived a disastrous marriage, which produced two children, but had a rather better stab at their care, though not without the intervention of Social Services. He lives in the cramped one bedroom flat in Streatham owned by his mother with his daughter Kayleigh. His ex-wife is on her third husband, has a life long dependency on Welfare and a history of neglect of her children. She is now demanding the son from the marriage is taken off her hands and moved in with the father. I feel a strong desire to help Kayleigh as she has shown a lot of courage and initiative to climb out of the pit. Maybe I can, because I was too young to help her father.

***

The winter of 1955 was one of the coldest on record. On one of the coldest days, my parents received a telegram from Redhill Hospital telling them my sister was seriously ill. They were on a waiting list for a telephone – in those days it took six months to get even a shared party line. My father trudged to the top of the road in heavy snow to put through a call. By the time he got connected it was all over. Shirley had died of pneumonia.

The loss of a child for any parent is a shattering blow. They need moral support sympathy and understanding. What my parents got was embarrassed people telling them 'it was all for the best'. No one meant to be callous. They did not understand. For them Shirley's very existence had been calamitous and my parents though recognised as grieving would surely realise in time that they had been relieved of a terrible burden. Some people did not even allow them that time. Two days after her death one of the neighbours called to ask if she could have Shirley's new clothes, as they would fit her youngest daughter. I do not think my mother ever got over the loss. Shirley's death broke her heart.

They broke the news to me the following morning and I burst into tears, but I was too young to understand the impact on my parents and that day seemed one of the longest of my life as they sat stonily staring into an empty fireplace in utter silence. My aunt Elsie's arrival with the familiar cake tin late in the afternoon offered some respite for me, though for my parents her complaisant acceptance of what had happened must have seemed intolerable. My aunt told me I must make it up to my parents for their terrible loss. I did not know how I was to do that. She left me with an overpowering sense of responsibility for my parents – quite a hard call for a nine-year-old.

Later that week the man from the Co-op funeral Society came. Shirley was to be buried in Thornton Heath Cemetery near where our grandfather was buried.

My parents chose a memorial for her with the words 'Bye bye pet' on the stone – another of her sayings. I was not taken to the funeral but I remember many Sunday visits to the cemetery to tend her grave. On one occasion pulling up a clump of grass from the base of the grave I dislodged a huge fat white grub double the size of my thumb. I did not tell my parents. For weeks I had nightmares of worms eating me alive, of graves opening and claiming me and of ghosts haunting me.

We had no light on the stairs and going up them to bed in the dark became an ordeal. Every shadow represented something sinister and I was convinced there was a lion under my bed waiting to eat me. One night, months later when the weather was mild enough for my bedroom window to be left open, a stray cat did climb into my room and settle under my bed. I heard his claws scratching on the linoleum and lay rigid in terror for hours till my parents came to bed and I was able to weakly call for them to rescue me. I can't recall all my other terrors, but I became increasingly nervous and tense. They had an expression for it, 'highly strung'. I noticed a new volume appeared among my father's substantial book collection. It was called *The Child: An Adult's Problem*. I can remember feeling quite hurt by the title and wondering if there was a companion volume entitled *The Adult: A child's problem*.

Like many solitary children, books became my salvation – a way of switching off and entering an imaginary world far away from the tensions and rows of family life. Despite a late start on the reading front I had not only caught up with my peers once I had mastered the basics, I now had a reading age well ahead of my chronological age.

There was a lovely old library in the park in Woodside with a stone cloistered entrance and I spent many happy hours reading my way round the junior library. I had made short shrift of Enid Blyton's famous Five and Noddy books early on, but the first books to have a big impact on me were *Alice in Wonderland* and *Alice through the Looking glass*. I identified with the solitary and opinionated heroine and her need to create some sense in a crazy world. I knew how she felt.

I also read my way through the Conan Doyle's Sherlock Holmes series and all the children's classics from *Treasure Island* to *Kidnapped*, all the Brothers Grimm and Christian Anderson stories, though one of the latter about a selfish girl who stood on a loaf which was supposed to be a present to her parents and was sucked down instead into the ground and tormented by vile creepy things renewed some of my earlier terrors and gave me bad dreams. My father's bookcase also offered challenges from *Pride and Prejudice* to *'The Quintessence of Ibsenism'*, which I later discovered was a rather dull essay on Ibsen by George Bernard Shaw, one of my father's favourite playwrights.

But the other major love in my life was my weekly dance classes at the Pembroke Hall, with the glamorous Sylvia Bryant under whose watchful eyes I took my first RAD ballet exams and learnt the rudiments of tap and modern stage dancing. I wanted with a great passion to be a ballet dancer and remember many trips with my parents to Sadler's Wells, Covent Garden and the Festival Ballet and on one memorable occasion to the Croydon Davis to see the Bolshoi Ballet on their first visit to England in 1956. Disdaining the overnight queues, my father got standing room only tickets by posing as Winston Churchill's secretary.

The Bolshoi performance was extraordinary; the male dancers seemed able to cover the whole width of the stage in one effortless leap that appeared to have them suspended in space. To me it was quite thrilling, especially the chance to see Galina Ulanova in the flesh. But the ballet star I idealised most was Margot Fonteyn. I think I realised early on that my physique did not match my ambition so I was in a state of acute embarrassment when waiting at the stage door for Fonteyn's autograph, my father in a very loud voice pushed me forward (this happened on more than one occasion) and asked Margot if she would like to meet her successor. Ever gracious, she would stop and ask me where I was training and wish me luck, but I wished fervently that my father could be more restrained.

Sylvia Bryant also taught acting and unlike many

dance teachers her shows were more than a succession of grade classes showing off their talents. She wove wonderful stories together and we were enjoined to utilise all our talents whether it was singing, playing the recorder, dancing or taking an acting role. The main problem with the shows was that they involved the making of costumes and this was my mother's undoing. A talented knitter who kept the whole family regularly supplied with jumpers, she could not sew to save her life and my costumes frequently unravelled.

In one show while still quite young I appeared as a grey squirrel till the large press-stud holding my tail in place came undone and turned me rapidly into a beaver. I also remember being one of the twelve dancing princesses in the production of the same name, but as this involved a tutu and full length ballet dress the dressmaking was passed to one of the more proficient mums. Looking back I am glad my mother was never one of those awful stage school mums who craved fame for their little darlings. She rarely accompanied me to examinations or sat in the wings or helped backstage. But I did wish she could sew.

Despite poor living conditions and all the traumas associated with my sister's disability, I have many happy memories of my childhood. There were kids up the road I sometimes played with like Lesley Green, Marilyn Jewell and Jean Thorne and we would climb the apple tree in my garden to sit on the garage roof. My mother told me I got worms from eating some of the apples. I also made tents with an old clothes horse and curtain, practised hand stands and cartwheels, learned to stand on my head (one of my father's accomplishments) and watched him do athletic tricks – he could hold his bicycle upside down above his head by the saddle with one hand. He did the same with our old pram one day and the wheel dropped off and broke my nose – I still have the ridge there to this day.

The garden although small, contained two sheds – one was the bike shed the other was for coal. I painted the coal shed with pink undercoat I found in there and announced that two mysterious people lived in the garden. Nancibal was a man and he lived in the bike shed (along with the torrid letters), Chylis was a girl and she lived in the rather gaudy coal shed. I made up many stories about these invisible characters.

Our neighbour still had an Andersons shelter in the back garden and I was warned never to try and explore it, as it was probably full of water and dead cats.

We shared a drive which this neighbour had monopolised as our family did not own a car. One day he returned to find that my father, having built a model village in our front garden, had rigged up a model railway line from the village down the drive and through into the back garden where a second model village complete with sand and a pond represented the 'sea side'. Casting aside his protests that there was no longer room to bring his car down the drive my father remonstrated with him. How else were we to connect the village to the sea-side? He had to be reasonable!

Our neighbours on the other side were an elderly couple called Mr and Mrs Lever. There was a gate in our picket fence and when in 1961 Mrs Lever was widowed, she would tap the back of her chimney with the poker when she needed anything and my mother would go across to help her. My mother told me that the Levers had anglicised their name from Levi because before the war they had experienced lots of anti-semitism. (I was later to find that Levi featured repeatedly as a first name in my father's lineage, though we have no evidence of a Jewish inheritance). Mrs Lever had raspberry canes in her garden, which she allowed me to plunder and two granddaughters who sometimes visited with their mum. These girls fascinated me as they came in party dresses and released into the garden would only run round the circular flower bed endlessly and could not be enticed to join in any of my imaginative play as it might mess up their frocks.

My father loved our small garden, which was usually a riot of colour. I had a small corner and grew a 7-foot sunflower, which my father claimed must be a record. My grandfather who laid out the original garden had a great love of trees and the garden possessed a poplar tree an apple tree and huge lilac and syringa bushes which lent scent and colour to a small space.

Open-air swimming was also popular with my dad – there was a lido at Purley Way and we would often visit on summer weekends. On one of these occasions still unable to swim I nearly drowned, when my father urged me to use the water shoot assuring me he would be there to catch me, and then got into an animated conversation with a work colleague and forgot all about me. I later learned to swim by default when someone took the stopper out of my rubber ring and I realised I had been swimming around without the aid of its buoyancy.

Making up stories, writing and illustrating them was one of my joys – a talent I inherited from my father who could keep me enthralled for hours with long serialised stories he made up out of his head. I still remember the one about the little white man, red man, brown man and yellow man who ran a school by the sea, all the children who lived at the school and the talking post box in the village. I wove a story around one of my dolls; I commandeered an old cupboard in the hall and turned it into her 'home'. I made furniture out of matchboxes and provided her with a biography. Her name was Cherry Riabochinska and her mother was a famous Russian ballet dancer. She lived in a flat in Soho and she was of course studying to be a famous ballet dancer herself.

Soho represented exotica. My father visited there regularly, attracted no doubt by the strip clubs as much as for the cuisine. He would return with deli food we had never seen before. Cheeses from Spain – he was to later bring a particularly rank one to a school garden party replete with maggots – tinned bamboo shoots – even on one occasion chocolate covered ants. These tins found a home behind the more utilitarian tinned cream, soups and carrots in our utility sideboard – (why my mother bought tinned carrots I cannot imagine because they were foul). One day he brought home a red pepper. We had never seen anything like it before. My gran was summoned to look at it and asked suspiciously what it was and how you cooked it. My dad had the answer. "Fry it with bacon and eggs" he said.

He also made me cooked breakfasts, with peppers and fried bamboo shoots the week my mother was rushed into hospital with appendicitis and he had to take over my full time care. Children were not allowed into hospitals as visitors, and I had to content myself with standing mournfully outside a window looking into my mother's ward and catching an occasional glimpse of her. I frequently experienced great bouts of anxiety when separated from my mother. I had a premonition that she might leave us anytime.

Every day my mother was in hospital I was late for school as my father was pretty bad at getting up in the morning and the fried breakfasts slowed things down even more. He rarely got to his office on time and once, torn off a strip by my mother, when, returning from night shift she found him still at home a good half an hour after he should have been at work, he swept his entire breakfast, boiled egg, egg cup, toast and butter, even the salt cellar into a bag and took it to work with him. Arriving in time for the mid morning tea break his exasperated boss asked what the hell he was doing as he re-assembled his breakfast all over his desk. 'What does it look like' said my father 'I'm having my breakfast'. When told this was quite out of order, he turned on his boss 'Look here my good man' he said 'It's bad enough having to come in here at all, let alone on time'.

It is a miracle how he got away with it, and can only be for one reason, he was incredibly good at his job and could understand the complexities of tax law far better than anyone else in his office. This enabled him to remain the office maverick – no one else could get away with what my father did. I only once saw him offer deference to anyone and that was to a doctor when he was seriously ill. Anyone else who tried to pull rank or put my father down soon regretted it.

At around seven, I got my first two-wheeler bicycle. It took me a while to get my balance and cycle with confidence but when I did my father announced he would take me on my first bike ride. He rode me from Croydon to Richmond Park – a not inconsiderable distance for a 7-year-old – the incentive being to show me White Lodge, the boarding school for the Royal Ballet. Arriving at the park I dropped to the ground exhausted and was soon sound asleep only to be nudged awake after twenty minutes by my father. 'I've just remembered you haven't any lights on that bike he said, we have to leave now'.

A tall angular man, thin as a rake, my father loved physical challenges. Athletics, and cycling were a great joy and he thought nothing of cycling 50 miles to the coast and back. Sundays could be something of an ordeal because in the summer months he would plan long elaborate walks in the Surrey or Kent countryside. The Green Line bus timetable would be scrutinised and we would be marshalled early for walks, which were often beyond the endurance of my mother and I. She would sometimes whisper to me that we would stop in the little tea shop round the corner and let my father explore on his own – for him a 20 mile walk was a mere stroll in the park.

He also loved climbing and would occasionally take himself off on lone holidays to Wales to climb Snowden or Scotland to tackle Ben Nevis. He had none of the gear associated with walkers and climbers today, just an old pair of leather brogues and a stout gabardine mackintosh. He was always losing the belt of the coat and would often utilise a length of rope from the washing line to act as a substitute. He was entirely oblivious of how he looked.

He also revelled in taking me on tours around London, a city he loved. Our tour would start at Southwark Cathedral, continue on to the Monument, Pudding Lane, St Pauls and by the end of the day we had taken in so many monuments, churches, museums and art galleries that I would be exhausted, not least because every road, every monument, required a detailed history and explanation of its significance and of all the eminent people who had populated the area over the centuries. Fred's knowledge of London was encyclopaedic and he revelled in sharing it with me.

He would talk endlessly to me about literature politics and ideas much as he would to an adult. I soon became a surrogate for my mother, who got less pleasure out of challenging theatre (Shakespeare she felt was to be endured) and who had minimal interest in politics, though she voted Labour all her life. Every year when my dad gave me the Daily Worker children's album as a Christmas present she would tell me to leave it behind when we visited relatives.

Deprived of a job that gave him any outlet for his talents my father maximised his leisure time. His literary skills were utilised writing fiery letters to the local paper about everything from dog shit on the pavement to the evils of capitalism. These letters were works of art that absorbed many hours in the evening and often dripped with irony and literary references. I found that on nights when my mother was working I could extend my bedtime by sitting quietly at the table drawing. My father intent on constructing the latest literary masterpiece for the Croydon Advertiser, the South London Press – occasionally The Observer, would be oblivious of my presence till a sudden glance at the clock would remind him that it was 11pm "What, are you still up?" he would ask. "Go to bed immediately – and don't tell your mother".

Like many families in the 1950s when TV was still a rarity, the Cinema was a major Saturday night entertainment and queues would often extend far down the street for the blockbusters with stars like Humphrey Bogart, Deborah Kerr and Burt Lancaster. There were two queues, one for the posh seats in the dress circle, which were 2/6d, and a much longer queue for the 1/3d seats in the stalls. We saw the lot, from Ealing comedies to the Hollywood epics and all the Rogers and Hammerstein musicals in glorious Technicolor, most notably *The King and I* with Yul Bryner.

There were two cinemas we visited regularly. The Davis in the town centre was very grand and doubled as a performance space for visiting opera and ballet companies. During the interval between films a magnificent Hammond organ would rise from the orchestra pit and the organist would play a medley while the ice-cream girls sold their tubs and choc-ices. Two films were shown each night, the main film and the B movie, which was usually a poor quality filler full of actors who had not quite made the grade. Ronald Reagan was a B movie actor. There were also cartoon extras of Bugs Bunny and Mickey Mouse and mercifully few advertisements.

The other cinema we visited was the Odeon near Norwood Junction train station. It was possible to enter the cinema at any stage in the course of the film, and if you had missed the beginning, you just stayed on to watch it again. Films were played on a continuous loop and it was not unknown for people down on their luck to spend the afternoon and evening in the cinema watching the same film come round several times because it was cosier than staying in some bleak unheated room. The back row saw a lot of action because under cover of the dark, couples could reach higher levels of intimacy than they were able to in the world outside, where 'nice' girls saved themselves for marriage and girls who did not 'wait' and fell pregnant were either marched down the aisle for a shot gun marriage or sent in shame to an unmarried mothers home where their off-spring were usually adopted.

The only other cinemas I remember were the flea-pit (as it was affectionately known) near Surrey Street market where I occasionally attended Saturday morning children's pictures – some of the films were serialised, so if you wanted to know how the film ended you had to return the following Saturday. There was also The Classic in South Croydon, which showed art house and European films and where I went much later as a teenager to see *Black Orpheus* and Truffaut's *Jules et Jim,* identifying with the enigmatic Catherine, the female muse of both men played by Jeanne Moreau.

My father also took me to a cinema some way from home, the last in South London to have gas lighting – I was about nine at the time – to see a Chaplin season. Here I saw and fell in love with *Modern Times, The Kid, The Gold Rush* and *The Great Dictator* and still think Chaplin's final speech in that film is one of the most moving indictments of fascism I have ever heard. It was in the same cinema I also saw the recently released footage of the concentration camps, the image of the mountain of naked skeletal bodies being shunted into a pit by a mechanical earth mover horrified me. I know many of my generation had the same reaction but most felt we understood why our parents needed us to see and understand those images, as a lesson in barbarism that should never be repeated.

Without a TV, radio was our main home entertainment.

We listened to *The Goon Show, Take it from here, Hancock's Half Hour, Monday night at Home* (with the eccentric Ivor Cutler), and I enjoyed *Jennings at school* and *Children's Hour*. My favourite by a mile though was *'Journey into Space'*. This had my dad and I enthralled and led to me leaving the Brownies (which I had decided was a silly organisation anyway, especially since I wasn't sure I wanted to pledge 'to do my duty to God and the Queen') but mostly because the timing was incompatible with the start of this engrossing space serial.

My mother used to listen to *Mrs Dale's Diary* a naff series about a doctors wife who had a cat called 'Captain' who must have been 102 he had been on the programme so long. It would always open with the words "I'm worried about Jim". Her favourite though was *The Archers*. It was broadcast nightly at ¼ to 7. She used to listen in her nurses uniform, while applying her powder and lipstick in front of the mirror because she had to leave at 7 to cycle to work. My father would irritate her by anticipating the closing denouement and singing out "da de da de da de da" before it ended. He took delight in anticipating the ending of dramas – like when he took me to see *The Mousetrap*, the longest running play in London and told me, correctly, and in a very loud voice, who the murderer was within five minutes of it opening. I'm surprised we were not evicted.

Holidays and days out were sacred to my father. He made sure never to miss a day at work during the winter whatever the state of his health or the weather, in order to claim what he regarded as his statutory sick leave when the sun shone. 'Never waste a sunny day' was his motto. As a civil servant he was entitled to an extra days leave for the Queens birthday. When people saw him sallying forth on a working day clearly heading anywhere but the office and asked 'What! You off work again?" His reply was always "Queens Birthday". Ironically, he was to die on her actual birthday many years later.

His first job with the Civil Service was referencing in Central London. He would complete this work in record time because he had discovered the Oasis open air swimming pool in Soho and would often be found there sun bathing on a lounger during working hours while he chatted up starlets like Vera Day or girls working at the notorious Windmill Theatre where they showed nude tableaux's every night – the theatre censors condition being that none of the girls were allowed to move.

Holidays to places like Barmouth, Tenby, Torquay, Fort William in Scotland, Dublin and Belfast, the Channel Islands and the Isle of Man were taken each summer. Then in my 10th year my parents got adventurous and we took our first holiday on the continent to a very basic holiday camp at St Aygulf in the South of France, a chance to visit Cannes, Nice, Grasse and Monte-Carlo. Package holidays were still very new in the late 1950s and I was only the second child in my school to have gone abroad. The following year it was Lido de Jesolo near Venice.

I can still remember travelling on the night sleeper and being woken at 3am by my excited father who wanted to let me know we were passing through the Simplon Pass and were in Switzerland. I loved Italy. The ancient buildings, the language, the beaches, the food, the grandeur and atmosphere of Venice and a memorable evening sailing boat ride to Cattolica. We also visited Trieste and Cortina d'Ampezzio in the Dolomites and even one day got as far as Naples. We were to return to Italy several times to explore Rome, Tuscany and Umbria.

I also remember my first Italian holiday as an example of my father's over-elaborate sense of thrift. Not one to travel light, he packed a tin of Nescafe and a can of evaporated milk into his huge bulging suitcase to which he attached by a rope, a tin kettle a primus stove and a couple of tin mugs. These were called into play on the overnight train. Locking himself into the lavatory he filled the kettle lit the primus and returned triumphantly some time later with mugs of Nescafé. Welcome as that might have been on a train without a restaurant car, I did not appreciate that we had to continue drinking the Nescafé when we arrived in Italy, which had some of the best coffee in the world.

My father financed most of these holidays, as his contribution to household costs was minimal. He brought the fruit and veg on Friday from Surrey Street Market, exotic tit-bits from Soho and paid for cinema tickets and trips to the theatre, which were numerous. This gave him spare cash for suits and cameras, so despite his salary being lower than my mother's he could afford things that were luxuries to other families. It was the women of the family who picked up the main bills. My grandmother paid the utility bills and my mother bought the food for the household and all the clothes and shoes for herself and both children. She frequently took out HP agreements my father was ignorant of, in those days women had to get their husbands signature to take out HP agreements but my mother was adept at forging his signature. My father believed the only legitimate credit was to purchase a holiday.

The man from the Co-op visited for weekly contributions from my mum, which could be translated into clothing coupons. At the time shopping for clothes and shoes in the Co-op was the equivalent of shopping in GUM store in Soviet Moscow. The clothes were dowdy, the shoes ugly. As I grew older and more fashion conscious it was the last place I wanted to get my clothes from but I was given no choice. By contrast, my grandmother was terrified of credit and getting into debt and would insist on paying the gas and electric bills on the day they arrived.

Despite having considerably more pocket money than many men of his class due to his living arrangements, my father kept a hawk eye on every item of expenditure down to the last halfpenny and would never ride where he could cycle or walk, or eat out when he could carry his own food and drink. We even took our own drinks to the theatre. The nearest we ever got to a restaurant was the occasional trip to the fish and chip shop. Taxis were for the dying. My father was not one to visit pubs (even though he had worked in them as a young man) and gave up cigarettes and pipe smoking once he had smoked the duty free allowance he picked up on our Isle of Man holiday.

My pocket money was 6d a week when my cousin got half a crown – 5 times as much, but this was supplemented by the sweets my parents brought home nightly. Extra strong peppermints replaced nicotine cravings for my father but my mother would buy a variety of boiled sweets each night – no doubt in celebration of the end of sweet rationing. Dental hygiene was minimal and no one insisted I clean my teeth night and day so the inevitable consequence was frequent visits to the school dentist. By my 10th birthday I had had several teeth extracted and a number more filled. Everyone in my father's family had false teeth before the end of their twenties. My mother on the other hand had all her own teeth, another small but significant class difference.

Growing up in the Edwardian era my mother had long hair all through her childhood – that was the expected style for girls. She hated it and couldn't wait to get it 'bobbed'. She assumed I would feel the same way. I did not and we fought over my hair length. I wanted hair long enough to sit on. Once when I had a mild scalp complaint she told me I had to have it cut but assured me it would only be trimmed. I was unaware that behind my back she was motioning to the hairdresser to make my hair shorter and shorter, until I saw the scissors cutting round my ears and realised my hair had been tightly cropped. I did not forgive her for a long time, and was unable to sleek it back in the conventional way for ballet. As soon as I took over washing my own hair I insisted it would be grown as long as possible.

There were certain things my mother did not stint on including well-fitting shoes. Coming from a generation who often had their feet stuffed into shoes that were too small she had reaped the consequences of hammer-toes and bunions. I was born with noticeable bunions on both feet and therefore getting comfortable shoes was even more important. In those days Clarks Shoe Shops had machines, which would x-ray your foot inside your new shoes to make sure the shoe fitted well and there was growing room. You could look through a glass viewer and see your bones picked out in garish green.

Despite the care taken with them, the shape of my feet plus my general lack of flexibility was to defeat my dream of attending the Royal Ballet School. I attended an audition at Barons Court in my 10th year and remember the moment when we were asked to take off our shoes and stand in a line to have our bare feet examined by Ninette De Valois. Walking along the line smiling encouragingly she got to me, and her smile froze. 'I'm not in' I thought and indeed that was the case. Pointe work was later to prove agonisingly painful.

Frequently bullied by my peers, I often tried to practice 'put downs' to my oppressors. One day on a radio programme I heard someone say 'drop dead' and that seemed a pretty neat 'put down' to me. One day I said it to my mother. She whirled round and grabbed me by the shoulders and vented her anger on me. "You said that to your sister once", she said, "and you got what you wanted didn't you? ". I was shocked rigid. Was I really responsible for my sister's death? Did I really have the supernatural power to make people die just by saying so? I was terrified the phrase would slip from my lips under provocation and that I would be responsible for more deaths, perhaps I had even damned my mother now? It was maybe the feeling that I had to purge myself from sin and this awful and unwanted power, which led me to seek spiritual re-assurance.

On our trip to Italy we had visited many ancient and beautiful churches. Watching the flickering candles in those highly atmospheric surroundings touched a chord. I decided I wanted to dedicate myself to Christ and be freed from my sins and this awful curse that had been placed on me. The thought of a man who sacrificed everything for the love of humanity, who lived a simple life and loved the poor appealed to me. So did the sheer theatricality of the religious services. My father, apart from telling me that Christ was the first communist, associated anything to do with the church with people like my Aunt Elsie and had no time for it. My mother was nominally C of E. She had been christened and married in a church and both my sister and I had been christened in a christening gown that had been passed down through four generations of the Halladay family. But outside birth deaths and marriages, she was a non-attender.

St Marks in Woodside was a high Anglican church, which adopted many of the catholic rituals like genuflection, making the sign of the cross, incense and Sanctus bells before communion – it all appealed to my sense of drama. I started attending services on Sunday mornings and sometimes Sunday school in the afternoons. I asked the vicar about confirmation classes and because I could not attend at the same time as the others, he offered to give me private confirmation classes. My father began muttering to my mother that I was going to turn into a bloody nun, but I was undaunted, took my confirmation and began to attend communion regularly. It was necessary to fast before communion and one morning I had a blackout and fainted. I remember coming to with someone pushing my head between my legs. I did not tell my parents.

It got to Christmas and I wanted to attend Midnight Mass. My mother baulked at the idea. I was only 10 and the church was a mile away. I insisted. Worried about me walking home alone in the dark she demanded that my father walk down and collect me. The idea of having to leave his armchair by the fire and turn out in the cold to escort me home from something he deeply disapproved of did not improve my father's temper.

He arrived early at a quiet moment just before

communion when the church was full of the scent of incense and the altar bells were being rung, a moment of silence, considered most sacred in the church service. I knew he was there because I heard a loud 'tutting' coming from the back of the church. I did not dare to look back. Then I heard his size 13 shoes echoing down the aisle and when he was level with me he said in a very loud voice, "Right my girl, I've stood here long enough listening to all this Black Magic and Hokey Pokey, you're coming home now". An intense shocked silence permeated the church. It was as if time stood still. I crept out with a lowered head feeling totally humiliated. I never went back.

Having squashed my religious ardour, my father did his best to divert me down other paths. I was not yet 11 but I had already seen some of the best theatre in Britain, I had supplemented my junior library reading with randomly dipping into his large book collection, sampling Chekov, Pushkin, Gogol, Tolstoy, Dostoevsky, Dickens, George Bernard Shaw, EH Morton, Palme Dutt, Stella Gibbons, Jane Austen and Ethel Mannin. Having disciplined myself to read *War and Peace* and *The Brothers Karamazov* in their entirety, I now believed I was capable of tackling anything and borrowed the three volumes of *Das Capital* from the adult library. I read and re-read Marx's impenetrable prose over and over again waiting for light to dawn. They were the first volumes to defeat me.

Now entering my last year at Woodside Primary School the 11-plus loomed. It was assumed I would do well. I was in the A stream and my continuous book reading had given me an excellent vocabulary and I could write and spell well. I was always in the top 4 for English always a step down from the top 3, Pamela Ashton, Janice Armstrong and Frances Newman. On one occasion I came third in English demoting Frances Newman to fourth place which made her burst into tears. She was a formidable artist though and I was much in awe of her colour sense and sophisticated visual compositions. At maths I did not do so well coming in 24$^{th}$ out of a class of 59. Still that was deemed good enough to make me potential grammar school material considering our year group also contained an equally large B and C stream. I was part of a group offered extra tuition in maths by the Headmistress Miss Delves and my mother had a reasonable anticipation that I would follow her to Lady Edridge Grammar School.

Other children were receiving private out of school tuition by parents desperate to ensure they did not end up at the unpopular secondary moderns. The pits was to be allocated to Davidson Road School at the end of our road, where a certain DH Lawrence had once experienced the true misery of secondary school teaching before the First World War.

The pressure never transferred itself to me. Throughout that time I remained disengaged from the whole process. I was a solitary dreamer, still affected by my sister's death and not able to understand what all the fuss was about. My parents never suggested the result could be important for my future education or job prospects and I went in to take the tests ill prepared and with no notion of exam technique or the need to finish the papers. I remember checking back carefully every thing I had done, slowly and methodically and had only got half way through when the time was up to hand in my answers. Many of the three dimensional tests baffled me and I was not prepared for some of the smart arse responses to questions like "What is the odd one out, a cat a dog or a wireless" I had answered a wireless because it's an inanimate object. Wrong. The correct and only answer was a cat because you didn't need a licence for a cat.

When the results came out I was told I had failed. I was shocked by my mother's distress. There were tears and scenes and I felt I had done something unforgiveable. My father's response was anger. He lambasted the tri-partite system that had failed his child, demanded interviews with the Education Committee, one of whom suggested that perhaps I was good with my hands since I was clearly not cut out for academia. He started a one-man campaign in the local papers against the iniquity of the 11+ and how a comprehensive system should be introduced forthwith. All the time I wanted to say to them, sorry I didn't realise it was that important to you or I would have tried harder.

The search began for an acceptable Secondary Modern. The nearest, Davidson Road was out of the question as far as my mother was concerned. My father didn't disagree – it had too many similarities to his own grim secondary school experiences. Ashburton School a newly built co-educational secondary was the next nearest but my mother had heard a rumour that a girl had got pregnant there so it was discounted straight away. The third possibility was Shirley Secondary Modern based in a leafy suburb some way from my home but just about acceptable in my parents view. There would be a battle to get me in there but they were prepared for that – or so I thought.

My mother developed other ideas. She knew I loved

dance and wanted a career in the theatre. Having failed to get me into the Royal Ballet School she looked for local alternatives. Prominent in *The Dancing Times* was an advertisement for Grandison College a theatre school in Norbury, which offered training in dance, acting and singing along with a secondary education. The Principal was an important sounding individual called Mrs Irene Grandison Clark. Miss Bryant my dance teacher was canvassed about the reputation of the school and assured my mother that Grandison provided excellent dance training. Mrs Grandison Clark was an important doyen of the ISTD (the Imperial Society of Teachers of Dancing) and many Grandison College pupils had gone into careers in the theatre and dance world.

My mother did not enquire further about the educational side of the establishment, or she might have discovered that the school was not recognised by the Ministry of Education and despite being headed by Miss Mary Pim, MA of Dublin University, there was a positive train crash of odd balls teaching a very basic syllabus below her. The credentials of the dance staff and singing teacher were impeccable however.

Grandison College took boarders and day pupils and its fees were not cheap. £20 a term when my father was earning about £10 a week and my mother £11 was a massive investment for them. On top of the basic fee was a long list of requirements. The school uniform came from one supplier, Dickens & Jones of Regent Street and included a grey Harris Tweed winter coat, a gabardine raincoat, a rust coloured blazer and a grey velour hat. Indoor and outdoor shoes were required, a grey pinafore dress, white shirt and a grey and rust tie and scarf. In addition to this, I needed two different kinds of dance tunics, ballet shoes, tap shoes, character shoes, tights, crossover, slacks and a T shirt for tap, a black circular skirt for National dance and all the text books needed for each academic subject studied. Private dance lessons and singing were extras – even the school lunches were twice the price of state school ones.

I could hardly believe my mother was contemplating sending me there, especially since it was clear from overheard discussions that my father had no intention of contributing financially, considering the whole affair the height of folly and well beyond their means. But my mother's obstinacy kicked in. She would do it – goddamit – if necessary over my father's dead body. Within a week I found myself being interviewed by the formidable Mrs Clark and Miss Pim before being offered a place in Form Three. There were only five forms in the whole school – Forms 1 and 2 were for primary age children, Forms 3-5 absorbed everyone else between the ages of 11 and 15 (the school leaving age).

Miss Bryant helped out. She knew an ex-pupil who had some items of uniform to sell, my mother made my school jumper and all the rest required a trip to Regent Street where the Grandison uniform rubbed shoulders with those of Roedean and other prestigious public schools. How she got the money together for all these acquisitions and paid my first term fees I do not know, but my mother was a determined woman and I was clearly a project she intended to invest in heavily. Throughout it all I was in a daze, unsure if I really wanted this, apprehensive, guilty, but also a little excited.

At Primary School the 11+ pupils were paraded in front of the whole school at the last assembly of term. The pupils were called one by one onto the stage starting with the Grammar school kids and descending to the secondary moderns. My name was the last to be called. Nobody had heard of my school. I would be travelling the furthest of them all in more ways than one.

# 1957
# GRANDISON COLLEGE

Going to Grandison was a huge cultural shift for me. From a local state primary with nearly 1,000 pupils, I was to attend a school some distance away with only 85 pupils in the whole school – just three of them boys. The average class size was fifteen to twenty. At primary school we had done a lot of sports and athletics and while I enjoyed the latter I hated ball games, so as far as I was concerned it was no loss to me that I never had to play netball again.

Instead, my daily timetable was to be punctuated with dance classes and many of these extended past the normal school day till as late as 7pm. Given that I needed to catch two buses on the most unpredictable routes in South London, it meant I was unlikely to get back on some nights till at least 8.30pm. Equally it would mean leaving home every morning at 7am. Over the summer my mother made sure I knew how to use the gas stove and make myself tea as I would be leaving well before she returned from her night shifts and well before my father woke to begin his day – cutting it fine as ever to get to his office by 9am.

The other major difference was the girls I would be associating with. Till now I had gone to school with kids from my neighbourhood so most of us came from similar backgrounds. Now I would be rubbing shoulders with children from the families of stockbrokers and wealthy businessmen. The majority of the boarders were children from Rhodesia and apartheid South Africa (all white of course) as Mrs Clark had connections with dance schools there. There were also boarders from Malta, Italy, Canada and America and one from New Zealand. There were a few kids there from working class homes, but the majority of these were on scholarships, carefully selected for their talents and expected to bring fame and glory to the school.

Looking at some of the diaries I kept while I was there, it is clear that I did not fit in, in so many ways. There is a sense of being overlooked, of not being offered opportunities. My father's reputation as a communist was not long in coming to the attention of the Principal and in this most reactionary of schools in the McCarthyite atmosphere of the 50s, I sometimes sensed I suffered by association. Mrs Grandison Clark used to mention she had seen my father's letters in the local paper and she made her views on trade unions, the Queen and the British Empire very clear. It might have been different if I had been one of the elect, a talented dancer, but my strengths, it was soon apparent, lay elsewhere, in areas of less importance to Mrs Clark.

There was also a shift in the relationship with my father. We had always been close as theatre companions and I had absorbed many of his ideas and interests. But his resentment of the money my mother was putting into my education became a continuous grudge, and the arguments between them quadrupled as a result. This left me feeling guilt ridden and unhappy. Especially when I was unable to fulfil some of their expectations. Many of their arguments would end with my father saying "we wouldn't have any of these problems if you weren't sending that bloody child to that bloody school" and more hurtfully "you are wasting your money – it's clear she's never going to amount to anything." Over the years my attitude to him hardened especially when I was accused of being 'lazy' or not trying hard enough to get holiday work. I think he was worried I was going to become an elite little snob, not entirely without justification, because in some respects I did assume some of the arrogance of my peers.

There were just two other pupils who started with me in September 1957. By some fluke we were all from working class homes. Paul Taylor was only the third boy in the school, an unprepossessing lad; he was a poor dancer and educationally well below average. However being male, he had an inbuilt advantage. Heather Hems the other new recruit was one of Mrs Clarke's scholarship protégés, though I did not know this at the time.

Grandison College was on a split site in Norbury, a prosperous suburb in South London. The main site on London Road consisted of a large Victorian House, which housed the 3 senior classrooms, an office and Mrs Clarkes private apartment on the first floor. There was also a Mr Clark resident there but he was a bit of a mystery man, as none of us had ever seen him. One girl claimed she had heard Mrs Clark order him back upstairs once. It was like living with a Mrs Rochester, though we never heard any mad maniacal laughter.

A conservatory at the rear of the 4$^{th}$ form connected the house to the foyer of the main Hall, a huge ballroom with a stage, which was hired out at weekends for weddings and celebrations and where some of our dance classes took place as it had a wonderful sprung floor. To the rear of the Hall there was a cloakroom and a further dance studio. At the far side of the hall was a kitchen where we could heat up our 1/3rd of a pint daily milk allowance* adding instant coffee during the cold winter months. Behind the kitchen were two changing rooms, which were no more than sheds attached to the main building and which acted as our chilly changing rooms.

The only route out to the Hall and studio was through the fourth form classroom. We knew Mrs Clarke was about to pass through when there was a muffled scratching at the classroom door. This was Marcus, Mrs Clark's ancient dribbly black spaniel who led the way and it was the cue for the pupil in the nearest desk to leap up and open the door for dog and owner. A pupil in the back row was similarly expected to rush to open the back door for the entourage to pass through. It felt like royalty visiting periodically and immediately quelled any noise or disruption in the classroom.

A second building 10 minutes walk away on a side road, consisted of three substantial Victorian villas connected together to provide accommodation for the boarders. The building also housed a kitchen, a dinning hall and another dance studio. To the rear were two derelict tennis courts. Every lunchtime we were lined up in a crocodile and walked round from the main school to the boarding school for our lunch.

In a school so small, new arrivals were subject to considerable scrutiny. I was unprepared for the first

---

* The Labour Govt. removed free milk for Secondary school pupils in 1968. Margaret Thatcher as Education Secretary in Ted Heath's Govt. removed it from all children over seven in 1971 earning her the nickname 'Milk snatcher Thatcher', Many ILEA authorities continued to supply it in opposition till the 1980s and 90s.

question whispered to me 'How many rooms do you have in your house?' My reply included the bike shed and the coal shed. I had already deduced this was some kind of test, confirmed by the whispering campaign, which followed on from the shocking news that Paul Taylor lived in a 3-roomed flat. This kind of naked snobbery abounded throughout the school. I was pleased to find out that Heather lived in a small villa in Wandsworth, the same size as ours and was mercifully down to earth and free of pretension.

The next shock was to discover the educational standards were depressingly low. The 3rd form, designed in theory for 11–12-year-olds contained, a 15-year-old who could barely write her name, a 14-year-old whose claim to fame was that she was the hands on the Nulon hand cream TV adverts (and consequently spent her entire time doing her nails), and a 13-year-old, who took none of the vocational subjects, and, riddled with acne, seemed to have an endless supply of popcorn in her desk (there was a tuck shop open during the breaks).

The other shock was the total lack of discipline in the schoolrooms. Wealthy pupils would disappear continuously out of classes for private lesson in dance or singing or just because they were bored. The boredom threshold was high because no one seemed to do any schoolwork. The only time all the private lessons were cancelled was when the school received a visit from the education inspector, as Mrs Clarke never gave up hope of getting the school 'recognised' by the Ministry of Education. Young as I was, even I could sense this was flogging a dead horse, but did have an advantage for the school insofar as they were not required to pay their teachers on the Burnham Scale. This was probably why we had so many unqualified, elderly or just plain mad teachers, all of whom had one thing in common, they were incapable of holding down a teaching job elsewhere.

There were only three people who could maintain order in the classroom, the two drama teachers, because the pupils tended to enjoy their subject, and Miss Pim the Head mistress, who could strike terror into the heart of the most obstreperous pupil. A tall and powerfully built woman with an immense chest, a livid complexion and a shock of white hair she was supported on improbably thin legs. When she sat down to teach she would heave her huge chest up onto the desk to give it some support. She was known to spit when she spoke – even more so when she got angry so the people in the front desks got regularly sprayed. Her regular drink was boiled water. When she got angry her complexion would darken to a deep puce working upwards from her neck into her face – it was like watching a kettle come to the boil. An impressive roar of 'HOW DAAAAAARE YOU', would follow – quiet terrifying,

Under Miss Pim was a phalanx of other less qualified teachers. There was Mr Stockdale who taught Maths. Rumour had it that he had come to us from Cane Hill, a long-stay psychiatric hospital. I was told he used to flick nose-bogeys at the class and ask peculiar questions like 'Do you like fried apricots?' He did not last long. Nor did a succession of English French Geography and Biology teachers. The exception was Miss Dixon who taught Art and was around for several years and saw me through an 'O' level in Art. She was a big benign lady with thick hair tied in a straggly bun, which shed hairpins and was always on the point of collapse, long charcoal-dirty talons, a large mole on her chin and a voluminous cloak. She taught me to draw trees and chrysanthemums. I could manage the human form passably well myself having drawn at home for years.

Miss Pim as the one academic constant, frequently stepped into the breach teaching not just History her main subject, but Religious Education and sometimes English. Despite her fearsome reputation she got on well with me. Not only was I dutiful, I liked History and could string two words together. It kind of singled me out. Over the years English was taught by a number of strange eccentrics, The were two ageing spiritualists well over retirement age who seemed to have stepped from the pages of Jane Austen, called Miss Kitty and Miss Elsie. Miss Kitty did the teaching, Miss Elsie just came and sat in with her sister and spied on the disruptive ones over her copy of *Women's Weekly*. The class could divert Miss Kitty by asking how her dead cat was getting on in the other life. On one occasion she had the fourth form on their knees praying for the cat. Later there would be a Miss Smith, an ageing relative of Mrs Clarkes who eulogised Kipling and the British Empire and got me to read the part of Lady Macbeth because I was the only one who could say the word 'breasts' without smirking.

The situation in the classrooms was in stark contrast to the dance classes, which were hard and rigorous and delivered by a series of sharp-eyed martinets, principally Miss Campbell who taught ballet together with Mrs Clark and Miss Jonas (known as Miss Anne) who taught modern stage and tap. No one ever answered them back.

The drama teachers, who were there when I first entered the school, were young and good fun. There were two of them called Miss Hughes and Miss Rhoda Leathers. By my second term at the school I had persuaded my mother to let me take packed lunches, so that I was a among a small group of school-lunch abstainers who stayed in the main school building when the others walked round to the other site for their lunch.

One lunchtime, Miss Leather joined us in the hall where we were picnicking and offered to play us some Boogie Woogie on the grand piano on the stage. We were having great fun before a scuffle of dog paws and a roar from the back of the hall announced the disapproving arrival of Mrs Clarke. She was not just disapproving she was incandescent with rage that we were in her hall where we had no right to be, during the lunch hour and worse still, our drama teacher (who should know better) was playing us what she regarded as decadent music – I think her response might have been different if it had been the Moonlight Sonata. About this time Sir Gerald Nabarro MP, a throwback from Empire, famously described, rock and roll as 'jungle music'. I have no doubt that Mrs Clarkes regarded Boogie Woogie in the same light. Miss Leather and Miss Hughes did not last out the term and we were henceforth informed that we had to join the rest of the school and eat our packed lunches at the other building.

I had turned rebel on the question of school lunches after enduring a term of quite inedible food served by Miss Pim and the cook Miss Thompson. Miss Thompson was a chain smoker who never took the lighted fag out of her mouth. Ash would form on the end of her ciggie and eventually drop into whatever was below her – frequently our rice pudding, which developed a grey tinge. The front of her otherwise white hair was dyed brown from nicotine stains.

Lunch mainly consisted of grey flavourless watery mince, accompanied by swede which had been boiled into submission for hours till it lost all texture and flavour and mashed potatoes which had received the same treatment. Pudding was either bread and butter pudding or the grey rice with a dollop of jam. Miss Pim's presence was to maintain order and act as gatekeeper because no one was allowed to leave any food. We became expert at forcing the maximum amount of food under our knives and forks so we could present an apparently clean plate to her on our way to the slop bowl.

Not being a boarder I was only dimly aware of other staff that were on the premises at night. The boarders spoke mysteriously of a member of staff who had a shrine with candles in her bedroom and who was suspected of practising witchcraft. There was also a matron but I seldom saw her. Apart from the class distinctions, there was another pecking order. Day pupils were ranked as 'outsiders' and the boarders represented a united front. Being constantly hungry however, they did occasionally cultivate daygirls to obtain a weekend invite to tea, where they ate ravenously.

My first dance lessons were daunting. The standard was exceptionally high, not surprising given the school was one of the leading dance schools in London, with a minority going on to train or dance with the Royal Ballet. Grandison regularly supplied children for West End productions like *The Sound of Music, Oliver* and *The Music Man*, for TV programmes and films like the *St. Trinians* comedies (which was a bit like drama mirroring life). Students from the school were also employed in pantomimes and summer seasons all over the country.

It took little time for me to realise that I would never be able to compete with the majority of the dancers. I was simply not flexible enough, I had the wrong shape legs and feet and although I had a strong sense of musicality, and did better at tap than ballet, I was never going to be among the chosen few. I later found that even in areas where I could more than hold my own, like drama, I was rarely put forward for auditions, the invariable excuse being that I was 'too tall'. I was neither short, blonde, or cute and that, it seemed, was what the producers wanted. I felt destined to be the eternal onlooker, spotting the names of Grandison girls in theatre programmes, catching glimpses of them on film, seeing them on TV credits.

Heather and I had started together in Grade 2 ballet but she was soon being fast forwarded through the Grade exams whereas I seemed to be fixed for unnaturally long periods in the same grade, even compared to children who seemed no more talented than I. In this environment my love of dance slowly leeched out of me. In some dance classes, in particular Modern Stage, I found the dance teacher Miss Anne a bully and I was at the butt end of much of her sarcasm even though every one else seemed to love her. I had to admit that some of her choreography was outstanding. She seemed to need to reduce those she picked on to tears and she would then be placatory. I would never succumb to this loss of face and so I became a challenge to her. I remember her bellowing at me "What's the difference between a bend and a stretch?" My mind went blank and while I was trying to phrase a reply she looked me up and down with withering contempt and said, with heavy emphasis, "And they call you bright". She gave me the only negative comment on my school reports that I was 'sometimes stubborn to correct my faults'.

Once a year we took part in a Royal Benefit at The Albert Hall for the Sunshine Babies Homes in front of its Patron The Duchess of Gloucester. I made only a brief appearance in the 1958 production and was envious of the children taking part in *'The King and I'* medley. Grandison had a singing teacher called Eric Palmer who had trained with D'Oyley Carte Opera and was devoted to Rogers and Hammerstein. I knew all their musicals backwards and had a strong singing voice. Trouble was singing was 'extra'. I must have appealed to my mother as I appeared in *South Pacific* the following year as a native of Bali Hai!

The 1959 programme also contained a distasteful number called 'The Hayride' which was based on the music of Louisiana Hayride, a parody on 'simple' rural black Americans and involved us 'blacking up' like junior versions of Al Johnson and singing 'we all is happy'. It was one of the few times Anne Jonas included me among the favoured set when I would have much preferred to have been ignored. At the end of the show we were all supposed to line up to curtsey submissively while the Duchess swept past us. My father's daughter, and a true republican, I hid rather than disgrace my family in this way.

Racism was endemic at Grandison – not surprising when so many hailed from apartheid South Africa. There were just two mixed race children in the school. One was Michael Bevan who was considerably more handsome than Paul Taylor and a better dancer. His rarity value and good looks protected him. The other was Hazel Carby, who became a friend of mine. Hazel's father was Jamaican and in the Royal Air Force during WWII. Her mother was Welsh. She was two years younger than me. At that time there was huge intolerance of inter-racial marriage and Hazel Carby, (who was later to become a professor in Afro American studies at Yale University) talks of the school being institutionally racist. This does not surprise me. I never met her father. He never came to events at the school and even when I was invited to Hazel's house for tea he was absent. I wish I had been able to do more to protect her there.

My main stand at the age of 14 was to agree to head the debate my drama teacher organised against the proposed Commonwealth Immigration Act of 1962, which introduced a voucher system of entry for British Commonwealth citizens who had previously had extensive rights to migrate to the UK. It was a bill promoted by the vocal right-wing Conservative Monday Club and was described by Hugh Gaitskell the leader of the Opposition as 'a cruel and brutal piece of anti-colour legislation'. There was only one person willing to act as my seconder, a Canadian girl called Susan Kraemer.

My father prepared me well with many cuttings from the national papers to illustrate my case, but despite this and Susan making a good supporting speech, we were roundly defeated by an the irrational and aggressive opposition. Its was only Hazel and another girl Janet True who later lent their encouragement and support after I was cut dead in the common room and accused of being a 'nigger lover'. I was to lose a further debate against capital punishment the following term as the 'hang them and flog them' brigade was predictably in the majority.

It says much for my staying power that I continued to work hard at my dance. The schoolwork seemed easy enough even though tackling homework at 10pm after an exhausting day at school and a long journey home was not ideal. I won the prize for coming top academically every year (hardly difficult) and felt relieved I had this to offer as a token to my parents since I felt an increasing pressure from them to know why I was not being 'put forward' for auditions.

Outside the school, the nature of my education had separated me more and more from the children in my locality. Early on I learned to stuff my velour hat with it's provocative rust ribbon into my school bag before I walked the gauntlet down the top end of Northway Road where some of the wilder kids lived. They were not above snatching it off my head and turning it into a football, as I found to my cost. I began to see myself detached more and more from my home and my family while having failed to find an anchor within the school environment that was moulding me more than I realised. My long hours also meant I was no longer available to socialise with the children who a few years ago I had climbed apple trees with and who no longer seemed to talk the same language

Heather, who remained a close friend throughout my time at Grandison, despite our obviously diverse talents, had the most ambitious mother I had ever met. Mrs Hems single-mindedly devoted herself to her daughter's career. She seemed more like Heather's agent than her mother, and Heather told me, when we met many years later, how critical her mother was of all her achievements

– never satisfied and always goading her on to do better. She decided when Heather was hardly out of nappies that her daughter was going to be famous, and for a time she also sent her son Graham to dance classes and competitive festivals – perhaps she had visions of them as the next Fred Astaire and Ginger Rogers.

I was invited over to spend the day with Heather at her home in Wandsworth on our first half term. Heather's grandma also lived with the family. She was a lovely homely old lady who ran the household. She did all the cooking and housework and made all Heather's costumes. Of Mr Hems and Graham I saw little and the whole house seemed devoted to Heather's career. The front room and living room had been knocked into one and were empty of furniture with the exception of a grand piano in the bay window. The floorboards were bare. I was enjoined to 'practice' with Heather in this studio, which took up two thirds of the family's living space and it was clear Mrs Hems imposed long daily practice sessions on her daughter. Combined with considerable natural talent, having an ambitious personal trainer for a mother meant that Heather learned early to perform. At one of the festivals where she was performing she caught the eye of Mrs Clarke and the offer of a scholarship to Grandison was made. I did not know this at the time and assumed that, like mine, Heather's family were scrimping and saving to send her there. I think all the scholarship children were told to keep the information very much to themselves.

1959 marked a turning point when we heard the school was to be relocated from Norbury to South Croydon. Parents were summoned to hear details of the move, and those that over-stayed their welcome were invited upstairs to the inner sanctum for a glass of sherry. It was there the *Croydon Advertiser* chose to take a picture of Mrs Clarke, looking acutely uncomfortable wedged between the two fathers she liked least, my father and Mr Kagan, both grinning inanely having partaken of one too many sherries and possibly a whiskey or two. Elaine Kagan was a well-endowed Jewish girl with a beehive hairdo and an impressive early cleavage. She decided before she left that she wanted to be a hairdresser (though I did later see her name listed in the cast for a TV series called *The Rag Trade* with Miriam Karlin). This was appropriate, as I believe her father had made a fortune as the owner of a sweatshop manufacturing Gannex raincoats. He drove a Jag; usually the worse for drink (these were pre breathalyser days) and would think nothing of flinging open the door of our changing room with a familiar demand that EEEElaine should hurry up.

The site move was a favourable one for me as the new location was much closer to my home and I could now cycle to school and save a fair bit on bus fares. Grandison was taking over a Squash Club at 107 Park Lane South Croydon and converting two squash courts in the grounds into dance studios. Room was found for all the boarders under the one roof with Mrs Clarke moving her own residence off the premises for the first time. A third small ballet studio had windows level with the top deck of passing buses, and we had a regular audience of curious passengers peering in at us when the bus stopped at the traffic lights.

Once again the fourth form was the walk through to the dance studio, and as the pupil with the desk nearest the studio, I was now on regular door duty for Mrs Clarke when she passed through. This gave her the opportunity to mutter in a low and disapproving voice that she had seen my father's latest letter in the Croydon Advertiser. It seems likely that her disapproval was shared, because soon afterwards, girls I did not like started to warn others not to speak to me, as my father was a Communist. My bicycle tyres were let down frequently, which did not help my sense of persecution.

Most of the staff accompanied us to the new site but there were replacements for some of the school staff. We had a Polish teacher called Mr Sierakowski to teach us Maths and Geography. He was virulently anti-Soviet and told me that Yuri Gagarin was not the first man in space; the Russians had faked it. The pressure of dealing with so many rude and disobedient pupils broke him in the end and when one girl, Jacqueline Taylor demanded to leave the room to go to the toilet because she had 'weak kidneys' his nerve snapped. Breaking a ruler across his thigh he pointed the jagged end at Jacqueline and chased her round the classroom, overturning desks, until the noise alerted Mrs Clark. We did not see him again and geography was then off the syllabus. Shortly after I was elevated to the fifth form, which was housed in a cabin in the garden and with some relief, left the disruptive fourth form behind.

By now, I had gained some resilience and some more friends who included a spectacular young dancer from Malta called Daphne Lungaro Mifsud. She had been trained in the Russian technique and even at 10 she was an accomplished performer. Dianne Spridell, Domini Winter, Angela Sandford, Fay Howarth and Jacqueline Hogarth (the $5^{th}$ form comic) were all girls I got along with. I was also friends with Suzanne Engels who claimed to be related to Frederick Engels and who unexpectedly departed after a short stay at Grandison, for the Royal Ballet School, though we kept in touch for a time after she left.

Margaret Cousins, our Drama teacher was instrumental in helping me turn a corner. At last I had found a subject in which I had the ability to excel. Mrs Cousins had an intensely charismatic personality. She could quell a disruptive class when she walked into a room, with a single look. She taught us how to breathe, to project our voices, to fill a stage, to analyse a character, how to move on stage, how to control and direct our emotions – everything we needed to bring to a role. I venerated her.

Under her expert tutelage I began to flower and to refine my ambitions. I began to dream of going to drama school and becoming an actor – Mrs Cousins own daughter Julia was studying at the Central School alongside Lynn Redgrave. Here was someone who could intelligently analyse the many plays I saw, who was friendly, approachable and brought out the best in, not just me, but all her pupils. She was very popular. For the first time I heard words of praise and positive encouragement. I was awarded the annual drama prize when I appeared as the mother in Christopher Fry's *Boy with a Cart* and remember it as an extraordinary experience, because having read the play just once I put the book down and announced I did not need the script. I was not only word perfect but I lapsed, unplanned, into a Suffolk accent, which I maintained consistently throughout the play. Even now I cannot really understand how that happened.

Unfortunately Mrs Cousins left us for pastures new shortly after the play, leaving her adoring 5th form quite bereft. Several of us started a correspondence with her, which she maintained for sometime, offering me some heartfelt advice and support more than once. Even today I regard her as my most influential teacher and I hope the remaining years of her teaching career were happy ones.

Having been redefined as a potential acting student some of the pressure was lifted off and I began to be offered character parts in choreographed dance productions and speaking parts generally. Hearing I was a strong reader Mr Palmer roped me in for the Nativity Play he had been asked to produce. This featured the normal array of carols, sung by a cast of Angels, Shepherds, Wise men, Mary and Joseph. I was to be the narrator who would stand behind a raised lectern in front of the stage, delivering the appropriate bible readings prior to the curtains opening onto the nativity scene. Hearing I was to have this part Mrs Clarke collared me one day and demanded to know if my mother could make me a cloak. When I expressed some uncertainty she became impatient "Good God girl you can't expect the school to do everything" she stormed. Why I needed to wear a cloak anyway I could not fathom.

Mr Palmer had his own idea of making a small wooden frame round Mary and Joseph to create a tableaux, and asked if any of the fathers could make this simple structure for him. My father volunteered. Mr Palmer never kept his appointment with my father to explain in detail what he had in mind and contented himself with a brief conversation over the phone. Big mistake. Maybe he was lulled into a false sense of confidence by my father's boast that he had worked back stage at the Lyceum Theatre before the war. All I remember is my acute embarrassment when, standing in full view of

Mrs Grandison Clarke, Miss Pim and assorted members of staff sitting in the front row, the air was suddenly rent with the sound of hammering as my father knocked nails into his contraption behind the curtain. I saw the whisper travelling along the row "What is going on? What is going on? What is going on? And then the reply coming back "it's Mr Roy, It's Mr Roy, It's Mr Roy. Once more my father had chosen a religious event to cause me the maximum embarrassment.

Another very good thing happened to me in the fifth form. For the first time since arriving at Grandison I had a ballet teacher who thought I had potential. Jillian Saint came to the school from the Royal Ballet and took on a group of us who had been held back to take our RAD Grade 5, the last of the children's exams, long after the fast track girls like Heather had entered and passed the professional Elementary and Intermediate exams, that followed the children's grades. The top grading for all the dance exams was 'Honours' and I had never managed to achieve or was expected to achieve this grade. One teacher Miss Davis, known for her dry comments had told me 'I was doing the best with what I had got' the inference being that this wasn't much. Now Miss Saint was telling me that I could get Honours for Grade 5. Encouraged to make new efforts, Miss Campbell and Mrs Clark gradually began to take notice and comment on my improvements. I worked throughout the term and into the next with a new will and energy but was not feeling too optimistic when on the day of the exam I was suffering from a serious head cold. I thought that had blown my chances so I was totally elated when, for the first time in my life, I found I had passed with Honours.

It illustrated what many educationalists had been

saying for some time in relation to the 11+ exam, that if you labelled a child a failure it created a self-fulfilling prophecy but if you believed in a child and raised their expectations there was no end to what they could achieve. Sadly for us, Miss Saint left to get married shortly afterwards. We learned with some consternation she was also going blind in one eye. I owe her and Mrs Cousins a huge debt for restoring my confidence in myself and helping me through the bumpy years of adolescence.

There was one other dance class I always looked forward to and that was National Dance with Joan Lawson. Miss Lawson was a world expert on National Dance and taught this subject at the Royal Ballet School. She was also a fluent linguist and could speak many languages. Mrs Clark was highly impressed with her ability to act as a skilled translator for the visiting Kirov Ballet. She had amassed knowledge of indigenous dance forms from all over the world and had travelled extensively to research dances first hand in some very remote corners of the world. I found her fascinating. There was less competitive pressure in this class and because many were social dances designed for the whole community, they were, with some exceptions, technically easier to master than other dance forms, so I was not disadvantaged.

Miss Lawson seemed to regard me highly because I was interested in the theory as well as the practise, particularly the genesis of the dance forms and how they reflected their national or regional cultures. However because I was known to be outside the elite dance core at the school, Judy Gridley, who was an excellent dancer, burst into tears when told she had to partner me for my Elementary National Dance exam. It seemed that despite the efforts of a few inspirational teachers, as far as my peers were concerned, I carried round a burden of failure on my back like a large hump.

In July 1961 I reached 15, the school leaving age having taken 4 'O' levels at 14. Unfortunately I only passed English Language having failed to do sufficient revision. Miss Pim was very disappointed at my poor performance in her subject but I was not alone. There were more failures than passes among the handful of entrants from Grandison. I had hoped to leave school in July and return in September as a dance and drama student, as this would reduce my fees considerably. Now this had to be deferred till my re-sits in English Literature, Art and History in November. I cursed myself for succumbing to peer group pressure and not revising sufficiently first time round, especially as they were the only subjects it had been possible to take. The remaining subjects had been so patchily taught we had not reached exam level. French Geography and Biology had disappeared off the syllabus (we learned no other science subjects) and the only other possible 'O' level I might have taken was Scripture, which did not appeal to me. I have since heard Susan Kraemer managed 'O' levels in French and Maths a year later, but she had been schooled elsewhere till she was 14, so that probably explains a lot.

Mrs Clarke and Miss Pim were completely opposed to me leaving school after Christmas and Mrs Clarke warned darkly that I would need 4 'O' levels to get into Drama school. On enquiry to Mrs Cousins, I found this was not the case, but reasoned that with luck, I would have 4 'O' levels anyway. Miss Pim said she wished to talk to my mother. My mother supported me, feeling there no good reason to prolong my time at school when they had little more to offer me academically. As a student however I could still continue my dance and drama training until I was old enough to apply to drama school. Luckily, I did pass all the re-sits and in January, wearing my own clothes for the first time, I returned to Grandison as a full time dance and drama student.

Being a student I found gave me a certain cachet I did not have as a pupil at Grandison. The students included girls who had not been educated at the school. They were usually more open-minded, often liked books and in many cases were significantly friendlier. One of them was Elinor Barnes, the schools first Beatnik who wore black clothes, white lipstick, played the guitar and had disconcertingly brown teeth as she had been born without teeth enamel. She introduced a new plan for stripping weight off her upper thighs by encasing them in polythene under her woolly tights so when she finished a dance class and stripped off the polythene, her legs would steam. The fashion spread among those sensitive about their weight, and there was a lot of rustling in dance classes for a while till the fashion wore off.

The student's relationship with the staff was different too. We were treated as young adults training for career opportunities and allowed to make more decisions for ourselves. One of my first was to drop Ballroom, which I detested. This was due to the fact that the teacher Mr Teddy Edwards had political views that would have found a home within the Third Reich. Daphne Newton, a particularly spiteful girl from Nairobi drew his attention to the fact that I supported the Ban the Bomb movement. "I hope you are the first they throw in prison", he snarled at me. He used to have to accompany me in ballroom exams, because I was too tall to be partnered by any of the other girls, which could explain the comment on the exam report 'a little tense around the shoulders'. Amazingly I passed the ballroom exams, which many others failed, gaining bronze silver and gold medals in my least favourite subject. I recently found a diary note about taking a book considered 'political' into my ballroom class and being told 'not to dare to bring it into this class again'.

I had already appeared briefly in the Cliff Richard film *The Young Ones* and now found there was more auditions coming my way, though these could be demoralising as we would travel up to places like White City for TV auditions only to have some assistant producer appear, give us the once over and then breezily tell us 'thank you, you can go' – a good induction into the cattle market world of acting. Twelve of us did make brief TV appearance though, introducing the horse act at *Billy Smarts Circus*, slithering around in the horseshit attempting to dance to the music of 'Dance ballerina dance'. The programme was pre-recorded to be shown at Christmas so the big top was festooned with Christmas decorations although the actual recording was made in late spring.

We had been photographed for Spotlight the casting directory and often worked through an agent in Streatham called Peggy O'Farrell. One day we were summoned to Mrs Clarke's office to be told that Peggy had said that if we were to work regularly we would need to be unionised. This displeased Mrs Clarke who made it clear she was utterly opposed to unions because she did not like the 'uneducated' dictating to the rest of us'. I was happy to join the union and wondered who

Mrs Clarke considered 'uneducated' given the parlous academic standards at her own school. Given how difficult it would be for newcomers to get an Equity card in the years to come, Peggy should have been offered grateful thanks for holding the door open for us, before the arrival of the 'closed shop'.

The school also suffered problems with the North/South divide. Our drama teacher Mrs Cox had a pretty vague understanding of regional accents 'up north'. We were given an audition piece from *Love on the Dole* set in Salford for an audition for *Z Cars* set in Liverpool. 'They want a Lancashire accent' we were told. Most of the staff and pupils would have been unable to distinguish between a Mancunian and a Liverpool accent to save their lives, though we did have two girls from Scarborough among the boarders. We were taught Received Pronunciation BBC English and even had elocution lessons. But things were changing.

Fed on a diet of Rogers and Hammerstein, Leonard Bernstein's *West Side Story* which had its London premier in 1959 came like a lightning bolt bringing in a very different kind of musical and dance form, just as *Look back in Anger* and *A Taste of Honey* were sending shock waves through the theatre. We were enormously favoured to receive master classes from a member of the Jerome Robbins Company in jazz dance using the music of Dave Brubeck, so different from the style we had been learning, which had its roots in the musical comedy of the 40s.

In 1961 my mother and I saw Albert Finney in *Saturday Night and Sunday Morning*. It was the first of a series of gritty black and white films about the northern working class, which would usher in a whole new genre of drama in both cinema and on television. At the time I thought Finney was from Tyneside.

Home was not without its share of gritty bleak drama too. Up to now my parents had got no further than verbal brawling, but one spectacular row culminated in my father hitting my mother across the face. She had a bad earache at the time and the blow hit her ear and caused her terrible pain. The word Divorce was bandied about (not for the first time) and my parents did not speak to each other for a fortnight.

This particular row seems to have been triggered because my father accused my mother of refusing to visit his family because she thought herself too good for them. When he stormed out, she asked me to cycle to Mitcham and visit my uncle as a proxy for her. I did so but I was appalled by my father's behaviour and refused to talk with him or cycle back with him.

Divorce was not easy then, especially for a couple with no money, who depended on a relative for a home. What was also very awkward was the fact that I had invited a friend to tea during the period when they were not talking; so all communication was conducted through me. "Ask your father if he wants a cup of tea", "Tell your mother no". Luckily Sandra my friend had parents on the verge of separating so she reassured me that it was much the same in her own home. But it was not easy.

My 1961 diary, which ran to 11 notebooks, is full of anger against my father. On one dramatic entry I had written. 'Sometimes he makes me wish I had never been born. I wish I was dead. Better still, I wish he was'. I yearned for a peaceful environment and spent long periods in my room trying to block out the conflict below. This was all a scene setter for the acute depressions, which were to plague my mother for the remainder of her life.

There was a flip side. When things were good they were very good. Cyril one of my father's old friends frequently visited us. An amiable good-natured man, he always helped keep the peace and I enjoyed his company too – he bought me my first CND badge. I remember wearing it, much like Sheila Rowbotham, describes in her autobiography*, as *'a declaration of wild extremity'*

Living close enough to central London we were lucky enough to see many ground breaking productions in the West End and in local theatres like The Pembroke and Streatham Hill. Between 1960–1962, I saw productions with some of the greatest names in the world of theatre and dance. The Lunts, Olivier, Michael Redgrave and a young Vanessa, Judi Dench, Peggy Mount, Alec McGowan, Paul Schofield, Tom Courtney, Lynn Seymour, Carmen Amaya, Antonio, Fonteyn and Nureyev. Everything from *The Changeling* to *Fings aint wot' they used to be, Chips with Everything* to *Uncle Vanya, The Lady from the Sea* to *La Fille mal Gardee*. Thanks to my father I was building up a wonderful portfolio of live performances. Thanks to my mother I was still able to pursue a dream becoming a performer too.

* *Promise of a Dream*

# 1962
# MY WORLD EXPANDS

1962 did not start well. After a surprisingly amicable Christmas I had looked forward to seeing the New Year in with my parents, but when I was going downstairs to share a Midnight toast with them, I heard a blazing row break out and retreated to my bedroom to make another gloomy diary entry. But things were about to change for the better and 1962 was to see a flowering in my social and political life.

Apart from a short lived holiday crush I had on a boy called John Bloomer, when we visited Scotland in 1960, and a few acutely self conscious gropes from boys at very contrived parties run by school friends, the only other male contact I had till then, was with a boy called Dave Cox who walked me home from an office party and returned to my house repeatedly to ask me out, though I was not interested.

Instead I took a shine to a 22-year-old Glaswegian called Jimmy McGlone, who I met at my father's office Christmas party and who clearly had designs upon my person, restrained only by my age and the proximity of my father. He had taken me out to drink Russian tea at the Kardomah coffee house, which I thought was very sophisticated and promised to call me after Christmas. He had literary pretensions gave me a Greek name which meant 'girl with the hair of a horse' (horses tail) and introduced me to Stendhal and Proust. I kept his number tight in my purse knowing my father thought he was a 'serial seducer' – he told me that Jimmy had made a girl pregnant back home in Glasgow just to scare me off. My mother later told me this was not true.

Jimmy and I meet again after Christmas but at my initiative. He took me to the London premier of Alain Resnais *Last year in Marienbad*, an obscure cult film with a dreary doom filled score, about a woman who may or may not have had an affair the previous year with a man she meets at a hotel – or was she raped – or did it even happen? It seemed an interesting metaphor for our short intense but oddly dysfunctional liaison, which had involved a lot of sexual wrestling. I knew then that it was over. Shortly after he left to return to Glasgow. Despite briefly considering myself a victim of doomed love, you bounce back very quickly at 15. I was to offer far more for my mother to worry about very soon.

By March I was attending CND meetings regularly, helping with the bookstall on Saturday mornings outside Trinity school and going on local demonstrations. Croydon CND was the largest group in South London and it contained many who were to become close friends and lovers in the years ahead. A rather formal well-dressed lady called Nora Reid was the secretary of Croydon CND, and Walter Wolfgang a middle-aged Jewish accountant, who had stood as a parliamentary Labour candidate for Croydon North East in the 1959 election, was the chairman. Doug Morton, a local haulier in the Communist party supplied the luggage lorries for the Aldermaston Marches and for motorcades.

But my social contacts came largely from the Youth CND group. Simon Hinkley was the chair, Bruce Reid, the strikingly handsome secretary. Tony Marks (Marco) was the group jester and the focus of much female interest. He was Jewish on his dad's side, and incorporated a smattering of Yiddish expressions into his speech even though he had no time for his old man, who made his money from the black market during the war and had deserted Marco's mother Bessie when Tony was very young. Marco was witty, intelligent, good looking and a great dancer. He was engaged to a girl called Pauline and was studying Sociology at Leicester University.

There was also a guy called Rusty with a big orange beard and big lascivious lips (who was to marry my sister in law a few years later) who was involved with the Committee of 100, Pam and her brother Pete Jones who dressed like a teddy boy, in rebellion at studying at Oxford, Len Law a printer, Jim Parish who used to give me lifts on his moped, a girl called Heather Pollard with a useful caravan at the bottom of her parents garden where we sometimes spent the night, June King who was something of a world traveller, Enid Atkins (one of the few with a car) Susan Hannam (who smoked and drank prodigiously even though she was only the same age as me) and the McShee sisters (Jacqui was later to earn fame as a singer with the folk group Pentangle), Peter Gillman (also at Oxford and later editor of ISIS) and his girl friend/later wife Leni O'Connell, Don Young, David Rose, Jack Kearney, Ray Meadows (who I went out with briefly), Abe (Mark Abrahams) and many, many more. Abe who was 8 years older than me, had been conscripted into the Air Force to do his two years National Service as he was born before October 1939 (conscription was finally abolished in December 1960) and still had his air force great coat. He played the trombone.

There was also an outer circle of people, who were

not campaigners but hung around with the social group at either The Star Jazz Club in West Croydon or The Woodman pub in South Croydon. People like Pete White and his brother Bob whose flat we used for parties and who tuned into the police car frequency on their radio so we would know in advance if anyone had reported our loud parties, and Mervyn Doy, a crazy man with a pig lorry.

Later I was to meet Terry Mandrell and Pat Fortune who lodged with Bessie Marks, Marco's mother. This was a world as different as possible from Grandison and for at least the first six months of 1962, I had an awkward foot in both camps. My CND friends who were mainly older than me, many at university, dressed down, largely in black. Levi jeans and duffle coats were de rigueur and the girls carried their gear in dolly bags (leather pull string bags) – all part of the fashion of rebellion. They rolled their own fags and drank Watney's Red Barrel. They were idealistic, intelligent, and articulate and they read books. They also loved having fun. They were the friends I had been waiting for.

Grandison Girls were more interested in clothes than politics, appearances rather than ideas. They wore pastel colours, flesh coloured nylons, pointed stilettos, lots of powder, lipstick and pale blue eye shadow, filed and painted their nails, sported elaborate bouffant hairdos and, on special occasions, drank Babycham with cocktail cherries. Black stockings were banned even for the students at Grandison. They were associated with bohemianism. Believing Miss Campbell had spotted me in Streatham one weekend as she swept past in a car when I was hitching up to London for a demo with a fag on the go and wearing the hanging offence black stockings, I thought I would be expelled. However she probably did not recognise me because it was never mentioned.

While Grandison girls were listening to The Shadows play '*Apache*' with their portable radios to their ears, I was skip jiving to Ken Colyer and Humphrey Littleton down at The Star Jazz Club and becoming acquainted with Jelly Roll Morton, Miles Davies and Charlie Parker (My first LP was Miles Davis's *Porgy and Bess* and I remember playing *Summertime* over and over again). On the commercial music front Little Eva and Sam Cooke were popularising the Twist as a dance craze, while Acker Bilk and Kenny Ball were commercialising trad jazz, but this was not to our purist taste.

Grandison Girls were 'nice' girls that thought sex before marriage was for sluts (although heavy petting was fine). Ban the bomb 'chicks' (yes, it was pre-women's movement) were clearly rather more sexually experienced, or at least pretended they were. If they used make-up at all, it was the Juliette Greco look – white lipstick with heavy black kohl eyes. I wanted to look like Greco and have a Paris Left-Bank life-style to match. I later learned Greco and Miles Davis had been lovers when he played in Paris.

My mother watched my transition from one camp to the other with considerable dismay. She had kept me supplied with voluminous skirts, can-can petticoats, stilettos – even a roll-on – all the fashions that were popular in the 1950s so I could hold my own in the fiercely competitive clothes conscious world of Grandison. The film *Breakfast at Tiffanys* had come out in 1961 and for a time I modelled myself on Audrey Hepburn and her slight understated elegance. Now all I wanted was a duffle coat from the Army and Navy shop, a pair of jeans and a khaki rucksack for the Aldermaston March. I also started knitting a very long black jumper.

The idea of me spending four nights away from home walking from The Atomic Weapons Research Establishment in Aldermaston Berkshire to Central London at Easter time was baulked at by my mother believing, that 'I would come home pregnant mixing with all those beatniks'. My father was more supportive having attended several CND meetings with me, and not having swallowed the same sensational stories from the News of the World.

My mother dug her heels in. There would be no duffle coat or sleeping bag supplied with her money if I insisted on going. Undaunted I stitched up two sides of my old feather eiderdown, took my school gabardine and wearing a cheap pair of suede casuals set off on April 20th to walk 54 miles. Ray Meadows had promised to call and carry my bag up to central Croydon on the morning of the march but he didn't show. Rather surprisingly both my mother and father rode into town on their bicycles carrying my bags to see me off. Our coach to Aldermaston left from Croydon Town Hall.

Ignoring Ray I found a place at the back of the coach with Abe. I found my spirits lifting throughout the journey. This was the first time in my life I had felt so happy. I did not know it then, but if I had, I would have quoted Wordsworth, *"Bliss it was in that dawn to be alive, But to be young was very heaven'*. Mark had brought his trombone and announced his attention of walking with Chelsea as they had the best jazz band. Our luggage was labelled with fuchsia labels – our group was Magenta 10 – as it was to be taken on in advance on lorries. We were told to look out for the labels when we got to Reading, where we were to camp for the first night. Every CND group had a different colour label for their bags. The logistics of organising the event were clearly phenomenal. Peggy Duff, the CND secretary was the logistical wizard behind it all.

The Campaign for Nuclear Disarmament had been launched in 1958 by a widely diverse group of people, academics, writers, scientists, church leaders, left wing politicians, Quakers, pacifists, artists, and environmentalists. Ever since the dropping of the A bombs on Hiroshima and Nagasaki in 1945, and the growing evidence of the dangers of nuclear weapons, fears of a nuclear war and the environmental damage caused by tests had been growing. James Cameron, who was one of a small group of journalists invited to watch the American atom bomb tests at Bikini in the Pacific in 1946, later wrote '*there is probably no subject that has had a more stunning and lasting impact on my future attitudes to almost everything than observing the Atom Bomb explosion in the Pacific. I foresaw something physically and spiritually disturbing and for once I was right*'.

It caught the mood of the post war generation, shaped by the dual influences of the Soviet invasion of Hungary and the British and French invasion of the Suez Canal zone within days of each other in 1956. While the degeneration of the Russian revolution into Stalinism typified by the Hungarian invasion brought an end to what Stuart Hall called 'a certain kind of Socialist innocence', Suez underlined the error in assuming that the lowering of the Union Jack in a few former colonies meant the end of Imperialism.

Against this background and the growth of the Cold War, with the Soviet Union entering the nuclear arms race in 1949, followed by Britain in 1952 and France in 1960, we suddenly saw ourselves in an unstable uncertain world, where for the first time, thanks to international ballistic missile delivery systems, we faced the possibility of a handful of world leaders annihilating most of the earth's population and leaving behind a poisoned and dying planet.

By the 1960s evidence of the continued deaths from leukaemia in Japan following the atom bomb explosions in 1945 and the growth of 'jellyfish' babies born to Pacific island women affected by the US nuclear tests, were becoming more evident to those who had the concern to find out – the information was not exactly handed to the public on a plate by the main stream press – the government's intent on misinforming being much as it is today.

Instead it was much easier to brand the opponents of nuclear proliferation and campaigners for unilateral nuclear disarmament as crackpots beatniks and weirdo's. Papers like the *Daily Mail*, *News of the World* and *The People* went out of their way to photograph the most outlandishly dressed, the most exhibitionist and there is no doubt the mass movement of so many young people did attract those who loved to party, dress outrageously and thumb their nose at the Establishment. Freed from conscription and many of the controls of our parent's generation, we were avowedly irreverent, experimental and determined to build a better world free of the insanity and risk of nuclear war.

Another major recruiter for CND had been the film of Neville Shute's 1957 novel *On the Beach,* released in 1959. Shute's post apocalyptic novel dealt with the experience of a mixed group of people in Melbourne awaiting the arrival of deadly radiation after a nuclear war in the Northern Hemisphere had wiped out all human life. CND leafleted to shocked cinemagoers and recruited many members as a result. Many of us began to wonder if we had any future to look forward to, and found that the 'four minute warning the British Government claimed they could give us to 'take shelter' in the event of nuclear attack, ludicrous by comparison. We often joked about what we could do with our last four minutes.

*The War Game,* a powerful TV drama produced three years later in 1965 was to depict a far more likely scenario than the completely unconvincing propaganda produced by Civil Defence, so convincing, that it was banned for two decades and only given a private showing in 1965 by the British Film Institute to relatively few viewers, myself included – the government being determined to avoid a mass public outcry that would have resulted from a TV viewing.

In the meantime the establishment continued to think of us as the lunatic fringe, exposing the country to the danger of Soviet attack by campaigning for Britain to unilaterally disarm and we were frequently told to 'go back to Russia'. The argument that Britain had to have the nuclear bomb to protect us belied the fact that the vast majority of nations of the world did not have this weapon and were not being 'taken over' as a result.

Some of the groups that derided us most were themselves unintentionally comical. A crackpot fascist organisation and a forerunner of The National Front, known as 'The League of Empire Loyalists" was led by Arthur Chesterton who had served under Sir Oswald Moseley in the British Union of Fascists. In 1962 they produced a poster in the style of a Music Hall programme, which we carefully peeled off a bridge on the first day of the march – careful being the operative word, as fascists were not averse to concealing razor blades under the corners of their posters to deter anyone attempting to remove them.

The poster announced *Canon Collins*[*] *Holy Loch Monster Circus – Red Star cast of Thousands – You wonder where the Yellow went?*[†] *They went on the Aldermaston March. Do not miss Bolshie Bertrand's* [‡] *Bloomsbury Beatniks-First class says Nikita Khrushchev, Do not miss Michael Scott's running act: Cold feet in the Sahara*[§] *Dr Soft Soper*[¶] *and the Great Unwashed-Weirdies of the World Unite, They wash nothing but your brains – Reading-Slough-Chiswick – here come the Michael Footlers.* The poster now hangs in my cloakroom – a framed reminder of some of the leading peace campaigners of the 50s and 60s and a golden moment in my youth.

The Aldermaston March represented a learning curve for me. I learned how to hold a banner and why it needed holes in the middle and 6 people to keep it steady in a wind. I learned folk songs by Woody Guthrie, Pete Seeger and Ewan McColl and protest songs like Rosselson's 'The Family of Man' and John Brunner's 'H Bomb thunder', which became an unofficial anthem of CND and was sung endlessly during the four days. I

---

* Canon John Collins was an Anglican priest and a founder of War on Want and The Campaign for Nuclear Disarmament

† Part of a toothpaste ad ending 'when you brush your teeth with Pepsodent'

‡ Bertrand Russell: philosopher. President of CND from its inception in 1957

§ Rev Michael Scott was one of the peace activists who tried to travel into French occupied Sahara to protest against nuclear tests by the French on African soil.

¶ Dr Donald Soper was an eminent Methodist pacifist who spoke regularly at Hyde Park corner

found my voice travelled better than most for shouting slogans thanks to my voice training. However it did seem to me a bit pointless to be shouting at cows in the Berkshire countryside – our only onlookers on the first leg of the march.

I talked as I walked and I listened a lot. I got into debates with Communists about whether the Warsaw Pact was defensive, asked questions about the permanent Arms economy, Stalinism, Trotskyism, The Movement for Colonial Freedom, the Civil Rights Movement, the anti-apartheid struggles, the Labour party position on unilateralism, what Quakers believed in and learned only too soon that a pair of suede casuals from Freeman Hardy and Willis were not adequate for walking nearly 20 miles let alone 54. By the end of the first day, blisters were beginning to form but I refused to let them deter me. Indeed I later noted in my diary that the walk on the first day 'was not tiring at all' and the weather was quite good.

We did not reach the marquees in Kings Meadows where we were spending the night until 7.30pm. There were a lot of press people milling around with cameras. By the time we had located our rucksacks and the right marquee I was ready for a rest. Seeing me shivering in my home made sleeping bag, Abe suggested I put my bag inside his voluminous air force sleeping bag to keep warm. We had only just wriggled into the bag when we heard someone say 'hold it' and looking up I saw a press photographer about to snap us bedding down. I have never got out of a sleeping bag so fast. That shot spread over the *News of the World* would have sealed my fate with my mother. Len and Jim had more upmarket coverage – *Reuters* took a photo of them cleaning their teeth.

Not anxious to give the photographers more interesting material, a group of us went out on a pub-crawl till closing time, ending up in a pub called The Reindeer. It was pitch black when we returned and I crawled into Abe's bag without anxiety this time. We were tired and the marquee was chilly so we clung together for some mutual warmth – there was little erotic about it, though I was initiated into French kissing which I can't say I liked very much.

Day two Reading to Slough, the march set out about 9.30am, although we had all been up, woken by the cold, by 6am. We lunched in a pub and watched the endless march go past. Later as tiredness kicked in, some of us stopped at another pub and then had real difficulty catching up with the Croydon contingent. I had never seen so many people and the thought that I was one of 100,000 felt really empowering. I later noted in my diary:

> *'Before we reached Maidenhead it started to drizzle and we were soaked by the time we got there. My feet like many others were beginning to give out and we still had about 10 miles to go. At last we reached Slough, the drizzle had increased and we were all very miserable. The police were supposed to direct us to Park School where we were staying the night, but instead, and on purpose they led us round Slough for another 5 miles. We were absolutely done in and traded some very sarcastic remarks to the police who could not*

*care a damn. When we arrived someone from St Johns Ambulance tended to our feet'*

By then my feet needed special attention, with blisters covering the whole surface of both heels, and they were taped up with foam. Later, with many of us bedded down in a classroom, a live wire we nicknamed 'Megaphone Dick' and his mates lifted our spirits with a comic rendition from some of the reading schemes they found in the classrooms. No one wanted a pub-crawl tonight. We were exhausted and soon asleep.

Day three: Slough to Acton and Ealing. My newly knitted black jumper disappeared before we left, never to be seen again. Because of the condition of my feet, and our general tiredness, six of us helped out with the baggage lorries and Abe and I kipped on top of some rucksacks on the 'Jade 2' lorry. We helped with some of the unloading at Acton and then were taken on to the Labour Hall in Ealing where we were to spend the night.

The weather was now very hot and we sunbathed in the garden reading all the reports of our 'goings-on' in the News of the World and the other tabloids. Later we caught the bus back into Acton and walked to Southall to re-join the March and Abe hooked up with a very good jazz band, so with revived energy and with some great music accompanying us we finished the day on a high.

Abe was bothered about our age gap though, because, as he told me, he was hardly 'pure and untouched'. So much for my mother's worries, I was with someone unlikely to seduce me or stay partnered with me for long. I found that did not bother me unduly. There were a lot of interesting young men suddenly in my field of vision.

The following morning my unsuitable shoes were not going to prevent me limp walking into London – though towards the end we did catch a tube to Hyde Park so we could watch the full length of the march enter for the rally. Later we walked up Whitehall where I was immensely pleased to see my parents who had came up to London to join the rally and I greeted them enthusiastically.

Despite their concerns for my welfare, I encouraged them to go home without me and joined the march going on to the American Embassy in Grosvenor Square where we held a ten-minute silent vigil and delivered a letter to President Kennedy. With the rest of the Croydon contingent we then made our way to St Pauls where our luggage had been left. The night ended in The Woodman in South Croydon but most of us dispersed early to sleep off the long four days.

Although I had learned a great deal on the march, I was aware that the campaign contained a vast range of religious secular and political opinions frequently in opposition to each other and I worried how so many disparate groups could be welded into an effective opposition to the nuclear arms race. Even then I considered the March was dissipating a lot of energy walking past fields and shouting at cows when I felt we should be doing something more confrontational and pro-active.

I was interested in the Committee of 100 founded by Bertrand Russell in 1960 who felt civil disobedience was needed 'in this time of utmost peril'. The Committee of 100 organised a series of sit-downs in Parliament and Trafalgar Square, the air ministry and later at the missile sites. Protesters were told to practise non-violence and to go limp if they were arrested and refuse to co-operate. Many were sent to prison. Russell was supported by eminent academics like Ralph Miliband and Stuart Hall and the original 100 signatures looked like a roll call of some of the most significant writers filmmakers and actors of the day. They included Lindsay Anderson, John Arden, John Berger, John Braine, Shelagh Delaney, Margaretta D'Arcy. Christopher Logue, John Neville, John Osborne, Herbert Read and Arnold Wesker. Despite the eminence of its supporters, I felt that unless we could make a connection with the general public who had been encouraged through the media to see us as some kind of crack pots, unless we could convince people of the risk to their lives from nuclear weapons, things would not change on their own. Later that year that risk was to be demonstrated as never before.

Meantime Easter holidays over, my alternative reality as a dance and drama student re-exerted itself although it was clear I was finding my time at 'this bloody school' more than irksome. Dance classes with the normal round of put downs and criticisms seemed increasingly intolerable, while the dialogue in the pub most evenings acted as a balm. Then there were meetings, parties and the jazz club at the weekend. My parents still exerted some influence insisting that if I went out on a Saturday night I had to stay in on a Sunday (which since I was often out all night on a Saturday was probably just as well) but as my mother observed I was changing out of all recognition.

Interspersed were visits to the theatre and the cinema with my father or my friends, two notable ones were, Brando in *Julius Caesar* and *'A Street car named desire'.*

I even produced the Wesker trilogy for my acting class and was surprised when my drama teacher told me her husband had been at the final rally on Easter Monday. She seemed equally surprised I had walked the whole way. My photo appeared in the Croydon Advertiser on a local demo, then on April 25 just a few days after Aldermaston we heard that the US had begun underground nuclear testing in New Mexico. There was a spontaneous demo in Grosvenor Square and more arrests.

Heather Hems was a bit fazed by all the sudden changes in my life. She had spent Easter returning to school for additional dance classes and found my transition to full time peacenik and my hints at a sexual sophistication, which at the time was largely illusory, a bit shocking. I thought her attitudes very Victorian. Although I was still loosely going out with Abe, it was clear I came second best to his trombone. I began to notice that the girlfriends of jazz musicians (women jazz musicians being a rarity) used to sit in gloomy isolation at gigs where their partners were playing and that being a musicians woman involved a lot of waiting around. Equally Abe at 24, needed a sexual relationship with his woman and had hang ups about my age, so it was clear he was going to look elsewhere before long and soon my diary was mentioning him arriving at the jazz club with a girl called Janet Shaw who lived near him in Tatsfield and them departing together.

We still shipped up together at all night parties, once at Len's home in Tatsfield when his parents were absent. In the early morning we made vats of spaghetti bolognaise laced with whiskey which I thought was so brilliant I repeated the bolognaise recipe at home (minus the whiskey) to my grandmother's great confusion. She was utterly perplexed by a meal that did not contain potatoes and muttered about my 'funny dinner' for weeks.

All was not happy laughs though. One or two of my pacifist friends talked seriously of suicide, several had depressive illnesses and at school one of the boarders from South Africa took an overdose. My mother also suffered from bouts of depression, when she would become completely inert. Two of the boarders were expelled and I have since learned that the practise of sneaking out at night with the old dodge of pillows laid the length of the bed to fool the staff was not uncommon. So I was not alone in my rebellion.

Then in mid May, Miss Jonas asked me if I would like to audition for a Summer Season in Great Yarmouth. I went up for the audition with Fay Howarth and having performed our two audition dances, was told by the casting agent she thought she could use me. I was then sent on in the afternoon to the Espinosa studios and learned some of the routines for the show, and was asked to do some pointe work.

They took my details and my measurements and said they would let me know. I was not optimistic I would be chosen. Since I was also apprehensive at the prospect of being sequestered for a three-month season in a small East Anglian seaside town where I knew no one, I was not too concerned if they turned me down, though I knew without question I would have to accept if it was offered to me. After all, wasn't that what all this training was about? I must have been borderline; because they waited till June 6th to get in touch and tell me they wanted me. Having got my parents approval I had five days before they started rehearsals in Great Yarmouth on June 11th during which time I had to go to London to have costumes fitted, arrange digs and say goodbye to all my friends.

I said farewell to many of them the same day on a protest demonstration near East Croydon station against Hugh Gaitskell the Labour Party leader who was visiting Croydon. This was a controversial demonstration. Many CND members were Labour Party activists and did not approve of the demonstration, which they believed would publicise the schism in the party. This schism was due to a reversal of the 1960 Annual Labour Party conference decision to support unilateral nuclear disarmament. Gaitskell the party leader was utterly opposed to this policy and had vowed to 'fight, fight and fight again' to reverse the conference decision. In 1961 he succeeded. Many in CND felt bitter at this rejection of unilateralism and many of our banners referred to 'Gaitskill'.

The decision was also to lead many of us towards the revolutionary left believing that the Labour Party and the parliamentary road to socialism was thoroughly flawed as a vehicle for change.

I can't remember Gaitskell showing up to face us, but while we waited I relayed the news that I was about to embark on my first professional season as a dancer, albeit on the end of a pier in Great Yarmouth with Yana, Jimmy Clitheroe and the Three Monarchs. I exacted promises of letters and Jack Kearney a diminutive Irishman who had taken a shine to me, took down my birthday date and promised to send me both letters and a present. I also got myself prominently photographed on the demonstration by the *Croydon Advertiser* sporting a fringe I had, rather unsuccessfully, cut myself.

The following day I collected my first Esher standard

contract from Shelagh Miller who had auditioned me, and found my way to Tom Arnold's costume store in Floral Street. I was to be the youngest of the 12 Fox-Miller dancers in a show called *Roundabout*. I also discovered Jill Ferbach an ex Grandison girl was in the show and engaged to David Conway the youngest of The Three Monarchs, a trio of comic accordion players who headlined at the Palladium. Les Henry (Cedric) the funny man of the trio arrived while I was being measured and spotting my CND badge, made a few facetious jokes about 'ban the bum', I had a sinking feeling that for the next three months I was going to be without anyone sympathetic to my point of few and the thought did not cheer me.

Later I posted two letters off to potential landladies in Great Yarmouth and in the evening accompanied my parents and grandmother to see *'A kind of loving'* at the pictures – a dramatic depiction of a clash of cultures – in this case between a young man considered feckless by his overbearing mother in law. I identified with Alan Bates – he was part of the new world!

On Saturday I got a letter back from a Mrs Bacon offering me digs at a rate of £2 per week – I was to get my own food. I would be earning £9 weekly when the show opened and just £4.10s a week during our first fortnights rehearsal. I would need to get a sub off my parents for the first week, as we would not be paid till Friday. I went to the CND bookstall at lunchtime to say goodbye to some of my friends. Jack had brought me some books to read and walked me home.

The next day my parents came up to Liverpool Street Station to see me off. I travelled up to Great Yarmouth with a dancer called Ann and Harold the Stage Manager.

We were met at the station by three more dancers Tessa, Lesley and Wendy. Ann was staying in digs with them. Tessa helped me back with my suitcase and then invited me to eat with them at their digs. They made a very small chicken go round five of us and warned me off eating canned peas. Smedley had a canning plant locally and a story had got around that a rat had been trapped in the pipe the peas travelled over and its remains had not been found for a month. If the aim was to put me off eating it was pretty successful. In the afternoon we visited the funfair and rode the Big Dipper. It was to be our last break for two weeks.

When I got back to my digs on Southtown Road, I found another girl had arrived who I was expected to share a room and a double bed with. Her name was Elaine Bramley and she was from Nottingham. She was 16. We were the youngest dancers in the show. Elaine had a long thin pale face and bright orange dyed hair, frizzy from frequent perming. She also had an impressive cleavage and disproportionately large breasts that she flaunted continuously – obviously regarding them as a major asset. I was self consciously flat chested and was not happy to have to share a room with this voluptuous siren – it made me unbelievably shy.

In addition to sharing the room with Elaine, 4 further girl lodgers from the local circus slept in two double beds in the front room, and had to pass through our bedroom and through a further single bedroom where Mr Bacon slept, in order to get to the bathroom. The lack of privacy was major.

Initially Elaine cheered me up. Having spotted my CND and MCF* badge, she informed me her dad was

---

* Movement for Colonial Freedom

in the Communist party. At first I felt fortunate I had been teamed with someone with whom I might have something in common. Unfortunately I soon discovered she had a malicious streak, was not averse to reading my diary and making scornful remarks about it, as well as making caustic comments about my figure or lack of it. Her politics were non-existent.

She had arrived with hardly any money and seemed to take it for granted that I would keep her till our first payday – she had this air of entitlement. She also seemed to expect to borrow my clothes explaining that she was from a large family and she was used to borrowing. But not lending it seemed. One day when she had gone out wearing my skirt, my headscarf and my lipstick I borrowed a college scarf she had purloined from a guy back home because it was chilly. You should have heard her create. The scarf was of 'sentimental value' she announced, and I was never to wear it again.

She also confused me with her contradictory behaviour, used as I was to uncomplicated friendships with men. She boasted about her virginity endlessly, while at the same time being as sexually provocative as possible, and she picked up the most disreputable men wherever we went. Once she stitched herself into her clothes to avoid a particularly ardent and muscular acrobat from getting into her knickers. She alarmed me by going into The Savoy, the most expensive restaurant in town, and ordering meals she had no money to pay for. 'It's OK' she would say – 'someone will pick up the bill', and they always did. We were chorus girls and chorus girls had reputations, however undeserved.

It was while I was at the Savoy with her one day, counting the change in my purse to decide what I could eat, that I met the Clark brothers – a wonderful black American tap duo appearing in another show. Steve Clark took an instant shine to me and offered to buy me a meal – he said he remembered what it felt like not to have much money. Later he drove me back to my digs in his red open top sports car and insisted on seeing me again.

We did meet again and I was invited back to his flat but despite his charm and persuasiveness I was just too young to cope with the advances of a man 22 years my senior. He did not give up and took to sitting outside my digs in his sports car waiting for me to come down and join him. My landlady was incensed, considering the presence of this elegant black man waiting outside the door was, 'giving her house a bad name'. She threatened to tell my parents about my 'goings on'. Her indignation was as much racial as it was a concern for my morals, which after all, were none of her damn business. I should have had the courage of my convictions and ignored her.

Steve might have been much older than me but he was very special. He and his older brother Jimmy were the last of the great black "brother" tap duos that honed their tap dancing skills on the streets of Philadelphia in the 30s and 40s taking whatever bookings came their way. Their skills took them to the Cotton Club in Harlem when Steve was only 15, but outside Harlem they faced huge racial discrimination like most black artists of the day. Rescued by Al Capone the mobster, who recognised their huge talent, they were booked into Vegas clubs run by the Mafia when Las Vegas was little more than a building site in a frying desert. Advised by Frank Sinatra they would face less discrimination in the UK they came over. Their first gig was performing for George V1 at

Windsor Castle with Gracie Fields and they went on to find a delighted following in the Northern clubs. They were regulars at the London Palladium and later opened a "University of Show business" in London counting Cliff Richards and Bonnie Langford among their pupils*.

Our team of dancers had eight numbers in '*Roundabout*' including a two-minute quick change, and there were two shows a day, six days a week. On top of this Elaine and I were selected by the three Monarchs to help them with a couple of gags, so we had an additional quick change. Our costumes were all second hand from the Palladium and large 'falsies' were sewn into every costume. We each had a new issue of two pairs of satin stilettos, a pair of Cuban heeled boots two pairs of fishnet tights, one set black, one flesh-coloured and some white pumps. In addition, girls with short hair were given a carefully matched hairpiece, as we were required to pile our hair onto our head in a bun. I had long hair and therefore was not deemed to require one.

Our costumes were varied. Sequinned tunics and tiaras for the opening number, sequinned ball gowns for the finale, a Charleston tube dress, a frilly white Carmen Miranda style Brazilian dress complete with elaborate turban covered in artificial fruit, a Harlequin costume with a huge unwieldy helmet, a ballet dress with a long flowing chiffon skirt, and sweat shirt and pants for a West Side Story style number. We had to provide our own stage make-up. We worked harder than anyone else in the show and were paid the least.

Top of our bill was Jimmy Clitheroe, a 50-year-old

* Steve now in his 90s, has outlived his brother Jimmy and resides in a home for retired theatre artists in Twickenham. He still plays the piano and dances.

midget who played a little cheeky Lancashire schoolboy. He had made his fame on the radio in a series called *The Clitheroe Kid* (named after the town in Lancashire he hailed from). He had a stooge called Billy Windsor. He shared top billing with Yana, a voluptuous blond singer once dubbed 'the English answer to Marylin Monroe' by Bob Hope, but who by 1962 was passing her prime. There was also a soubrette called Wendy Wayne, two acrobats, a singing quartet called The Jones boys and the Three Monarchs who held the show together.

My skit with the Monarchs involved me coming onto the stage wearing a fringed bra, a black wrap around mini skirt and a cowboy hat and carrying a lighted candle. A fishing line held by the stage manager just off the stage was attached to the skirt and hat. Each of the 3 Monarchs aimed a toy gun at me and with the first bang I had to surreptitiously blow out the candle, with the next bang Harold, pulling on the line, whipped the hat off my head and the third time my skirt was whipped off revealing a pair of pink frilly drawers. I then had to scream and run off the stage.

Elaine followed me on wearing brown trousers and had to say on enquiry that they came from John Colliers. Cedric would then come on trouser-less and say he was John Collier. It was the kind of humour embodied in Donald McGill postcards – hardly sophisticated – but it seemed to go down well with the holidaymakers of Great Yarmouth.

The theatre was at the end of Britannia Pier, sporting the normal array of one-armed bandits, candyfloss, fairground rides and fish and chips stalls. At the end of the pier were speedboat rides and we would occasionally be taken out free of charge if business was slack. At the entrance to the pier was a chimpanzee in a cage. It was a miserable life for him but he exacted a small revenge on those who offered him peanuts. Inserting the peanut under his foreskin he would use it as a catapult hurling the nut back through the bars at unsuspecting tourists. If he got a hit he would shriek with pleasure. We learned to give him a wide berth.

Just along from us was the Wellington Pier theatre. Their show featured Harry Secombe, Des O'Connor and I think the Clarke Brothers. Also appearing in Great Yarmouth that summer were Lonnie Donegan and Frank Ifield who had just had a number one hit with '*I remember you*'.

We saw little daylight during the rehearsals, which given it was a fearfully cold summer was not much of a loss. I sent home for my winter woollies and bathed in the sea just once in three months. My diary records how hard the rehearsals were and that Shelagh Miller the choreographer was *'nasty to Elaine and me and cuts us out of everything possible – me more than anyone'.* It was obvious we had been the last and reluctant choices to make up the dozen required for the troupe. My diary also reveals that the dancers were rehearsed on Saturday evening and Sunday afternoon and so did not have a single day off before the show opened.

Carol Mather was the head girl of the troupe and acted as a mother hen to us all.

Having worked with Yana previously, she confided that Yana was bi-sexual, and might find a pretext to get the girls to take their clothes off for her. She advised us not to get caught in a room with her alone. (Elaine was later asked to take her top off and model a bikini)

Yana travelled around in a white opened topped saloon with six white poodles and her manager, a woman who had an artificial hand. She had a personalised number plate YG1, (her real name was Pamela Guard) and had apparently offered the car to Yuri Gagarin when he visited Britain in 1961.

The Jones boys played a rather dull medley of songs – the most dramatic being the song from *Exodus*, which has since become something of a Zionist anthem 'This land is mine – God gave this land to me'. Wally, one of the four, reminded me of a little brown bear. He was particularly friendly and had worked as a chef. Later in the run I offered to knit him a black sweater and thanks to some last minute help from my mum, he actually took receipt of it after the show was over.

Gradually the show was pieced together and the more I saw of the finished product the more inane it seemed – especially the lyrics of the opening song. Add that to living with Elaine and the miserable weather, and my sense of alienation was complete. There was a new release out by Carol King that summer called *'It might as well rain until September'* and the lyrics summed up my mood perfectly. I was also enduring till September and could find no redeeming features in this bleak rain washed corner of Norfolk.

When the opening night came, followed by a first night party with all drinks on the house, I decided to drown my sorrows. I downed 15 drinks, all of them shorts and the next thing I remember is being on my hands and knees on the pier and wondering why the sea was coming up to meet me. My next memory was lying on the floor of a taxi but after that nothing till the following morning when I woke with the hangover from hell to find a gladioli on each stair which I had plucked from my first night bouquet.

My grim faced landlady stood over me while I downed a glass of Andrews at her insistence, having turned green at the sight of Elaine emerging from the kitchen with a fried breakfast (I swear she did it deliberately). I was sick as a dog for what seemed hours, but it cleared my head. However for several weeks afterwards even the smell of whiskey made me queasy and I don't think I drank alcohol for the rest of the run. I am surprised I didn't end up in hospital. I put it down to my tough Roy genes.

Carol Mather came to stay at our digs. She was originally in a caravan with Carmel another dancer but decided it was too inconvenient. She was given our room and Elaine and I moved into a front bedroom with a view out onto the road.

This put us at serious risk of being thrown out when two of Elaine's 'boyfriends' took the opportunity to scale the drainpipe and let themselves into our bedroom with the collusion of Elaine. I was never consulted and loathed the juvenile drunk who was brought along to partner me. I had wrestling matches with this idiot who just wanted a quick grope – he was not capable of anything else. We were not found out, but Mrs Bacon did catch them pissing up against the wall of her side entrance and ticked us both off.

My parents came up for my birthday in July and to see the show. At last I was 16 – the legal age of consent! Everyone made a fuss of me at the theatre. They had organised a whip round to buy me some luxury cosmetics as a present. Oxo one of the stage hands contributed a bottle of port (this must have been one of my tipples on opening night I guess) and Blondie and Ian, two of the other back stage crew left me a box of chocolates in my dressing room. I was very touched given that I was hardly on especially friendly terms with anyone, with the possible exception of Carol who I liked a lot. My parents gave me a watch and Jack Kearney sent me his copy of the complete works of Shakespeare with a note inside 'the best volume on my bookshelf". He signed it 'SM', which he told me later was short for Sebastian Melmoth, Oscar Wilde's nom de plume. That was my favourite present by a wide margin – I still have the volume today.

The following day there was lunchtime mayoral reception for the show biz fraternity in town, so while I attended my parents visited Norwich and I did not see them till after the evening show, which they said they enjoyed very much (?) I guess any show with your daughter in it is a good show. Sunday, the last day of my parents visit, we took a coach trip to the Norfolk Broads and I realised this was the first time I had managed to escape Great Yarmouth. Later, surrounded by young chorus girls, my father, in his element, managed to make a short cine film of us, featuring Elaine in a bikini bending down provocatively to show off her cleavage in a close up – no scruples at all. Monday we saw them off on the train and I vowed I would make better use of my weekends.

By dint of asking around, I found that some of the cast drove back down to London after the show on Saturday night, returning early Monday in time for the matinee. I resolved to ask for a lift and this was how I came to spend a Sunday back in Croydon and down The Woodman, where I regaled my friends with the strange goings on in the world of variety. Marco was also down that weekend and invited me back to Bramley Hill for coffee.

This was the first time I met Terry Mandrell, though I am sure he did not welcome or even remember the meeting. He was working shifts at the Wonderloaf factory in West Croydon at the time and had come off a shift dog-tired and put himself to bed not long before we arrived back. This did not please Marco who loved to tease and persecute his rather stuffy lodger. Insisting I came into their shared bedroom he shone an angle lamp into Terry's face, wrenching him up by the hair and demanding in a mock German accent 'wake up British Tommy – answer the questions British Tommy'. This went on for some time and the more Terry pleaded with Marco to leave him alone the more he felt the need to provoke him. I think I intervened in the end.

All I can remember of that first meeting is someone in winceyette pyjamas with thick curly brown hair and a very correct teacher-like voice. As someone with a very underdeveloped sense of fun he was a perfect foil for the anarchic exuberance of Tony Marks. Before I left, Marco announced he would be coming up to see me and I nurtured that possibility. Ray Meadows and his friend Arthur also announced it would be a 'rave' to turn up so I anticipated at least two visits.

Given the hours we were putting into the show it might have been assumed that the cast would be keen to join Equity. Elaine and I signed up, but few others bothered, and as we were the only ones to express interest in being the Equity deputy and representing the company at the variety meeting in London, it was decided we would both go. So we got our late lift down to London after the Saturday show, the dawn bus from the Embankment and shipped up at my parents in the early hours of Sunday morning. A few hours sleep and we were back up to London for the meeting but I remember little of what was discussed.

That evening I took Elaine down to The Woodman to meet my friends. She clearly made an impression on Jack Kearney who later described her in a letter as 'your beautiful and charming comrade'. Marco invited us both back to Bramley Hill again, and confirmed his wish to visit.

But before then we were to make a move. A number of us were unhappy with our digs and resolved to see if we could rent a house to share, which would give us more freedom to invite visitors. Carol was appointed as the oldest and most respectable to do the negotiation (so much was impossible for the under 21s then) and managed to get us a 4 bed-roomed house in Windsor Avenue which, we were told, had once been the home of Vera Lynn. We even had a garden with a resident tortoise! We were delighted, not so Mrs Bacon who threatened to write to my parents, who, having seen the overcrowding in our digs, would have been the last to object to our move – especially with Carol in charge. Tessa and her boyfriend, Elaine and 3 other dancers moved with us – unfortunately that still meant we would all be sharing rooms and beds, but at least we could entertain now.

I remember little of the visit by Ray and Arthur his friend, who hitched up to see us. Ray was anxious to tell me he loved me – he had already sent me a letter Kerouac style telling me '*I think you are way out beyond the Van Allen belts, a real cool chick like a gasser a real thinkalot goodlooker with mooneyes shining like a pond at night with hair like wow*' and illustrated it with lots of quirky pictures, but by now I was no longer interested and just thought he was being daft. Arthur seemed in a bad humour as soon as he arrived even more so when they came back from seeing the show. I can remember him snarling at me, 'Can't you get any bloody jazz on this radio'. They departed early.

More interesting was the weekend visit from Marco who came up on the back of Len Law's scooter. Throughout the Saturday he kept us regaled as we showed them both round the town and seemed delighted when I was the only one to pick up his reference to 'sabotage' when we saw a coffee bar-owner reprimanding one of his staff*. I harboured expectations that he was especially interested in me, and if this was the case, I was prepared to throw caution to the wind. But no, when we returned to the house after the show he disappeared. I found him in the bedroom with Elaine who was in the process of calmly removing her bra as I came into the room. I felt really betrayed but it was clear he had been planning this all along. I hoped against hope that Elaine, the professional virgin, would repel his advances, but this seemed unlikely. I had certainly not intended to.

Len and I made a makeshift bed in the lounge but I think we were both disappointed by the outcome and spent an uneasy and uncomfortable night. Before he left Marco also offended Tessa's Northern Irish Unionist boyfriend by painting a CND symbol on the tortoise. The boyfriend was livid and described it as a desecration. All in all, a less than satisfactory visit.

Only a few other memories of that time survive, like the ritual shampooing of the hairpieces, which were hung on the line to dry every Sunday, looking as if we had all been scalped and the sharing of the bath water.

---

* From Wesker's *The Kitchen*

The first in added Dettol to the bath water before the next person and so on. The day I pulled the short straw and was woken in the small hours for the last cold milky white bath with pubic hairs floating on the surface, I decided I was cleaner without bathing.

The tradition of sending up the last night, gave us some great opportunities. We blacked out our teeth in the ballet number and Elaine doctored the skit with the Monarchs by saying she got her trousers from Dorothy Perkins. We also unstitched the falsies from our Brazilian costumes because in the middle of the number, two of the Monarchs had to appear dressed like us and Cedric had to accuse the other one of pinching one of his falsies. When he got to the line "You've got it, I know you've got it", we all yelled out, "No he hasn't, but we have" and threw all the falsies into the audience. One landed on the conductor's head. Cedric's comment was "I always thought they were funny girls".

The leaving party, (held the night before the last show), was hosted by us at Windsor Avenue. Wally came early and did the catering with me and we lit fires in all of the rooms. The whole cast and backstage crew came along, apart from Yana, Les and Ann (who was having an affair with Lonnie Donegan's drummer). Jimmy Clitheroe had managed to evade his mother for the night and was last seen under a couple of chorus girls, our dresser Cassie got very drunk on Gin, tried to flush her shoes down the toilet and then put herself to bed next to a fornicating couple. It was the nearest we got to La Dolce Vita! Memories yes, but not ones that left me wanting more. I was happy to leave it all behind when late September came.

We were all offered an Autumn TV gig, which

was appealing in an industry which rarely supplied continuous work, but I had had enough and decided that working on half-wit variety shows as a chorus girl was not a future I desired. The season had earned me some money, and a professional contract but I wanted a more intellectually challenging future in the theatre.

# A NEW RELATIONSHIP, A ROMANCE AND A MISSILE CRISIS

Two days after the end of the show, I was back at Grandison with my Elementary Stage and National exams looming. I was still half-heartedly going out with Abe, and Jack Kearney was making a play for me, inviting me back to the house he shared with his enormously large family, attempting and very nearly succeeding in seducing me. Then one night I met up with Terry Mandrell at the new YCND centre for a folk night. We volunteered to do the washing up together, went for a drink and then he walked me home. In the pub and all the way home he talked to me about his mother's menopause. I can think of few subjects more likely to turn off a young woman, but kissing me at my front door he said, rather breathlessly, "we must do this again". I was left with the impression he was distinctly odd.

Shortly after I was selected to audition for pantomime with 11 others from the school. We had a dance choreographed by Miss Campbell especially for the occasion and were taken on as a job lot. I was not unhappy about this. I had always liked pantomimes and remember when I was young insisting my parents got seats near the front of the stalls so I could rush onto the stage when the comic asked for volunteer children from the audience in the penultimate scene.

This show was only 3 weeks away from home as opposed to 3 months, I would be with people I knew and I would be earning. The pantomime (*Cinderella* with Mr Pastry) would tour two weeks in Shrewsbury over Christmas, a week in Maidstone and a week in Sutton where we could live at home. We were given a date in late October for a costume fitting in London.

But by then I had far more important things to worry about than a costume fitting. Between October 16th and the 28th the country held it's breath while the United States and the Soviet Union held a military stand-off in Cuba which brought us to the brink of a nuclear war. Kruschev the Russian premier had stationed nuclear missiles on Cuba 90 miles from the American mainland and for 13 tense days it looked as if neither side would back down.

Every morning I woke with the fear of nuclear annihilation and on the final weekend thousands of us gathered spontaneously in Trafalgar Square. Vanessa Redgrave cancelled her first night; I jettisoned my costume fitting – what was the point if we were not going to be alive the following week? Finally Kennedy backed down and a face saving compromise was agreed, where in return for the Soviets withdrawing their missiles from Communist Cuba, America agreed not to invade Cuba and promised privately to withdraw its own missiles from Turkey. But it had been a close call. International relations became a little less confrontational but the risks from nuclear weapons and nuclear accidents remained. I got ticked off for missing the costume fitting though.

The missile crisis over, I began to hang around more with Terry. Affectionately nicknamed 'Stumps' by Marco, he was shorter than me, 5'4 in his ex army wool socks, which reeked due to his overactive hormones and an inability to appreciate that they should be changed daily. They were so stiff with sweat when he took them off they would stand up on their own. Mrs Marks called him 'the bottler'. I resolved that I could only sustain a relationship with him if he recognised the problem and did something about it.

Terry was desperate for a relationship (the socks had almost certainly played their part in deterring potential girl friends), but not any old relationship. He wanted to settle down. On our second meeting he told me I had good child bearing hips. I should have run a mile. He was a Cambridge PhD student researching early trade Unions and the London Corresponding Society but he seemed to live permanently in Croydon. He said this was because he did not want to be 'seduced" by Cambridge but also because much of his research was in London at the Institute of Historical Research. A milkman friend in Cambridge signed his lodging chits, as proof of residency was required to claim his grant.

His father was a skilled instrument maker and his family (he was the eldest of five) lived in Stevenage and like so many of our generation, he was the first one to go to University. Like me, he had also failed the 11+.

Early on he worried about my suitability, he asked Marco's opinion as to whether he thought I was the kind of girl he could take into a Senior Common Room.

"Almost certainly not" was Marco's estimation. I was young, wild, poorly educated with a vast vocabulary of expletives – a Rita waiting to be educated but certainly not moulded. Marco's advice was to 'sleep around more' before he started looking for serious partners. Not bad advice, but Terry did not take it.

While he had a handsome face, his body was out of proportion, something as a dancer I was very conscious of. He had a long body, short legs and a big bum. I was soon to discover he looked better with his clothes on than off. He took everything very seriously, carried an air of authority and smiled infrequently. He often looked as if he had swallowed vinegar – and indeed he was addicted to pickles. Looking at his gloomy visage on Peter Gillman's wedding photo, I thought he would have made a good undertaker. Leaning on a wall on the far right of the picture, he looks as if he had strayed into the wrong ceremony. He was extremely staid and set in his ways and therefore seemed much older than his years (by about forty). But on the plus side, he gave me a sense of security and complete confidence in his commitment. Not that I shared it at this stage, but I figured Terry would do until someone more interesting turned up – and I had a fair few others in my sights.

And there were opportunities and great parties to attend – some of those involved many of us hitching up the M1 to Leicester to see Marco, who lived in a rambling old house with several other sociology students and an old communist landlord called Parkinson. Terry and I also went up alone, though we were only given an old mattress on the floor to sleep on – Marco offered us a CND flag as a bed cover – there was nothing else. I thought it was funny-Terry, predictably was not amused.

But being staid had its advantages. Terry acted as a buffer zone between my parents and me. He got on straight away with my mother but he found my garrulous father a real trial. My father thought him a pompous little git and his air of superiority irksome.

Both Terry and I had joined the International Socialists

group as we felt involvement in the peace movement was not enough. We were concerned about many other issues, racism, colonialism and social class inequality. One of the 50 varieties of small left wing groups, IS appealed both because its members seemed to have a sense of humour and a realism about its own size and importance. It attracted some formidable intellectuals and punched above its weight and size in political analysis.

Although I had joined IS, I remained committed to the anti-nuclear movement, attending the CND Annual conference in 1962 and writing a report for Socialist Worker which they captioned 'CND offers no lead', I could see we had to set the politics of peace in a wider context. I was interested in the Permanent Arms Economy theory that the nuclear arms race provided capitalism with a solution to the problems of overproduction, a sort of military Keynesianism. IS also identified the USSR as a State Capitalist regime, which had long since abandoned its revolutionary credentials. Most of the Bolsheviks who opposed Stalinism were now, like Trotsky, either dead or rendered powerless in gulags or mental institutions.

My dad, whose political activism had been largely confined for some years to writing vitriolic letters to the local paper engaged in a debate about Stalinism and the Soviet Union with Terry who spent some time piling on the facts about how Uncle Joe had betrayed the revolution. My father listened, rather sadly I thought, but then said as a final rejoinder, "Well I don't care what you say, I think Stalin was a very misunderstood man." Unlike many who had left the CP after the invasion of Hungary in 1956, my father still needed his icons.

As a 'regular' boy friend Terry succeeded where

previous ones had failed and finally relieved me of my virginity. As a virgin himself, it was hardly the significant event I had hoped it would be, more a Peggy Lee 'Is that all there is?' moment – especially since, practising considerable economy, Terry preferred coitus interruptus to spending money on sheaths. Unmarried couples were excluded from Family Planning in those unenlightened times – you had to show evidence that you were getting married before you could get treatment or supplies.

Although the pill was technically available from 1961, the take-up was slow and it was not till 1974 it was prescribed free to all women. Still Terry's economy was to give me a few heart stopping moments when I feared pregnancy – I even took some pills I bought in Soho on one occasion, but they were completely useless and luckily, as it turned out, I was not pregnant anyway.

My parents must have developed deep suspicions about my love life because my father took to arriving unannounced at Bramley Hill on his bicycle, to see if he could catch me in bed with Terry. I found ever more complicated excuses to explain why I was staying out all night, the most successful being that I was at a party and had been offered a lift home but was worried the driver was drunk – that always worked and I was urged to stay where I was, risks to life and limb ranking higher than risks to my chastity.

My mother tried persuasion. She wrote to Terry appealing to his maturity, saying she thought I was growing up too soon, that I was under-age for propping up the bar at The Woodman and expressing a concern that I was letting my dancing slide. I can appreciate her anxiety now, seeing her five-year investment in an expensive dance training potentially coming to nothing.

It may have been a contributory factor in the deep depressive illness she was beginning to harbour. There were even dark hints from my father that they were considering making me a 'Ward of Court'.

The person whose attitude surprised me the most was Bessie Marks. Oversleeping one morning at Bramley Hill instead of creeping out before Bessie was up, I woke with a start to find her standing over us in a dressing gown with a cup of tea. Too late to burrow under the covers and pretend I was not there, I was astonished when she calmly put the cup down and said 'I didn't know you had a visitor Terry, I'll get another cup'.

Just as calmly, invited by my parents to tea one night, she didn't bat a hair when Fred, who loved to embarrass people, produced his blue films. 'You must have had a good light to take them in Fred' she commented after a particularly torrid scene – my mother was shocked 'Good God he didn't film them" she said. Marco, like his mother, had no inhibitions whatsoever – he was embarrassed by nothing, which is why he always got on so well with my dad. He told us Bessie used to pack black market condoms during the war for his father.

I may have overcome any problems with Bessie, but Terry walked me into a positive minefield. I had visited his parents once. They could not have been more different from mine. Honor and Bob lived in a council house in Stevenage, which was clean as a new pin. Honor was a compulsive cleaner who had been in domestic service, and I am not sure I impressed her as suitable for her graduate son, the apple of her eye. I was 6 years younger and a 'chorus girl'. I had a loud un-modulated voice and I swore. I was not at all domesticated and when Bob asked Terry down the pub for a few pints and made it clear this was a men only invite, I showed my resentment. I had no interest in babies or settling down – and why should I? I was 16 and the world was just opening up for me. In short, I was not a 'nice' girl.

One thing that certainly did make an impression on me was that throughout the weekend his parents did not quarrel once. I had never been with my parents for more than a few hours without a row. I had not known it was possible for a married couple to survive this long without a heated exchange and the notion of emotional restraint was quite alien to me. However I was quite unprepared for what Terry did on a subsequent lone visit, which certainly raised the anti – he confided to his mother that he was sleeping with me. She went ballistic. His father was summoned and elicited a promise from Terry that he would not sleep with me again unless we were to get engaged.

I was incredulous and angry when he told me what he had done. How dare he! How could I face his parents now? I suspected they blamed me as a bad influence on their son. As far as I was concerned the relationship could just jolly well end there – if this was a backhanded way of blackmailing me into an engagement he could go to hell.

The touring pantomime supplied me with a perfect cooling off period. Even better, before I departed, a quiet unassuming girl called Mandy Bateman (with a suitably modulated voice) approached me and said she was interested in Terry and would I mind if she made a play for him? As far as I was concerned that was just fine by me, especially if it meant I would never have to face the censorious Honor and Bob again. Who knows? Maybe my next boyfriend would have sweeter smelling feet.

I wrote to Diana Moss the secretary of Shrewsbury CND who helped me locate some digs. Diana lived in a graceful Georgian house called 'Innisfree' with a large walled garden replete with ducks and geese (at the time I was ignorant of the Yeats allusion but I certainly found some peace there). Her house was no. 14 Sutton Road. She would almost certainly been friends with Hilda Murrell who lived at no. 52 a committed environmentalist, rose grower and anti-nuclear campaigner whose later life was to be anything but peaceful.*

The winter of 1962 was one of the coldest winters on record and deep snow had turned Shrewsbury, an attractive market town, into a Christmas post card setting. The digs Diana had found me near the cinema hosting the Christmas pantomime, proved pretty cheerless. My land-lady put me up on a divan in her formal downstairs front room which like most front rooms of the time was devoid of heating, and told me supper would be supplied for me each night on my return from the theatre. This turned out to be a flask of cocoa and a couple of pieces of white bread smeared with 'sandwich spread'. For a week I slept and rehearsed in my woolly tights – I did not take them off all week and piled my coats on the bed to try and keep warm.

Diana rescued me and invited me over on my first

---

* In 1984 Hilda was murdered in highly mysterious circumstances, which point to an involvement by the British security services. She was about to submit damning evidence to the Sizewell enquiry and had a nephew in a key position in naval intelligence during the Falklands War. The case was a forerunner of the later death of David Kelly in equally unbelievable circumstances. They both had information the govt wanted suppressed. Hilda's death has been the subject of plays films and books. See *A Thorn in their side* by her nephew Robert Green
ISBN 978-1-78219-428-6

free evening for home made soup – a Godsend – and introduced me to her lodger. He was an art student called Roger Curtis, tall, slim, attractive and involved with YCND. We bonded immediately and he insisted on walking me back through the deep snow at the end of the evening, despite being incapacitated by a hand injury, which would require him to attend hospital a few times during my stay. He was anxious to make good use of the time available to us and arranged to meet me at the stage door the following night.

The other girls were amazed, as they knew no one this far north. 'Where did you get him?' they all wanted to know. My kudos went up considerably. I also found that my summer season, (deathly dull as it had been), had given me a level of experience and confidence on the stage which some of the younger dancers did not possess. Freed from the low expectations of my Grandison teachers, the show promoter had no hesitation in featuring me prominently in all the dance numbers, with the exception of the audition piece choreographed by Miss Campbell, which had been shoehorned into the show and showcased the usual suspects. I was also asked to understudy Dandini and offered a line 'Hurray for the Prince, Hurray for Dandini'. It was hardly Shakespeare but it was a start.

It seemed absence had made Terry's heart grow fonder. He sent me a letter on Christmas Eve from Bramley Hill expressing some critical reservations about getting involved with Mandy and told me that he missed me one hell of a lot. He expressed himself to me in a way no one had before. It was my first proper love letter. He wrote:

*I thought this evening of phoning your folks up and wishing them all that Xmas cheer and then I suddenly realised that you wouldn't be there and it hit me right in the stomach and I ached. I had a sudden vision of you, smelt you, touched you, saw you move and stretch and smile and I wanted to be with you. Just with you'.*

Heady stuff for a sixteen-year-old, suggesting Terry was hardly contemplating a break from me, even if he did recognise in the letter that there were many factors that might work against a continuing relationship. It left me feeling flattered confused and full of uncertainties.

One of those factors was Roger. Over the next few days we took long night walks along the snow covered banks of the river holding hands, caressing and talking endlessly about the world, about politics, about ideas. It was very innocent and touching and I felt increasingly drawn to him.

Christmas Day I ate dinner with my landlady Mrs Rostrom, but then spent the remainder of the day with the Moss family and Roger at Sutton Road. Boxing Day I had a matinee and Diana brought her children along to see the show. I was aware I would only see Roger sporadically over the remaining week, given his hospital appointments and my work schedule but I hoped that by the time I left Shrewsbury after the New Year, we would have established a bond which would not be broken by distance, though I was unsure how we could sustain the relationship either. Terry had said jokingly in a PS to his letter that he didn't mind me talking to strange men as long as they were not too strange or friendly.

My feelings for Roger were already going well beyond friendly and I was bothered by the slightly proprietorial tone of the letter.

On the 30th December I received another letter from Terry sent from his parents home and describing in detail – more than I wanted or needed to know – the course of his short affair with Mandy which was iredeemingly over. He talked about her so disparagingly and with such arrogance that it made me feel very sorry for Mandy, who had been swiftly claimed by a guy called Peter Morgan at a Christmas party and was presumably now recovering from any illusions she had harboured about Terry. After the sweetness of the first letter it shone a cautious light on any future involvement with Terry, which he would clearly want on his terms. He did say in the letter that he could not see why I should wish to tie myself with an old fogey like him (though he hoped I would) and on the basis of this letter I tended to agree – even though he signed off with 'much love'.

The night before I left Shrewsbury I spent with Roger. We sat up talking till late and as I did not want to go back to my digs he put me up in his room. He originally put me in a separate bed but I persuaded him into mine before too long. We cuddled together for the remainder of the night but we did not make love. I could feel he did not want to rush things with me though it was clear the desire was very much there on both sides. I wish we had.

The Maidstone part of the tour passed in a blur, I remember a party and talking to a guy from the Merchant Navy about the complexities of personal relationships and then as a sequel, sitting up till very late talking with Inez, the girl who had taken an overdose, about sex before marriage. I showed her Terry's first letter, and I think this persuaded her that having sex before a wedding ring was put on your finger was not necessarily disastrous or damaging for a girl's reputation. We had been brought up with the morality of the fifties, but this was now the 60s and things were changing.

Before I left Maidstone I got another letter from Terry. He was house sitting for the Gillman's in West Wickham. He said how much he felt a vacuum in his life without me and was waiting impatiently for my return. I had talked to him on the phone passing on the sailors words of wisdom, that he was probably confusing his first experience of sexual intimacy with love, and although he admitted this might be so, he said I was beginning to assume a very large portion of his life, his thinking and the motives behind his actions (which was a reference to the treatment he had shamefully meted out to Mandy).

He wrote *'You have moments of incredible charm and delicacy – the way in which you turn your head and smile. Be careful how you use it, you can charm away a man's soul. You can also give a man chance to hope where none exists. I am afraid that I have even lost my interest in other women.'* This was pretty sophisticated word seduction, but then he must have sensed my uncertainty because he followed this with, *'Do you feel the net closing in? Are you caught? That is how I would feel if someone cared as much about me as I claim to care about you. But that is probably because no-one has ever cared that much for me.'*

What was I to do? I had thought things were so clear-cut when I left. I had been ready to move on. I had found someone I wanted a relationship with and now this. Terry suggested I tell my parents I was coming home a day later so he could spend a night with me before the show started the last week of its tour in

Sutton. Rather reluctantly I agreed, maybe to see if I could end his illusions about me.

Sutton the show was on home ground. Mrs Clarke came along and made a point of coming backstage after the show and congratulating me on a fine performance. My parents came. Terry came with Bessie (late) and missed my one and only line. OK it wasn't Shakespeare but it was the only line I had. I did not appreciate then that much as Terry was enamoured of me, the world of the stage was part of the 'effete and artificial world' he saw himself rescuing me from.

# 1963
# BLACK DOG DAYS. LOSSES, SPIES AND BIG CHANGES

1962 had been a very significant year for me, my social life had expanded, I had got politically involved, been on my first Aldermaston March, completed two seasons as a professional dancer, attracted the interest of several men, lost my virginity and, most importantly, we had collectively survived the Cuban missile crisis. My confidence in myself had grown by leaps and bounds and I no longer felt so vulnerable. What I had not done was spare much time to notice what was going on at home.

Up to 1961 I had spent most of my social life outside the demands of ballet school with my parents. We had holidayed together and I had supported my mother as a buffer zone against my irascible father. I had abandoned this role in 1962. Every minute I was not at college I had spent cultivating my social life and keeping away from family quarrels. I was growing up.

My mother would have been fifty in 1962, pre-menopausal but considered old then (still is for many people) and I think she felt she had little to look forward to. She had contained her grief at my sister's death, concentrating all her hopes and dreams on my future and paying a high price in doing so, both literally and in endless fights over money with my father. She had lots of debts she had kept hidden.

Now I was moving away from her and no longer needing her support. I was talking of leaving Grandison and auditioning for drama school, but I think she could see that Terry had an agenda of his own which, if he got his way, would include an early marriage and probably the end of my career on the stage. He had started to talk of 'Sydney waiting for Beatrice' – I think he had me marked out as a future historical research assistant.

One day clearing out a blanket chest my mother found a tiny sock that had belonged to my sister. I do not know how many hours she sat holding that sock but she had a kind of catatonic shock and could not, would not move. The doctor was called and diagnosed severe depression and my mother was put on medication.

When I was a small child my mother had worked as an SRN at Queens Hospital – a geriatric hospital housed in an old workhouse. Elderly people feared it and said you only came out of Queens in a wooden box. My grandmother had made my mother promise she would never be sent there. My mother would often come home and tell me how many dead bodies she had laid out the night before.

Patients that died at night would be left on the ward till the following day and occasionally confused patients who nocturnally wandered would put themselves back to bed with a corpse. When people asked me if I wanted to be a nurse like my mother I would recoil in horror at the thought.

When I got older my mother left Queens and tried working as a District Nurse and in private care homes, but she did not like these and eventually went back onto night shifts at Bethlem Royal, a psychiatric hospital. The hospital, also known at various times as St Mary Bethlehem and Bedlam, had a history going back centuries and the word bedlam meaning uproar and confusion is derived from the hospitals prior nickname. By the time my mother was working there, Bethlem had been moved from a succession of sites in Central London to a huge rural estate called Monks Orchard in West Wickham. The grounds were full of wild cats and sometimes my mother brought a kitten home for one of my friends.

The work was far less onerous than at Queens. The more serious cases of mental illness were treated at Cane Hill an old isolation hospital in Coulsdon, and in the 1950s and 60s Bethlem Royal took the less serious cases of depressive illness and notoriously, treated homosexuals with aversion therapy. Till homosexuality was decriminalised in 1967, being gay was considered a mental illness. Nausea was induced by apomorphin when the male patients were shown slides of homosexual sex activity. Electro shocks were also used. The patient could control the shocks by switching to slides of heterosexual sex. It was barbaric and it claimed lives, most notably Alan Turing the father of the computer and a war hero.

My mother loved the gay men in the hospital because they were so considerate, always keen to make her a cup of tea and offering to 'keep an eye on the ward' if she fancied taking a snooze. It was a far cry from dealing with incontinent confused elderly patients or laying out dead bodies.

I remember visiting the hospital one day and my mother and I having a game where I had to guess who was a nurse and who a patient, not always easy. However when an exceptionally tall woman who looked like a transsexual with garish red cupid bow lipstick, thick foundation and a beauty spot bore down on my mother and asked to be introduced I was sure I had got it right this time. 'Patient' I whispered. "Oh no" said my mother "she's a senior sister"' Nicknamed 'Cynthia' after the comedian Hilda Baker's stooge ('she knows you know, she's quite conscious really' was Hilda's catch phrase), no one ever told her why they called her Cynthia. She didn't mind she said, because it was a pretty name.

Nursing was an escape from domestic problems. My mother was exceptionally good at her job and had many nursing friends, most particularly a woman known as 'Mac' and Hilda Gilchrist who would sometimes call into our house after a shift. She chain-smoked and was very garrulous. Her eldest daughter was in the peace movement.

The medication prescribed for my mother did not seem to help. Her depressions deepened – she later described it to my father as like a huge weight bearing down on her that she could not dislodge. She was put on the sick and finally admitted as an in-patient to Cane Hill and prescribed Electro Convulsive Therapy (ECT). Cane Hill was an inappropriate option for her. It contained long term institutionalised mentally ill patients, people who pissed themselves and stood in the middle of the room howling like a dog. But as she was a nurse at Bethlem it was felt it would be worse sending her there as a patient.

I instinctively felt how wrong this was, but this was not an era when doctor's decisions were challenged. I tried to help in practical ways like taking over the family washing – "why don't you take it to the launderette?" Terry wanted to know. He had no idea what it would be like asking my father for the money. I hand washed everything instead, putting it through the mangle and hanging it in the garden or on the kitchen airer to dry, did the ironing (which had devolved to me some time back) the washing up and some of the cooking.

As there was no longer the money to pay my fees at Grandison, I relinquished my place. I had exams pending but when I contacted my old dance teacher Sylvia Bryant she very magnanimously told me she would take me on as a student free of charge. She said I could help with the juniors and make tea or something. In fact she never asked me to do anything to pay my way. I was inordinately grateful to her. She knew my mother had lost a child and felt a real empathy for her. I was delighted to be returning to her studios in Wallington – it felt like coming home and I found this small studio and its handful of students really pleasant company.

Returning to Miss Bryant's also provided me with a little pocket money as one day she received a call asking if one of her dance students could model for a group of nuns. The nuns in question were taking a teaching diploma at Roehampton Catholic Teacher's Training College and specialising in visual arts. Their course required them to do a course in Life Drawing, but anxious to avoid exposing these young brides of Christ to nude models, the college had asked for a dispensation from the examiners.

It was agreed that they could draw a ballet student in leotard and tights as an alternative. This explained how I came to be posing for a group of nuns every Friday – one of my more bizarre art modelling jobs. Every week I was invited to the staff dinning room for an elaborate lunch of fish washed down with white wine. They had difficulty in the afternoon keeping me awake – I had a tendency to slide off the stool with the after effects of a cooked lunch and alcohol.

Sylvia Bryant also helped out the Wimbledon Light Operatic Company, by arranging the choreography and staging for their productions. She asked three of us to take part in one of the productions to add a little colour. The production was entitled *'Passion Flower'* and was based on Carmen. We were asked to do a short flamenco. It was one of the most miscast productions I have ever known. The romantic lead was Don José, a stout little Welshman about 5'2' and not a day under 40. He had a powerful voice, but when he hit a top note his eyes crossed in the middle. Carmen was 6'2" exceptionally tall and thin (she was known as 'Olive Oil' after Popeye's girlfriend and indeed walked like her.) She was a peroxide blonde so to add authenticity she dyed her hair black. It came out bottle green. It was just as well we were supplied with fans so we were able to hide some of our mirth when they were on stage singing a love duet.

My modelling money did little more than pay the fees for my forthcoming dance exams, so I cycled to Wallington to avoid asking my father for the bus fare. Since my mother had been admitted to hospital he had become impossibly irritable and resented any expenditure outside of feeding me. He had never coped well with stress and just took out his anxieties on those nearest him. He was a mass of brooding resentments. Unfortunately I would bear the brunt. Worse still, he had uncovered a series of HP agreements he had known nothing about and he was incandescent that my mother had got into this kind of debt. In those days married women had to get their husbands signature to get credit. My mother had clearly been forging his.

As soon as I had obtained my exams I resolved to get a job to pay my way and apply to drama school. Failing that, I would gain another 'O' level and apply to Goldsmiths, who at the time offered a drama teacher diploma with only 5 'O' levels as an entry requirement. Getting independent as soon as possible seemed vital.

In the midst of this I got a letter from Roger in Shrewsbury. Suddenly that romantic interlude seemed a million miles away. He was feeling the same way. His letter began

> *'I'm feeling pretty depressed now and it seems to get worse as the memory of you fades more and more. I just don't know what to say except that I just can't get you out of my mind and there appears to be no way of bridging the gap between us. I suppose that you aren't particularly bothered about me now that you are back with your friends but I find in this living hell you are one of the only reasons I have to go on living. I never realised that anyone could have such a profound effect on my life so quickly but the more I miss you and the more it hurts, the more I realise what those few hours we spent together really meant to me. I realise that what I am writing will appear terribly insincere but I stress that this is just how I feel about you.*

He went on to say that he was giving up various commitments to spend more time getting YCND going in Shrewsbury and that this was mainly as a result of meeting me as he found my enthusiasm for CND quite inspiring. He ended by saying he missed me terribly and was dying to hear from me and that he hoped we would meet again *'before man decides to make our earth into an empty blackness.'* He urged me to write or send him a photograph – he said it would be a change to look at something without bitterness-he offered no explanation for the reason for his bitterness. A Valentines card – one of only two I ever received followed shortly after.

Did I reply to him? To this day I do not know if I did, but the chances are that I was so consumed with misery myself, trying to help at home and at the same time stay out of my father's way, cycling 6 miles to dance school and back and trying to improve myself sufficiently to pass my ISTD Elementary ballet, and pursue my drama training, that I did not know how I could hold out a hope of resuming what was so special to both of us. I did not even have the bus fare to get into town let alone a train to Shrewsbury, but I did take an exhausting cycle ride up to Cane Hill with Susan Hannam to look for my mother. She was inert in bed. Turning to me she looked at me blankly. 'Who are you?' she said. She had just come round from an ECT session.

Terry was around and I took some comfort from meeting him when I could. He loved analysing people and decided that my mother's breakdown was mainly my father's fault. My father saw me as mainly to blame. The truth is never that simple. There were a whole set of complex reasons and the suppressed grief at the loss of my sister would also have played a part too. Now with me on the cusp of leaving home, she must have felt she was losing both children and that there was not enough to sustain her in the years ahead.

I started to spend more time at 24 Bramley Hill to get away from my father. Bessie Marks's large rambling flat was part of an old mansion next to St Andrews Vicarage in a beautiful old part of Croydon. Marco used to make late night raids on the vicarage garden to remove their croquet hoops and on one occasion the signpost on the gate. He was intent on persecuting the vicar.

The flat consisted of a long high ceilinged bedroom with huge windows shared by Terry, Pat Fortune and sometimes Marco, a bathroom with peeling red walls, a small sunny dinning room, a tiny gloomy kitchen overlooking an internal well and a massive sitting room with a huge marble fireplace which must have been a ballroom at some stage. There was a mirror image room in the opposite flat, which was later to be rented by Pat Fortune and his wife Rosemary after a hasty marriage when Rosemary got pregnant. Keeping the flat warm was not easy, as a small army of paraffin stoves attested, which is why Bessie lived mainly in the small dinning room.

Below Bessie were several basement flats. Roy Barnacle, who called himself an antique dealer, rented the flat at the rear. He had taken over most of the derelict garages to the rear of the house to store his acquisitions. He had a very large family and there were always lots of little Barnacles running round the back garden usually minus nappies or pants. The flat reeked of dirt, so badly it was a nose holding job when the door opened to reveal a filthy cluttered hall. Barnacle supplied me with my first item of furniture, a small bamboo desk that he covered in dark green leather for me. It cost me £8 and I paid him in instalments. I managed to fit it into my tiny bedroom at Northway Road because when the room had been decorated the year before, I had asked for the door to be re-hung so that it opened outwards. Acquiring this small desk was my first symbolic step towards independence.

My mother came home but her 'recovery' was short lived. No one had provided her with counselling or one to one support. In these days women of her age were often written off as 'menopausal' and there was little attempt to find the underlying causes of their depression – just ECT, and then back home. Terry's mother had received the same treatment. It seemed that doctors took the view that if they could get women back functioning, which to them meant doing the household chores, they were 'cured'. Terry asked if we could talk to the consultant, as he was anxious to propound his views. It did not help, it was clear the doctor was uninterested in the views of the daughter's boyfriend.

In March my mother was admitted again. The day she was admitted I received another letter from Roger. He told me he was coming down to London the following Saturday and would love to meet me. He said he knew he hadn't written for months but that was not because he was not thinking about me. He asked me to give him an opportunity to explain. He was coming down with a group from the youth centre to the Festival hall and asked me to meet him outside the National Gallery at 2.30pm.

I did not know if that would be possible. I had no one to hitch with and in the circumstances felt I I was as likely to get the money for a train fare to London from my father as a one-way ticket to Timbuktu. I let it lie. That Saturday morning I hand washed a huge family wash, perhaps hoping that this deed would earn me a few Brownie points with my dad, but he came home in a foul and resentful mood. He started to cook the dinner, banging pots and pans around and shouting orders. He slammed the food down in front of me and then proceeded to verbally lay into me while I was eating. I cracked, angry at the injustice of it all and thinking miserably of where I would rather be. I screamed that I didn't want his fucking dinner and ran out into the hall.

He pursued me. He rugby tackled me on the stairs, hit me hard – the first time ever – and demanded I return and eat my food that he had paid good money for. Nausea welled up in my throat. I told him to stuff it. He put his hands round my neck and started to shake me. At that moment the telephone rang. My father answered it. 'It's for you' he spat. He stood over me resentfully while I picked up the receiver. It was Roger, confused, unsure but pleading with me to come into London and see him. All I could say, with my father breathing angrily in the background, was 'I can't'. I could offer no explanation I just kept repeating 'I can't'. Eventually he rang off.

I ran out of the house and walked all the way to South Croydon crying my eyes out. It was the last time I ever heard from Roger, though in a sequel a few years later my parents visited Diana Moss on a trip to Shrewsbury and she told them I had broken Roger's heart. I still wish, even now 54 years later, that I could meet him and explain. Roger represented an alternative life I might have had – though who is to say?

By April I had taken the last dance exams I planned to take. I decided that I would apply to drama school for September. I sent off applications to RADA and LAMDA and was given audition dates in May. I would need to prepare a piece from Shakespeare and a contrasting piece from another play. I spent ages pouring over my volume of Shakespeare conscious that hundreds of wannabe actresses would be doing the potion-taking scene from *Romeo and Juliet* or the quality of mercy speech by Portia. I wanted something really obscure. In the end I bolted together a speech of Cressida's from *Troilus and Cressida* in my desire to do something different and, I hoped, memorable. Unfortunately I gave the play only the most cursory study – a bad mistake as no speech appears in isolation. For my second scene I chose the trial scene from Brecht's *Caucasian Chalk Circle* where Grusha angrily denounces Azdak the judge.

Terry had moved by now to Peter Gillman's home in West Wickham. He had a tape recorder and I would go over there to practise recording my audition speeches in peace and quiet. Peter had recently lost both parents and inherited their semi-detached and a couple of cars. Overnight he became the wealthiest member of YCND though in circumstances no one could envy. He had recently got married to Leni and they were still completing undergraduate degrees, Leni at Reading, Peter at Oxford. They rented a house equidistant to the two universities in Wallingford so they could live together during term time and asked Terry to move in to look after the West Wickham house in their absence. Over the frozen winter of 1962/3 he had his time cut out dealing with burst pipes. I went over to see him when he was there alone but was less keen when the Gillman's came back for weekends.

It was clear that Peter Gillman did not like me, and if I was in any doubt about that, he wrote to Terry telling him in no uncertain terms that they regarded me as an unsuitable partner for him, that I was discourteous and lacked social graces. He clearly saw me as an intellectual inferior. At a time when most of his friends had few if any possessions he guarded his with zeal. He would leave notes which said things like 'when we were last home we noticed a chip on the third blue tinged fruit bowl down on the left. Could you explain this?' I found them scary and intimidating and could not understand why Terry liked them. I guess that he was protected by his potential Cambridge doctorate. He, at least, was their kind of person.

Other friends of Terry's were much more welcoming. Anthony Tuck (Spider) a very tall thin and gently humorous man and his delightful wife Jennifer encouraged us to spend occasional weekends with them in their flat near Clapham Common. Terry and Spider had been students together at Lampeter College in mid Wales – no women just a lot of sheep – Victor Brox Hickling, who was to become a legendary Blues singer was also at Lampeter with them and he and Annette, his very elegant Nigerian wife and later children would enter and re-enter my life for many years. I remember the first time I saw Annette. She came to a party of ours in an elegant white evening dress straight from Ronnie Scotts where she had been singing – the ultimate in cool and confidence. Spider had a battered Bond – a 3-wheeler car you could drive with a motorbike licence. They called it Esme after Salinger's 'From Esme with love and squalor'.

I learned to cook properly for the first time by watching and assisting Jennifer who produced the most exquisite food on a very basic budget. Jennifer had been to art school and decorated their flat with huge flair and sophistication. For the first time I began to appreciate how good design and simple but clever use of light and colour could transform a living space. The Conran revolution of Heals and later Habitat (the first Habitat opened in May 1964) was beginning to transform the homes of the baby boomers, while canny purchases of discarded Victoriana, like iron bedsteads and Victorian chairs and chests, could also be purchased at a snip, as our parents generation were intent on throwing out all at that 'old stuff' in favour of G plan, studio couches and record players on black plastic legs.

Our visits to Clapham also gave us an opportunity to watch *That was the week that was* on TV. We did not have a television set and neither did Spider or Jennifer but there was one in the empty flat downstairs and Spider would go down early to get it warmed up and shout us up the stairs as soon as it started. It was the first satirical show to appear on Aunty BBC and was like nothing we had ever seen before. I still remember the very first time I saw it back in 1962. We were in Don Young's parents house, the TV was on in the corner and suddenly I heard Millicent Martin say in a very clear voice 'your flies are undone'. I was transfixed – I thought, no one is allowed to say things like that on the television. But risk taking was on its way in and deference on its way out. Although it was to take till 1968 for the theatres to be free from nearly 400 years of censorship imposed by the Lord Chamberlain, the new director of the BBC Hugh Green was keen to 'prick the pomposity of public figures' and appointed Ned Sherrin to do just that.

Sherrin utilised a whole welter of satirical journalists and comedians who were waiting to take on the establishment. *Private Eye* had just been launched and *Beyond the Fringe* had been a storming success on both sides of the Atlantic. TW3 arrived in the wake of the Profumo affair, a sleazy scandal involving a Tory minister, the prostitute Christine Keeler and Ivanov a Soviet spy and after that no politician, or public figure was safe from TW3 who also targeted the monarchy, racism in the American South and Apartheid South Africa, religion, the class system and the decline of the British Empire.

In America the Civil Rights movement was attracting our attention and we were dismayed by the election of the racist Governor Wallace in Alabama in January, determined to oppose 'negro rights'. Medgar Evers a leading Civil Rights activist, who was working to get black people registered to vote, was murdered in July 63. Millicent Martin in a savage parody of the American red necks and the KKK, appeared in a Black and White Minstrel style show number on TW3, crooning *'Let me go back to Mississippi – it's the place that I love best – where the Mississippi mud, seems to mingle with the blood, of the niggers that are hanging from the branches of the trees'.* Sometimes as Brecht had found, shock and parody were the best way to fight the indefensible. But this full frontal approach on British TV was new.

From America the distant rumblings of the feminist movement were heralded with the publication of Betty Friedan's *The Feminist Mystique.* Too late for Sylvia Plath, the dark introspective poet who committed suicide at the beginning of the year when her marriage with Ted Hughes collapsed. Too early for us politically aware young women, still struggling to update the1950s female role models, even if the Beatles had burst on the scene with a more upbeat and cheerful version of love. Like the mini skirt new values were creeping up on us each year.

In Vietnam the Viet Cong won their first victory in South

Vietnam and the American involvement increased. The Vietnam War was to become an increasingly important subject of future protest. April also saw us preparing for the 1963 Aldermaston March. I fostered a hope that I might see Roger marching under the Shrewsbury banner, but if I did I was not sure what I would be able to say to him. Already things had moved so far along with Terry.

This year the Committee of 100, conscious that their campaign of sit-downs and passive resistance had raised insufficient public awareness intended to challenge the Official Secrets Act by exposing some of the governments undercover operations in the event of a nuclear war. They wanted to show how the secret command posts (known as Regional Seats of Government) were incapable of dealing with the chaos that would result from a nuclear attack. Disillusioned occupant(s) of at least one RSG had leaked to the West German magazine *Der Speigel* and to the Committee of 100 the information they were now making public. Nic Walter, was the only activist who was ever identified and only then after his death*

In March 1963 based on this information, a group called Spies for Peace had broken into an underground Regional Seat of Government RSG6 at Warren Row Reading and stolen official documents, showing a network of RSG's covering the whole country as centres of military government in the event of a nuclear attack on Britain. These were located in Catterick, Cambridge, Brecon, Dover, York, Reading, Kidderminster, Edinburgh, Nottingham, Dartmouth, Preston and Armagh in Northern Ireland. The HQ (code name CHAPLIN) was

---

* See *Damned Fools in Utopia*: Nic Walters and David Goodway

in London. They were also linked to a military HQ at Aldershot.

The RSG's were camouflaged concrete bunkers with an operational staff of several hundred. They had facilities for generating electricity, pumping water and disposing of sewage, several months supply of fresh water, fuel, segregated dormitory accommodation, a 24 hour canteen and even a bar so the inhabitants could drink the world above them goodbye. The bunkers also contained the most sophisticated communications systems, dozens of tele-printers and a radio signals department for use in the highly likely event that the normal telephone system would be destroyed.

The staff included politicians, civil servants and scientific officers, under a camp commandant. There were offices for The Treasury, The Central Office of Information, the GPO, the BBC, the Board of Trade, the Ministries of Heath, Food, Supply, Transport and Power. The largest civilian dept was the scientific section dealing with bomb data and radiation risks, run almost entirely by Oxford dons. None of this information was in the public domain.

The RSG's had been activated several times for trial simulations of a nuclear attack. Exercise Parapluie which took place over weekends between April and June 62, was based on absurdly low estimates of 7 bombs dropped on England. One of these the Birmingham Bomb (estimated at 5 megaton - the Russians had already exploded a 60 megaton bomb the previous Autumn) produced radiation levels so high all military personnel in the region were ordered to go to ground for 48hours. What happened to the civilian population does not bear thinking about. The RSG communication centre degenerated into chaos – messages were transmitted up to two hours late and there was total confusion about where they had come from and where they were going. This happened during a purely imaginary exercise, which assumed nuclear destruction on an absurdly small scale.

Fallex 62, a full-scale rehearsal had followed on 15 September. Thousands of reservists received practice call-up papers and the RSG's were manned on the same day. On 17 September the hospitals were evacuated, 19 September the regional commissioner assumed full governmental powers and became the dictator of his region. On the same day imaginary evacuation of heavily populated areas began chocking all the main roads. On September 20 all the ports were evacuated. During this imaginary build up the Civil Defence Corps pretended to distribute the, as yet, unpublished Householders handbook telling people to get in 14 days supply of food and water (where from?) and to stay under cover for 7 days (then what?). Large heavily populated areas like London were called Z Zones and abandoned to their fate. The imaginary war started on September 21, which by an extraordinary coincidence was when all the preparations were complete.

Meant to test the military preparedness of NATO as well as the emergency civilian services, it proved a widespread disaster revealing the extent of the devastation as 15 megadeaths. One megadeath represents a million dead by nuclear explosion. Commenting on the exercise in *Der Speigel*, the West German Minister for the Interior said afterwards, 'under the present circumstances nobody has a chance' – and this was even with the authorities presupposing an absurdly long preparation period. Despite evidence that every hospital in the region would be destroyed and most of the major towns eliminated, the 1963 White Paper on Defence was to tell another story "In general, the plans were basically sound and practicable" it announced.

The subsequent pamphlet entitled *Danger Official Secret – RSG 6,* sent to the press and distributed discreetly on the Aldermaston march outlined all this and blew the gaff on the whole tragic farce of NATO. It proved what we already believed, that there was no defence against nuclear war. When the march reached Reading a breakaway group invaded the RSG and set up a picket. I remember a suspicious number of plain clothes men on the march that year (they were the ones with the polished boots) asking if we had 'one of those pamphlets'. The incident soon sparked a new song sung to the tune of Harry Lauder's 'I've got a lassie' – it began

*We've got a secret,*
*An unofficial secret,*
*And we'll publish it for all the world to see,*
*They've got a shelter*
*A nice official shelter*
*They call it an RSG.*

Spies for Peace got front-page coverage in the media but a government D notice prevented follow-ups. In July the Beatles produced a new song '*Listen, do you want to know a secret?*' It seemed prescient. I did see the Shrewsbury CND banner on the march. I don't recall seeing Roger.

Later in the year some of us also travelled up for an anti-Polaris Demo in Glasgow. Henry Miller, Terry and I stayed with Paul and Monica Foot and I remember Terry and Henry scouring Saucihall Street for a pub they could take me into since most seemed to be exclusively for hard drinking males. The one we ended up in had a number of expressionless young couples with pints and whiskey chasers lined up in front of them which they seemed to be silently downing with a relentlessness that was disconcerting. I was reminded of the famous Degas painting of the Absinthe drinkers. They had the same look. Glasgow was also the first and only place I saw women slumped in doorways at mid-day almost comatose with drink. The demo by comparison seemed very earnest and middle class. Am I imagining it or was there a chant that went "30,000 Scottish boilermakers say Nay to Polaris". Watching a video of the demo now is fascinating. I recognised a friend or two and there was a jazz band on the Holy Loch boat with couples skip jiving.

Aldermaston over, I decided I needed to get a job. My exams were finished and my auditions were looming for drama school. Passing a curtain shop called Swainsons in South Croydon, I saw an advertisement for a shop assistant, applied and got the job. The wages were poor £5.00 per week for a six-day week from 9–5.30 – after deductions I got £4.15s. My main duty was tea making, adding hooks to the curtains made in the back workroom, answering the phone, serving customers and labelling and sorting remnants. My father who had been encouraging me to get a job was miffed. He told me he would lose his child tax allowance now.

Apart from myself, the staff consisted of an elderly woman who did all the invoicing and typing, two women who made the curtains and a young woman who came in for occasional days work, travelling all the way from Aldershot for the privilege. I could not imagine why she would travel so far for such a dull job. I concluded she must be in love with the boss. Mr Swainson measured the curtains ordered from rich customers in deepest Surrey, and went out to hang the finished articles. Lined red velvet was the most popular choice.

I soon discovered that my boss was a member of Moral Rearmament, an evangelical anti-communist organisation previously known as the Oxford Movement, started by an American churchman Frank Buchman. The Moral Rearmament movement members had been given draft exemption during the war, much opposed by Earnest Bevan, and Buchman was said to have sympathies with Hitler. His organisation placed emphasis on recruiting the rich and powerful and was deeply conservative. Although I wore my CND badge to work I kept silent about my opinions in this hotbed of Daily Mail readers.

I was a reluctant wage slave and had a problem arriving on time. I spent far longer than I should in the back kitchen at work ostensibly making tea but actually practising my audition pieces and I dreamed of escape to full time drama school in the autumn.

I was conscious, indeed had been gently forewarned that 16 was a very young age to be applying and that drama schools usually were more interested in students who were 18 or over, but I was undeterred. The day for my audition at RADA came and went, followed by an audition at LAMDA. I was undecided how I had performed but felt I might not have done myself any favours with the pieces I had selected, as they did little to show me off to advantage.

Amazingly I was to get an almost instant feedback on the RADA audition as shortly after Patrick Fortune met one of the RADA examiners at a social event. He would by then have seen several hundred applicants. He remembered me immediately though – Ah yes the girl who did the Troilus and Cressida speech – so I was right it had stood out. He said he thought I was 'promising', perhaps a little young? LAMDA seemed to think the same. I was sent very kind letters letting me down gently and suggesting I should re-apply in a year or two. 'Go away and have a couple of abortions and come back with some heavy life experience' was how Spider interpreted it to me.

This left me with a bit of a dilemma. I wrote to Mrs Cousins asking for advice. She said the same. Get a job, get lots of experience with related evening courses or Am Drams, contact Mrs Bird the current drama teacher at Grandison for practical help and reapply next year, only this time widen your net to include schools like Guildhall, Central, Webber Douglas and Rose Bruford in Sidcup (David Rose from Croydon CND was about to go to Bruford to train).

She told me not to get demoralised, and that she thought I had potential as an actress ('and I do not say that to many people'). She also expressed a great deal of concern for me – she said I was very young to be dealing with all the problems at home (I had told her about my mum's illness) and suggested we tried to get together soon. She even said if I was short of money she could always whip up the odd pound. I was deeply touched. Her own daughter Julia was graduating that year from Central alongside Lynn Redgrave and Mrs Cousins said Central would be a good choice – perhaps better than RADA, where she had some reservations about the training.

The Aldermaston march that year had attracted much international support. Grigoris Lambrakis, a prominent Greek pacifist had marched with us at Easter. He was an MP for the United Democratic Left in Greece and had voiced strong opposition to the Vietnam War. On his return to Greece he planned to take part in the first pacifist rally from Marathon to Athens. The police banned the rally and arrested many demonstrators including the young composer of the film score of *Zorba the Greek*, Mikis Theodorakis. Using his parliamentary immunity Lambrakis marched alone carrying the peace banner he had brought to Aldermaston. The police also arrested him. On May 22nd shortly after delivering a keynote speech at an anti-war meeting in Thessaloniki, he was clubbed to death by two far right thugs while the police looked on. 500,000 people rallied at his funeral to protest against the right wing government and the monarchy.

Queen Frederica of Greece was due to make a State funded visit to Britain in July. A third cousin of the Queen and Prince Phillip, she had been an enthusiastic member of the Hitler Youth in the 1930, was known to be inherently undemocratic and notorious for her unconstitutional interventions in Greek politics and clashes with democratically elected governments. On July 11th a demonstration was called outside Claridges in London where she was staying, to protest against the continuing imprisonment of Greek communists many of whom had been resistance fighters against the Nazis during the war. Many had been kept for many years in barbaric conditions in Greek gaols. In the aftermath of the Lambrakis murder and alarmed at the growing power of the extreme right in Greece, a number of us decided to take part.

Queen Elizabeth was to collect her guests for a

reception and was booed by the crowd. Insurrection indeed! Up till then, my experience of the police on demonstrations had not been positive but I had never experienced violence at their hands. I went on the demo in open-toed sandals. Big, and never to be repeated, mistake. Finding myself with Enid Atkins in the front line of the demo after the police cut across our ranks, we linked hands with the others. A line of police bore down on us, intent on breaking our line. Seeing my naked toes a policeman brought the heel of his boot down hard on my big toe nail and ground it with his heel. The PC next to him punched Enid in the stomach with the words 'in any civilised country they would turn the gas on people like you' – a statement that might have been warmly endorsed by Frederica.

Not only was the violence a considerable shock, but the attempt to stitch up the demonstrators was even worse. One demonstrator charged with insulting words and behaviour likely to cause a breach of the peace, had his case thrown out of court when the police quoted a fictitious road junction where he was arrested.

Even worse was the attempt to fit up Donald Rooum a cartoonist for Peace News who was arrested by the notorious bent copper Harold Challenor. "You're fucking nicked my beauty. Boo the Queen would you?" said Challenor before punching Rooum on the head. At the police station Challenor added half a brick to Rooums possessions with the words "There you are, me old darling, carrying an offensive weapon – you can get two years for that."

Rooum a member of the National Council for Civil Liberties, had studied forensic science. He refused to touch the planted brick and handed his clothes to his solicitor for testing. No brick dust was found and Rooum was acquitted. Not everyone was so lucky and many were arrested on the perjured evidence of Challenor and other Police Officers from West End Central, which was earning a reputation as a centre for bent and nasty coppers. *

The following day I hobbled into Swainson's minus one toe nail and with my foot bandaged, in time to hear the secretary telling Mr Swainson how disgraceful it was that this hoard of leather coated thugs had beaten up the poor police and booed the Queen. Her source? The Daily Mail of course.

I ditched Swainsons, initially for a job on the light assembly line, testing TVs at Phillips on Purley Way, because they paid £7 10s per week, but I didn't last long. The early hours combined with a clocking on system did not sit well with the late hours I habitually kept. I do remember the supervisor showing me the cloakroom and telling me, "this is the 'in' door and this is the 'out' door and whatever you do, do not confuse the two – it's a rugby scrum in here at 4pm – someone had an arm broken". Indeed it was. I can recall women smuggling their coats up onto the factory floor and waiting for the clock to jump round to four (Factory clocks do jump as

---

* Challenor got his comeuppance in 1964 when he was charged with conspiracy to pervert the course of justice. His defense was insanity. Deemed unfit to plead he spent a short time in hospital diagnosed with paranoid schizophrenia. Three other detectives were sentenced to three years. A later parliamentary enquiry was criticized as a whitewash allowing police corruption to continue unabated in the Metropolitan Police Force. 'Doing a Challenor' entered police slang as an expression for avoiding prosecution by retiring sick from the force. It is estimated twenty six innocent people were charged by Challenor and 13 served time because of him. He was later immortalized in a number of books. Joe Orton modeled the character of Inspector Truscott on him in his play *Loot*.

Currell Brown was to observe in his surreal depiction of factory life '*Small creeps Day*') By one minute to four, one arm was in their coat sleeve. Watching the action when the siren sounded was like watching a speeded up film. The most extreme example of alienation I had ever seen.

Following Mrs Cousin's advice, I scoured *The Stage* for acting courses I could take. I noticed an evening course at the Actors Workshop, based at Dinley Studios off Baker Street, run by an American Actor called Robert O'Neill. O'Neill had been trained at the NY Dramatic Workshop of Erwin Piscator. Piscator originated epic theatre, later adopted by Brecht and he also developed mnemonic documentary theatre. His students included Marlon Brando, Walter Matthau, Tony Curtis, Harry Belafonte, Eli Wallach, Rod Steiger and Tennessee Williams. O'Neil had trained with Raiki Ben Ari at the NY workshop, a Russian born actor/ director who had founded the Habima Theatre in Moscow, a Hebrew language theatre company in the 1920s. That seemed like a pretty impressive legacy so I applied, was interviewed and offered a place for the September term. This would involve me in a two year 3 evenings a week course plus rehearsal time. Apart from fees there was the train fare to central London to find. Clearly I would need better-paid work.

In the meantime we planned a holiday in Wales with Rosemary and Pat Fortune (surprisingly not objected to by my parents). Memorable because Pat nearly killed us when the brakes on his Austin failed as we were plunging down a narrow road which led to a sheer drop over a cliff, and for Terry, usually even tempered, having a serious strop. Having sprayed me continuously with buckets of seawater when I was trying to sunbathe, I chased him and picking up an old sock from the beach swung it at him. It was heavy with sand and slapped him round the face. 'That's it' he yelled in fury, 'we are finished'. I remember thinking how silly he looked as he stomped off in high dudgeon. Needless to say the mood passed but I should have noted that Terry did not like to lose fights. We also visited Lampeter his old college. One of the ancient professors took flight when he saw two women entering the quadrangle and fled to his upstairs turret. "That's Dicky – he's frightened of women" we were told.

Come September I switched employers again as evening acting courses were incompatible with early factory shifts. My next job was with Bowyers Dairy in West Wickham checking on the order books for the 16 rounds-men. It was then I discovered how many were on the fiddle – never with the customers who had a predictable milk order but only those that ordered random additional items like a bag of potatoes or a bottle of orange juice. I was later to read a sociological article in *New Society* specifically on fiddles among milk roundsmen, so the pattern must have been widespread. While I was there, one of the rounds-men over played his hand and was sacked for thieving, but not before he had stolen my entire weeks wages too. The company were very good and even gave me some compensation. They also gave me a ham at Christmas, which I passed on to my mother and acres of silver foil remnants from the milk bottle tops, which made pretty effective decorations.

My acting course was based heavily on the theories of Stanislavsky and we were told to read his book *An actor prepares*. Lee Strasberg's tutelage of actors like Marylin Monroe Paul Newman and Jane Fonda and Marlon Brando and Steiger's training in this technique had caught the imagination of the new generation of drama students. I found the techniques fascinating. They made a lot of sense, though the preparation required for each part was a little unnerving.

The class was a mixed one containing quite experienced actors and complete newcomers. The level of commitment was exceptional and working in mixed rehearsal rooms with the noise permeating through from other floors did not hinder our concentration. There was a fair bit of star spotting as actors like James Fox regularly used the building. We were taught to critically evaluate our own performances and give feed back to others as well as evaluating professional actors to distinguish between those who always played themselves and those who internalised their character. O'Neill had a particularly high regard for Alec Guiness and a very low regard for Patrick McNee star of the TV series *The Avengers*. "He should be called Patrick McPee", he said, "because he stinks". The series also launched the career of Honor Blackman and Diana Rigg.

We were soon paired for two-handers. One of my first scenes was playing Rose in Graham Green's *The Living Room* (the play opens with a toilet flushing – it was changed by the theatre censor into the sound of a sink tap running) Unfortunately the girl I was teamed with lived in Hendon so rehearsals were expensive and involved a fair bit of travelling.

I also decided to try and get some film work and contacted Peggy O'Farrell who was happy to have an ex-Grandison girl on her books. She told me to get some new photographs sent to her for Spotlight. Since using a professional photographer was expensive, my father fixed up for me to get my pictures taken by a colleague of his who was an award-winning member of Croydon Camera Club. We arranged a couple of sessions in the autumn and the first went well.

The second session was arranged for November 22nd. However when I arrived at their flat his wife answered the door in tears. "We cannot take your photographs" she said "We are too upset. President Kennedy has just been shot". November 22nd was also the date when Stanley Kubrick was due to open *Dr Strangelove*. The premier was cancelled and the film did not open till the New Year. *That was the week that was* changed its programme to a straight dedication to Kennedy. Both in the US and in England the shock of the assassination was profound.

Not everything in November was doom and gloom, the Beatles in solid ascendancy appeared at the Royal Variety Performance where John Lennon famously asked the audience in the cheaper seats to clap along to *Twist and Shout*, "while the rest of you can just rattle your jewellery". I loved their music and was beginning to reflect this in the fashions I wore. Mini skirts, long leather boots, a black leather peaked cap, a Mary Quant style black linen mini-dress and a bright red PVC raincoat. Biba opened that year, a beautiful boutique with chocolate brown walls bringing a new look to young women and Carnaby Street brought flamboyant and throw away party clothes. We couldn't usually afford these but we raided jumble sales for old fur coats, threaded melon seeds together to make long necklaces and in the warmer months walked barefoot. Much to the regret of some of my male friends, tights were beginning to replace stockings and suspenders-much to the relief of us women who found them much more comfortable and easier to wear.

Ever since the incident with my dad I was focused on the idea of moving out and was determined to do so as soon as possible. Simon Hinkley was going out with a girl called Pauline Swindells who had a large bedsit in West Croydon. I loved going there. It had exactly the right Bohemian quality I was looking for – a large divan bed in the middle of the room, strategically near the ancient gas fire which had a pull down section for boiling a kettle, Candles in wine bottles, a large selection of LPs propped against the wall and a general air of comfortable neglect. We would call it romantic squalor now.

Pauline had a job as a secretary at the BBC, so could afford to rent this space with an adjoining large kitchen/diner, but my current wages were inadequate to support myself and rents in Croydon were not cheap. Terry and I began to hatch a plan to rent a place that might be big enough for all four of us to share. This would make it viable financially and enable me to tell my parents I was sharing a flat with Pauline – they did not need to know about the others.

The hunt for a flat was now on but we faced fierce competition. To ensure a chance of securing a coveted flat, you needed to get up early to buy *The Croydon Advertiser*, scour the 'To Let' sections and be following it up with phone calls by 8am. I was kept out of the negotiations and left it to the others who were older and had more impressive incomes. In 1962 gender sharing was verboten. Only 'married couples' could get rooms. To assist the 'temporary-marrieds', Woolworths did a flourishing trade in rolled gold wedding rings which cost 2/6d (12.5p)– the gold wore off after a bit and they went a bit green but they were fine for the short term. I purchased one in anticipation.

# 1964
# INDEPENDENCE AT LAST – AT A PRICE

Early January 1964 due to the valiant efforts of Terry and co. we secured a wonderfully capacious top floor flat in East Croydon at 8 Fairfield Road. We had two double bedrooms, a single bedroom a good size living room a basic but large kitchen that led out onto a fire escape, a bathroom and a loo. By outer London standards we had done exceptionally well.

I relished the move, not because it involved moving in with Terry particularly, but because it freed me from the oppressive atmosphere at home where family tensions had become unbearable. Sometimes with my key poised to let myself into the house at Northway Road, I would hear the sound of the vacuum cleaner and turn round and go out again. My father would be doing the vacuuming and winding himself up into a fit of righteous indignation about the filth in the house.

The family rows afforded me a prompt. I announced shortly after Christmas that I had decided to move in with Pauline Swindells in the New Year. Little was said, just a shocked silence. I remember packing and lugging two suitcases up the road early one morning (I had already arranged the transportation of my small desk). Met by one of the neighbours, she jokingly enquired whether I was leaving home. "Yes" I said. Her face was a picture. Girls of my class without the option of escape to University usually went straight from home into marriage. I was 17 and ahead of my time.

I was deliriously happy living in an argument-free environment. Terry and I had a room with twin beds. These could be pushed apart if my parents visited. Simon and Pauline were pretty laid back and I liked them both. We shared the cooking and shopping and took to using the fire exit to access the flat. This was due to discovering the woman on the middle floor had a serious drink problem, and if we came up the inside stairs she would fling the door open and insist we came in for an 'insy winsy drink' x 5. There was also a large garden at the rear.

Art modelling and working as a char was the combination that seemed to provide the largest income, and fit in with my life style – all cash in hand. I was reading *The Stage* regularly looking out for work and among the small ads was one for Domestics Unlimited. The agency offered cleaning jobs by the day for out of work actors – I could never get my head around the euphemism of 'resting'. As the agency employed actors daily rather than weekly you could take time out for auditions whenever you needed.

One of my first cleaning jobs was in Chelsea in the rather bijou home of an architect. I was told his wife was sick in bed and having given me some instructions about how to use the floor polisher on the extensive wood floors downstairs, he asked me to check on his wife regularly to see if there was anything she needed. I found his wife sitting up in bed with both her wrists bandaged and stitches visible across her throat. I quickly apprised why I was there and popped upstairs frequently to keep an eye on her, interspersed with a bit of floor polishing.

Examining his bookshelves I found a copy of Henry Miller's *Tropic of Cancer*. Only a few copies of this novel had been smuggled into England at the time and while there was no actual ban it was difficult to get hold of, so having done my 'wife checks' and the floor polishing, I would curl up and dip into Miller's Parisian erotica. Given I did the minimum of cleaning I was surprised to receive rave reviews from the architect. I can only assume most other actors were appallingly undomesticated.

The art modelling idea came about when it occurred to me how many art schools there were in London. I drew up a list. St Martins, Sir John Cass, Slade, Royal Academy, Camberwell – all these gave me regular work plus loads on the outskirts Reigate and Redhill, Guildford, Hornsey, Ravensbourne, Croydon – there were even private art classes that needed models. I canvassed them all and soon had a full diary of modelling assignments. I offered clothed poses initially – these would usually involve a 4 week portrait class so you had to keep a note of what you were wearing and make sure you turned up in the same clothes every week. I would also pose as a ballet dancer in leotard and tights but quickly learned the error of my ways when I was asked to pose with one leg bent at the knee at right angles to the lower leg. I had to hold the pose for an hour without a break. I can still remember the excruciating pain in my left knee as I tried to massage it back to life in the breaks. It is the knee I still have problems with – I swear it started then.

One of my bookers was Peter Oliver, a middle aged art teacher who ran a private art class in the heart of stockbroker Surrey. He would pick me up at a Tattenham

Corner train station and drive me the rest of the way in his sports car, pausing at a tiny cottage reminiscent of a Beatrix Potter illustration to pick up Mrs Beddells a lovely old lady in her 90s and one of the most talented artists in the class, a real Grandma Moses. Peter had done well as an artist finding fame and fortune in the States, producing ancestral portrait galleries for wealthy Texans who wanted an instant lineage for their elaborate mansions. He described the techniques he used to 'age' them and create a cracked surface on fake 'ancient' paintings.

The art class was exclusively female and possessed of serious money. Once when there was news of a puma on the loose, Peter asked one of the class members if it had attacked any of the deer in her park. 'God knows' she said 'there are so many of them'. Her next-door neighbour was Peter Sellars. Every lunchtime, these wealthy ladies took me to the pub, bought me wonderful pub lunches and a couple of shorts. In the afternoon I would have to be propped up as I slowly listed to the side in a snooze, replete with food and booze-much as I did at Roehampton with the nuns.

It was Peter who finally persuaded me to model nude. I was exceptionally reluctant as I was still very self-conscious about my boyish figure, but he was very persuasive. Given the art class was composed entirely of ladies over the age of 50, I eventually agreed. The only art school where I refused to do life modelling was Croydon, on the basis that there was a greater chance of meeting someone I knew. However the system was not entirely fool proof. One night down The Woodman this guy kept staring at me saying "I'm sure I have seen you somewhere before". Then, just before closing time he proclaimed, "Got it! I didn't recognise you with your clothes on!" Marco was mightily amused. After that I became known as 'the common or garden body exhibitionist.'

My most bizarre modelling job was at St Martins. Potential models would queue outside the school and the art teachers would come out and select which ones they wanted. I was usually lucky as there were few young models. One morning I watched two bag ladies rifling through the waste bins at Charing Cross station only to see them later join the art model queue. One of them confided in me that they were regulars – "I can lie down on a mattress all day (I don't do standin') and its warm in there". That morning they were looking for a group. I was selected to model with the bag ladies and Quentin Crisp – the original naked Civil Servant. At that time few gay men dressed as flamboyantly as Quentin so it was great fun to be arranged at his feet while he sat on a podium staring out like Boadicea with his hair in an immaculate mauve quiff. He did not deign to talk to us.

One day coming into the flat I heard a drawling American voice reading poetry on the radio. I was transfixed. "Who is that?" I asked Pauline. "Sylvia Plath" she said. Plath who had committed suicide the previous year was recorded reading her poem *Daddy*. I thought it was brilliant. The following day I was modelling at Sir John Cass Art School near the Tower of London. I used to take my sandwiches down at lunchtime, to listen to Donald Soper speaking at Tower Hill – he was better than a Music Hall artist – no heckler ever got the better of him. There was a bookshop nearby and I went and bought Plath's anthology *Ariel*. Her laconic dark poems struck a chord with me – they still do.

Simon had plans to start Croydon Film Club, which would show a season of classic films including Eisenstein's *Battleship Potemkin* and Luis Bunuel's *Viridiana*. I thought it was a great idea, but Terry was less than keen, as returning one night he found Simon had borrowed the blankets off our bed to hang up in the church hall for black out. I thought it was funny, but Terry had a limited sense of humour about such things.

The other problem was convincing my parents that I really was just living with Pauline. They said they were coming on a visit, so we spent a long time removing any vestige of male occupation – taking the after shave and razors out of the bathroom tidying away any male clothes even steaming off a label on a cake tin with Simon mother's name on it. Just before they arrived I looked through Pauline's bedroom door and saw a used condom under the bed, we removed it in the nick of time.

My father was certainly suspicious – it was a spacious flat for two girls. I think my mother wanted to believe it was just the two of us – ironically it was my old Gran who told her "I reckon they're living together". My father took to popping in late at night. One night he rang the doorbell about midnight and Simon had to pull on his jeans and answer the door – we were both asleep. Pretending he was just about to leave, my father said "Well I'll walk down the road with you then". Simon was forced to accompany him and then double back, run up the fire escape and hammer on the door for us to let him in cursing my father roundly.

Since 1963 a Limited Test Ban Treaty had been signed between the US the USSR and the UK, which prohibited nuclear tests in the atmosphere, outer space and underwater (though not underground). Much of the energies young people had brought to CND began to diversify into other campaigns, and this year there was just a one day rally in London at Easter instead of a four day Aldermaston March.

Increasingly we were involved in campaigns against the Vietnam War and Apartheid in South Africa, supported the Civil Rights movement in America and disrupted BNP rallies. We were also involved in lots of local campaigns around trade unions and local housing issues such as slum landlordism, typified by the notorious Peter Rachman who brought in thugs and savage dogs to evict tenants who could not pay his extortionate rents. The delayed launch of *Dr Strangelove* in January, was a blackly comic reminder of how easily an accidental nuclear war could still be triggered though. Robert O'Neil my acting teacher was in the cast.

A number of small left organisations were working within the Labour Party to influence policy especially as this was General Election year, and that included the International Socialists. Terry and I joined Croydon South Labour Party with Pat Fortune and others in IS but we were in a minority on crucial votes even though we had delegates to the General Management Committee from the Young Socialists from several of the wards.

The Co-operative Party were entitled to two delegates to the GMC, but rarely sent anyone, as the membership seemed to be very elderly. "Well there's nothing for it" Patrick told us, "you'll have to join the Co-op party". Terry and I dutifully, but without enthusiasm, attended our first Co-op meeting after signing up. It was worse than we feared. There were several people knitting in the meeting and a few asleep. When it got to the item where they had to elect delegates to the GMC we felt too embarrassed to put ourselves forward. We should not have worried. After a long pause someone turned to us and said 'Perhaps these young people would like to stand as delegates?' We managed to feign mock surprise and were duly voted in, which gave us the majority we needed on the GMC much to the shock of the right-wingers in the local party.

My life was full now, with acting school claiming much of my time, working and politicking claiming the remainder of my life. We attended a series of 12 weekly lectures on Marxism by Tony Cliff, aka Ygael Gluckstein at Ruskin House in Croydon. Cliff, a volatile stout little Jewish man in his 50s, had moved to the UK from Palestine in 1947. He was the founder of the Socialist Review group, which became the International Socialists. Prone to confusing metaphors, one of the worst was his definition of the contradictions of capitalism as being like 'Olive Oil stretched between two cliffs'. This turned out to be a reference to Popeye's girl friend, straddling two cliffs and being pulled in different directions by Popeye and the villain. Cliff watched a lot of daytime children's TV. His lecture series was endlessly entertaining and also energised my political awareness.

The IS group was still small enough for the National Committee to meet in the front room of Cliff's Islington terrace. Attending national meetings and conferences, I met leading members of the group, which included John Palmer, Paul Foot, Michael Kidron, Cliff's brother in law, and most memorably, Jim Higgins who had wit and wisdom beyond measure. Jim and I got on like a house on fire because he cut through the earnest and boring sectarian shit and took the piss out of it, while at the same time knowing more about the minutiae of factional politics than anyone else I knew – certainly he was one of the few who could challenge Cliff on obscure political references.

Local IS meetings were held regularly in the flat next door to Bessie's at Bramley Hill where Rose and Pat Fortune now lived. Rosemary was pregnant and I would go and help her prepare the tea for the 'comrades' – usually involving a hunt for the right number of cups. Janice their daughter was born about the same time as Alan, son of Henry Miller, not the *Tropic of Cancer* Henry Miller, but an amiable academic friend of ours with chronic halitosis, who was linked to the New Left Review Group.

Sue Miller brought her baby to the meeting one day and when I had finished serving the tea I had to take refreshments to the breastfeeding mothers in the next room. As I opened the door on three breast-feeding mothers all lined up and feeding their babies on the narrow bed, I was met with the overpowering odour of shit from a dirty nappy. Sue Miller pulling her exceptionally plain child off a huge blue veined breast turned and asked me "And when are you going to start to breed?" I backed out of the room in horror. 'Never' I thought.

Very few women at that stage played an equal part in political organisations. It was almost taken for granted that we would be the child-rearers, the makers of tea, the people who ran the crèche at Political conferences. I found some of the debates obscure in the extreme and though I purchased Cliffs book on Russia and State Capitalism I found it unbelievably dull and almost unreadable and could not understand why my male comrades could get so excited discussing which left tendency had what 'line' on some obscure point of doctrine.

To admit as much then would have been heresy indeed. I was always too intimidated to stand up and speak myself, conscious always of how little I had read and how little I knew. Acting school kept me outside the political inner circle as well and gave me an alternative point of reference. For many of my political friends, politics was their whole existence.

One weekend my dad came up to meet me at the flat to tell me Grandma had died. My mother had taken her up a cup of tea that morning before going up the road to collect Grandmas pension. When she returned she found my Gran collapsed back on the bed in the act of pulling on her stockings. It must have been instantaneous. Thrombosis was given as the cause of death. She was 84.

My parents organised the funeral. Grandma was to be buried with Granddad in Mitcham cemetery. Her coffin would be laid out in the front room the day before the burial and my mother confided she was not looking forward to sleeping in the house with her mother in a coffin in the room below. The coffin stayed open for neighbours and friends to pay their last respects. It was the first dead body I had seen and while I hovered apprehensively at the door, Mrs Lever, our old neighbour, brushed past me and leaning over the coffin, kissed the corpse. I could not bring myself to do it.

The funeral was impersonal. The minister hesitated before he made the speech about committing 'her' body to the ground-he obviously couldn't remember whom he was burying. Despite a Christian service, Grandma had not seen the inside of a church for many years. I felt detached from the whole thing. There had never been a strong bond between us. She had been a constant presence in the lives of my parents; it would be odd but probably beneficial for them now, living without her.

Under the terms of my grandmother's will, my mother was to inherit one third of the value of the house and her brothers the remaining two thirds. Both brothers were prosperous and the house at Northway Road was not worth much. They magnanimously relinquished their shares to my mother, in recognition that she had been looking after my grandma for the last 17 years. For the first time in their lives my parents were property owners and had double the living space. They made a few improvements – added a conservatory to the rear, bought a new carpet for the front room and knocked down the garage, which took up a large chunk of the garden. They were never going to have a car – my mother said my father had the wrong temperament for a driver. She was undoubtedly right.

I made good friends with some of the actors at theatre school. One of them, Verity, visited me at my flat. She arrived with her waist length hair loose and flowing down her back, a mini dress and bare feet. Her brother Nic was also at the Actors Workshop and had just got a part in Peter Shaffer's new play *The Royal Hunt of the Sun.* She was rather critical of my flat mates who she said seemed to leave a lot of the housework to me.

Terry was more than critical. He became obsessed with Pauline's indifference to the vacuum cleaner and clearly found the slightly Bohemian charm of our set up very irritating. His impatience grew, so that when our first six-month lease expired, he decided he wanted us to move on. This was tricky, as I could no longer use Pauline as the cover for our living arrangements.

We decided to tell our parents that we were engaged and had found a suitable flat – Terry had already located one near to Bramley Hill – and because these were in such short supply we had decided to snap it up before we were actually married. This must have been a blow to my mother – her daughter cheerfully admitting to 'living in sin', only just 18 and actually, in truth, with no intention of marrying either.

The flat Terry had located was in a square called The Waldrons and the house was a beautiful old four-storey Georgian mansion with a vast unkempt garden. Unfortunately there were major damp problems in the basement flat which was to be our home. The smell of damp hit you when you walked in. The back bedroom had a wardrobe against an internal wall, but leather shoes and bags left in there went mouldy in weeks. Slightly damp washing was soon flecked with spots of black mould, which could not be removed. There was a cupboard off the kitchen where the meters were sited, which was like a subterranean cave and slugs were frequent visitors to the kitchen floor.

The entrance to the flat was at the side of the house down some stone steps, which led into a large square flagged lobby; a single bedroom, a double bedroom and a separate toilet were to the left of the front door and a kitchen, bathroom, and living room to the right. There were bars on all the windows, which made me anxious about us locking ourselves out – there was no way we could get through the windows – or so I thought at the time. We were later to have a burglary – someone found they could access the flat by removing an insecure bar in the toilet window and took things from our bedroom while we were asleep in the same room. On their way out they knocked over a two-foot high cast iron doorstop in the shape of a man, which had the words 'J H Kellogg' on the base. How we slept through the toppling of Mr Kellogg onto the flags I do not know. We did wonder if this was the cornflake millionaire, but I later discovered it was his evangelical brother. The flat had charm even though it was hellishly damp, it was affordable and most importantly it was just round the corner, via a short footpath, from our friends in Bramley Hill. We moved in July.

In the flat above us was an Indian couple with a toddler and a baby. Their flat was built over a walkway through to the garden and the bedroom walls had black mould growing up them. Their doctor had advised that the baby was not to sleep in the bedroom, as it would be injurious to its health. We were lucky, the weather that summer and into the autumn was largely dry and sunny, so the flat was tolerable.

My 'living in sin' had inevitable repercussions on the home front. My mother suffered another bout of severe depression and my father blamed this entirely on me. From almost the first day that we moved into The Waldrons, he began telephoning nightly to tell me how worried my mother was about my living arrangements and demanding to know when we were going to get married. The calls turned into a barrage when she was hospitalized. I was accused of being uncaring, of being responsible for my mother's suffering, and this began to have an unnerving effect on me.

I was very young, I was not ready to get married (although I had once in a weak moment said I would marry Terry) but I was not in love with him. I was fond of him, recognised his strengths and his talents, saw him as a good friend, but I had not seen us as long-term partners. I was playing house, but I wanted my life to expand farther than being the wife of an academic and 'breeding'. I still wanted a career as an actor, and saw very clearly that this would come into conflict with Terry's aspirations, which were for a supportive academic partner and mother of his future children. I had regrets about leaving the much more flexible living arrangements I had in Fairfield Road.

In the end the pressure was too much. Neither of us had a particularly high opinion of the sanctity of marriage and had seen plenty of open marriages and relationships among the revolutionary left to know that there were plenty of different kinds of ways of living now. We figured it was only a piece of paper – we were living together anyway – if it made my mother happy we would do it.

Ironically, because I was under 21, my father had to sign a licence giving us 'permission' to marry (in Scotland you could get married from the age of 16 without parental consent, hence the popularity of Gretna Green for weddings). It seemed ironic he was granting his 'permission' when he was the one applying all the pressure to get us married. We fixed a date for September. My mother made a wedding cake and had it professionally iced. September came and saw my mother back in hospital. We cancelled the wedding. More bombarding phone calls from my father followed. We re-arranged it for 10th October 1964, hoping my mother would be fit by then.

In the meantime, the politicians were setting their own timetables. Both the Labour and Conservative Parties had changed leaders the previous year. Alec Douglas - Home (Lord Home), a tweedy aristocrat, had superseded a seriously ill Macmillan. He was a compromise candidate for the Tories. He seemed totally archaic and ineffectual and was regularly lampooned by *Private Eye* as 'Lord Gnome'. Following the death of Gaitskell the previous year, Harold Wilson had been appointed the leader of the Labour Party with George Brown his Deputy. George had a drink problem and once, famously, appeared on a news programme so drunk that the Labour Party had to issue a statement the following day. It said Mr Brown was 'tired and emotional' last night. It entered common parlance as a metaphor for drunk and incapable.

The Tories popularity had been on the wane since the Profumo scandal – I can still remember my father chortling over a cartoon of two prostitutes chatting on a street corner with one saying to the other, 'Life's better under the Tories'. Douglas-Home had deferred announcing the date of the General Election till September to try and improve the Conservative's image. He finally fixed the election date for mid October – five days after the date for our wedding.

Croydon North West had always been a safe Tory seat so the Labour Party was fairly relaxed about the Labour Candidature for this constituency. The local party with the support of some far left votes, elected John Palmer; a leading member of IS to stand. For the first time we had a revolutionary candidate standing for the Labour Party in Croydon*. A tall man, verging on the portly, (a

* The Labour Party did not repeat this mistake. When John tried to stand in the 1966 election and told the selection committee he reserved the right to defer from official policy on issues of conscience, Reg Underhill the Asst National Agent told him there were only two issues of conscience the Labour Party accepted. Drink and Religion.

result of much fine wining and dining and long evenings in the pub), John Palmer was a magnificent orator and possessor of a first class intelligence. He was the financial editor of *The Guardian* and on the National Committee of the International Socialists. He hailed from an Irish Catholic background and when inebriated would sing Irish Republican songs for hours. Marco was appointed to be his agent and they set up office in a campaign caravan opposite Croydon General Hospital. I had not known John that well before the campaign, but I helped out whenever I could, delivering posters and knocking on doors. John seemed a bit of a loner. We never saw him with a partner. Terry and I joked that we should maybe fix him up with a woman. It was a joke to come back and haunt us.

With the chopping and changing of the wedding dates my relatives had bowed out of the revised date for our wedding. My mother was still in hospital. My father insisted she wanted us to go ahead anyway. I was asked about wedding presents. I said I didn't know – I really wasn't thinking much about this wedding. Nearly all my friends bought me a casserole pot for a wedding present. We accumulated 13 – I could have opened a shop. My mother had spent the money she found in an envelope of Grandmas, marked up for my wedding present. Later, when she was out of hospital, she presented me with a hideous Lloyd loom laundry basket in lilac with a satin seat covered in purple cabbage roses that she had bought with her co-op tokens as 'grandma's present'. I declined the offering – I couldn't help it, I thought it was hideous. I would have preferred a choice – though it is doubtful I would have found anything I liked at the Co-op.

I got married in a fawn sweater dress I had bought from C & A's, a dark green leather coat and green leather shoes. Our witnesses were Henry Miller and Barry Hindess (a Sociologist friend of Terry's, also doing a PhD). Terry's parents were late as their car broke down in the middle of the High Street and Bob arrived with his hands covered in motor oil. My father brought the wedding cake in an old pudding basin with a handle. He also bought a portable tape recorder and when he pressed the wrong play back button and disrupted the ceremony he was ushered out.

The wedding was attended by dozens of friends in yellow and red rosettes who had come straight from a Labour Party motorcade. Heather Hems came, so did Walter Wolfgang and Nora Reid. I had no time to get another wedding ring so I got married in the Woolworths one. We put it in a matchbox and then couldn't find which matchbox it was in, so several boxes had to be emptied onto the registrar's desk. Terry had registered my address as 8 Fairfield Road and my occupation as a drama student. This drew a few titters from Marco. Outside we were photographed with a clenched fist salute. 'Not much sense of occasion' muttered my father.

There would have been even less sense of occasion without Sue Miller. She had been to catering college and she took me to Surrey Street market the day before to buy boiling fowls and rice to make a risotto. Without us knowing, she and Henry also went out and hired some glasses and bought a few bottles of Asti-Spumante, or we would not have had a toast to offer those who followed us back to The Waldrons. As it was, I quite liked the informality of it. The wedding cost us £2.10s. My father pissed me off big time though by thrusting a microphone under my nose and asking me if I loved Terry. Bit late I thought, I didn't hear you ask me that before you propelled me into this marriage. My father had turned out to be as conventional as hell, more concerned with what people thought than in my happiness.

In the evening Terry and I went to a political debate between John Palmer and the Liberal Candidate. John was in fine form, as he had been throughout the election campaign – to such an extent that he said he had given himself a few nightmares worrying he might win. He did not need to worry. Harris the Tory retained his seat with 46% of the vote but John had narrowed his lead with 33%.

We were in Croydon Town Hall for the count, wondering if after 13 years the Labour Party would finally pull it off and wrest power from the Tories. It was a close call – rather too close as Labour emerged the victors with a majority of only four, which would compromise their ability to implement an election pledge to nationalise the steel industry, as two far right Labour MPs Woodrow Wyatt and Desmond Donnelly were opposed to it.

The most shocking election result was in Smethwick a small foundry town near Birmingham in the West Midlands, where Peter Griffiths the Tory candidate wrested the seat from the standing Labour MP Patrick Gordon Walker. Griffiths, trading on local anxiety about the housing shortage, blamed this on immigrants. His campaign was associated with the disgraceful slogan "If you want a nigger neighbour vote Liberal or Labour". Although the Conservatives denied creating the slogan, Griffiths did not distance himself from it either, saying it was 'a manifestation of popular feeling. I would not condemn anyone who said that'.

Griffiths dismissed Gordon Walker as a middle class toff from Hampstead who did not understand the fears of ordinary working class people. Gordon-Walker had also voted against the 1962 Commonwealth Immigration Act. After the election he was taunted with cries of "Where are your niggers now Walker?" What made matters worse, was the lack of a strong support from the local Labour constituency, which had been operating a colour bar in their clubs!

The following year Malcolm X was to make a trip to Smethwick at the invitation of the Indian Workers Association to show solidarity with their cause. He visited Marshall Street where Griffiths had tried to get the council to compulsorily purchase empty houses in order to sell them to white families only, (a scheme that was scuppered by the Labour government). Malcolm X compared the treatment of black and Asian families in the Black Country to the treatment Hitler meted out to the Jews. When asked what could be done about it, he said he would not advise waiting round while the racists constructed gas ovens. He never returned to find out if they had. Nine days later on his return to the States, Malcolm X was brutally assassinated.

We decided two days after the election and a week after we had got married to throw a party at the Waldrons to celebrate the Labour victory – our flat was to become famous for its parties. At the party a drunken John Palmer began to make advances to me. I did not resist. He told me how much he was attracted to me and how much he wanted to sleep with me. He was staying the night. "What now, tonight?" I asked him. "Yes" he said. I made a bed up for John on the floor in the living room and told Terry what John had said. "Well maybe you should go next door" he said. "Are you serious?" I asked "Yes" he said. "I don't want to own you - don't get cold".

I went next door. Did Terry imagine John had passed out with the drink? Far from it. I spent a torrid night of sex with our erstwhile Labour candidate - it was the most exciting sex I had ever had - but then he was only the second man I had ever slept with. It was not so much what he did with his body, but what he whispered in my ear. He said he had lusted for me for months. He verbalised his erotic desires so effectively, he could have left me on an orgiastic high without even touching me. The man was one hell of an orator, even in bed.

I was unsure how we would cope breakfasting together, but we did and John departed telling me he must see me again and that he would write to me. So, began months of a strange double life, played out in the full knowledge of the man I had just married. I assumed that no one else would be told. I reckoned without Terry. He decided to tell Pauline Hibberd all about it. Pauline was Marco's new woman and the one he wanted to marry. Pauline was very undecided if this was what she wanted. I was hardly a good advertisement for married life either.

On the surface I was Hazel Mandrell, with a new husband who was busy filling our nest with coir carpeting, arranging books on temporary shelves made of wood planks and bricks and generally doing cosmetic things to improve our space. On evenings when it was possible, John would meet me at Wimbledon Station and take me for meals in fancy restaurants where I felt out of my depth because I did not know which knife and fork to use. Up until then, the only restaurant meals I had eaten had been at West Croydon curry houses, where egg and chips was always on the menu for the late night Irish labourers and we took it as a badge of honour if you could consume a whole Vindaloo.

Now I was with this worldly journalist eight years my senior and with considerably more affairs under his belt than I had given him credit for. Each night would start quietly and genteelly in a restaurant or pub and end in fast and furious snatched sex wherever it was possible, on the common, in churchyards, once on a suburban train between stations. I felt a passion I had never felt before, certainly not with Terry. John wrote 'when I am with you nothing – nothing seems real'. For me it had the quality of a dream too.

I disregarded the fact that he was much older, that he was no Adonis – after all he had seduced me with words and I was too enamoured to care about appearances. So I was confused and upset when he asked me if I thought there was something wrong with me because my breasts were so small – this from a man prematurely balding, with a double chin, a beer gut and a microscopically small dick. This was my first, but certainly not my last encounter with the male double standard. The fact that he thought he could make comments like that about a woman's body while being so apparently unaware of his own physical inadequacies made me wonder if men ever appraised themselves naked in full length mirrors. Sadly we had been socialised not to fight back – yet. It just filled me with dismay and added to my sense of inadequacy.

In the midst of this dual life came a call from Beverley,

Terry's sister. She was 16 and in a real panic. She had been sleeping with a local boy and was pregnant. She had already had many fights with her father who regarded her as promiscuous and she could not face her parents with the news. She asked to come and stay. The boyfriend, far from standing by her, had left the country. He had joined the Rhodesian police force, which says a lot about my sister-in-laws taste in men.

Abortion was illegal then. Many discrete enquires were made and we were told it was possible to arrange a termination for her at an exclusive Harley Street practice, but the cost would wipe out Terry's whole grant for a term. There seemed no alternative. Beverley went to London, had the termination and came back traumatised. We had this girl with engorged breasts, leaking milk and calling herself a murderer and crying all the time. After a few weeks she sought solace with Len Law who moved himself in for a time, then she started an affair with Rusty who also moved in. Bob was right – she was fast.

I was working at the time for a trade union in London, The Society of Telecommunication Engineers. Ironically it was in the same building as The Guardian, and I was always on a look out for John. I worked long hours, but someone had to bring home the gravy. As Beverley was home recuperating, she cooked for us in the evening. For some reason Terry seemed to need to goad us both. He told Beverley she was lazy because she was not working, he told me I wasn't helping Beverley enough with the housework. We were beginning to resent each other before we compared notes and realised he had been winding us both up.

Terry kept accumulating a pile of his stiff socks in the

bath and when I wanted a bath I just chucked them on the floor. Previously we had sorted out our own laundry but one day when he had no socks left he asked me when I was going to get around to washing them. "You want me to wash them?" I asked in disbelief. Pulling himself up to his full 5'4" he retorted, "You don't keep a dog and bark yourself". The fact that I was keeping both him and his bloody sister at the time did not seem to have occurred to him.

The situation with John was getting out of hand. I felt utterly trapped. Living in an overcrowded flat with Beverley and now Rusty, who I found intimidating and peculiar, I was desperate to escape a marriage I felt I had been forced into. The cruel fate that had given me my first taste of passionate love, only a week into my marriage, haunted me. I took an overdose. There were only 20 aspirins in the bottle but I hoped they would do the trick and I took them all.

Nothing happened. An hour went by. Still nothing happened. I felt I was in a scene from *Look back in Anger*, standing ironing Terry's shirts while he watched TV unconcerned. Eventually I told him I had taken twenty aspirin and he leaped up and began slapping me on the cheeks and walking me up and down 'to keep me awake'. That seemed a little pointless since I was already awake and ironing. He made me drink strong coffee but he did nothing else. It was when we went to bed that things started to happen. I experienced a continuous singing in my ears as my blood pressure rose. I sat up all night with pillows banked up behind me. In the morning I was still here. I did not know for a long time what damage if any I had done myself, but I was later told it could have triggered the hearing impairment I was later diagnosed with.

I had to confront John and express my desperation. I wanted him to resolve it, to tell me he would rescue me from my unfortunate marriage. In the course of the conversation I told him I had felt so desperate I had taken an overdose. He went white. "Christ", he said, "You have just taken years of my life". Without another word he frogmarched me to the bus stop, piled me on the bus and told me our affair was over.

I was more desolate than I had ever been in my life. Terry was not home that night, but I assumed the other two were in the flat. I went to bed and muffled my desperate sobbing. I did not know how I could go on. In the morning I found that Beverley and Rusty were not there either. I wish I had known – I would have rent the place apart with howls of remorse. The man I thought loved me so much had turned out to be a moral coward.

Beverley was getting serious about Rusty now and settling herself into the left scene in Croydon. Despite having a large wardrobe of clothes she would borrow mine surreptitiously. I could not stand Rusty. He had a way of looking at me that made me want to squirm. I heard he had bouts of mental illness and had been unable to take his Finals and been allocated a 3rd. One day I came back and he was asleep drunk on our sofa. He woke up when he heard me and told me to go out and get him some more Guinness. "No" I said. He followed me into the kitchen, grabbed a knife and chased me round the flat. Luckily he passed out on the sofa still clutching the knife. I told Terry they had to go.

Beverley now joined me working as an art model in

London. She and Rusty were looking for a home. She started to accumulate saucepans, china and glasses, but she always used mine in the flat. Why burn your own saucepan when you can burn someone else's? Eventually they found a Victorian terrace to rent in South Croydon. It was a great relief when they moved.

# 1965
# MORE BIG CHANGES: THE BOOMERS BEGIN TO SETTLE DOWN

"Death of a ruling class tug" shouted the *Keep Left*[*] seller outside Ruskin House. It was late January 1965 and Winston Churchill was dead – remembered less on the far left as a war time hero than as the man who, as Home Secretary, brought out the troops against the miners in Tonypandy in 1910. The great and the good all gathered for his funeral on 30th January.

Ian Craib[†] moved in with us when Beverley and Rusty finally moved out. Ian and I got on well. He was introspective and prone to bad depressions but he was also funny and empathetic. We were both active in the Young Socialists and the IS group and Ian was editing a youth paper called ISKRA (The Spark). Terry was teaching part time at Balham and Tooting Technical College now, to supplement his grant. I was still modelling and attending

---

* *Keep Left* was the youth paper of the Socialist Labour League. IS was locked in sectarian disagreement with the SLL, led by Gerry Healey a brutish bully of a man. Much later, accused of improprieties with young female comrades, Jim Higgins wrote that while he could believe Healey (who he thought had a close resemblance to the Mekon in Dan Dare) was capable of grievous bodily harm, grievous bodily charm seemed unlikely. See Brian Behan's chapter *'Nationalization'* from *With Breast Expanded* for a hilarious description of the SLL.

† Ian was to become Professor of Sociology at University of Essex. Before his premature death in 2002 he gained an international reputation for his theoretical links between sociology and psychoanalysis

acting school. Tennessee Williams featured heavily in our performance pieces. We must have performed his entire repertoire. I also remember an outstanding performance of *A taste of Honey*.

Over in the States, Lyndon Johnson was sworn in for a full term as President, and vastly escalated the war in Vietnam, drafting a disproportionate number of young black Americans into the war machine and sending them to fight alongside white GIs who, as Martin Luther King was to point out, they would not have been allowed to sit with in the same school rooms back home. In April Australia, under Menzies, also sent troops to Vietnam, including many of aboriginal descent. Wilson was under pressure from America to send troops, but aware of potential rebellion in his own party, conducted a balancing act while providing back stage support in resources and training.

The civil rights marchers made repeated attempts to march from Selma to Montgomery, but were met with violence and a church minister was murdered. Eventually they succeeded at the end of March. By August LBJ had passed a Voting Act that removed qualifications, which had debarred black people from voting, but within days there was rioting in Watts over police harassment, which ended with more deaths. Loraine Hansbury the promising young Afro-American playwright of '*A raisin in the sun*' died suddenly from a brain haemorrhage. She had been writing a new play entitled '*Young Gifted and Black*'. Nina Simone dismayed at the death of her friend and mentor took the title of the play and turned it into a song-it was to become the anthem of the Civil Rights Movement.

Much of our protests that year revolved around

opposition to the Vietnam War and race issues-it was the year Rhodesia under Ian Smith declared UDI (Unilateral Declaration of Independence), setting up white minority rule of 220,000 white Rhodesians over 4 million Africans. There were demonstrations against the South African all white cricket team outside Lords (they had de-barred D'Olivera the most talented coloured cricketer) and regular demonstrations outside Rhodesia House. Vanessa Redgrave had organised an effective boycott of Equity members against theatre tours to South Africa, The Rolling Stones had cancelled a tour, Marlon Brando had called for a similar film boycott, and there was a campaign to have them removed from the Olympics and other major sporting events. We individually boycotted Cape fruit and wine and were to do so for many years.

It was also the year when Wilson issued an Immigration White Paper. The Smethwick election results had indicated to the Labour Government that the immigration issue was a potential vote loser, so they reversed their total opposition to the Commonwealth Immigration Act. They reduced the number of entry vouchers dramatically, with only 15% going to Commonwealth countries, which meant that white immigrants from countries like Australia and New Zealand had a disproportionate allocation against immigrants from India and Pakistan.

The White Paper clearly had a racial element to it and it created a rift, which saw many of the revolutionary left reappraising their membership of the Labour Party. This was hardly mitigated by the passing of a Race Relations Act later in the year, especially when Wilson looked as if he was backsliding on a pre-election pledge to ban arms sales to Rhodesia. We had not forgotten that British-made Black Saracen tanks had been used in the Sharpeville massacre in 1960. It looked as is the government would still honour existing arms deals.

CND organised some fundraising concerts this year, one at the Fairfield Halls – a huge concert Hall and theatre complex, which had opened in Croydon in 1962. On the cast were Donovan and Julie Felix. Beverley had a big hand in the organisation. Later that year we were to hear Dizzy Gillespie and Duke Ellington at the same venue. George Melly also appeared in a London CND fundraiser his only fee a bottle of whiskey before the performance. As part of his act he included a performance poem from Alfred Jarry's *Ubu Roi*, which included the following lines, which he exhorted the audience to repeat

*Look, look, the wheel turning*
*Look, look the bourgeoisie trembling*
*Hola! Holes in the arse!*
*Long live old Ubu!*

I was enlarging my education by attending IS summer camps which were held in Chigwell North London. More used to catering for Boy Scout troops, the accommodation was arranged in fairly Spartan single sex bunk bed dormitories and a warden patrolled at night. Knowing this, the comrades sensibly divided themselves. Those with children and families tended to go to one dormitory, couples to another, the third reserved for those live wires and single blokes likely to party the night away, as this would be the dormitory the warden would raid due to the noise level.

Terry could be annoyingly abstruse on occasions and would not take my advice about where we slept. He parked us on a bunk bed in the noisy dorm where, at the height of the nighttime celebrations, the warden paid a visit. He demanded to know who was our leader, which produced a chorus of "we have no leader", then, spotting me, he insisted I had to move.

We protested and Bill Thompson enquired querulously what kind of pervert he was, preventing a man sleeping with his own wife. That cut no ice with the warden, and I had to bundle my stuff together and move. I was furious with Terry. This was the second time he had embarrassed me this way, the first being when he had insisted we used the Gillman's double bedroom at the West Wickham house when they were absent, only for them to burst in on us late at night. The following day Tony Cliff intercepted us at breakfast. "My, I have heard of some disgusting thing in my time", he said, "but for a man to sleep with his own vife – that really is disgusting"

During the year, while Pauline was making up her mind whether to marry Marco, he took a PGCE at a Maidstone college with another friend Peter (Tubs) Read, a tall rotund rugby player – hence the nickname. They shared a bungalow in Maidstone and the local Labour Party was invited to use the place for committee meetings. Facing the front door at the end of the hallway was the toilet. Marco, lacking any inhibitions, rarely closed the toilet door. The committee members rang the front door one day and on being told to come in as it was not locked, were confronted with Marco sitting on the john with his trousers round his ankles. "Welcome comrades" he cheerfully announced "I will be with you in a moment" After that they used the kitchen door at the back.

Despite her reservations, Pauline decided to take the risk, and sometime in the early spring, she and Marco were married. Pauline had prosperous parents living in the leafy suburbs outside Croydon and they had a conventional formal reception with a marquee in the grounds of her parent's house. Some of her more traditional relatives looked somewhat discomposed by the speech of Tubs Read the best man, as he hinted darkly at Marcos disgusting personal habits. He did not outline what they were. Just as well.

Pauline was an immensely striking girl, with a wonderful bone structure, a willowy frame and a laconic manner. She sucked her thumb and wound her hair round her fingers when she was lost in thought, and much of her thinking seemed to concentrate on the state of her health. She was a walking study in hypochondria. I have often wondered if she had a premonition, because her life was to be tragically cut short a few years later, but not due to illness. Underneath this child/woman persona, beat a fierce intelligence and she was to excel at the London School of Economics.

Marco got a job as a lecturer in Sociology at NW London Polytechnic. He was assisted by a technical error. He had partied hard while he was an undergraduate and obtained the standard 2:2 'party' degree, which usually precluded graduates from grant aided research. When he received his degree certificate he found a typing error had awarded him a 2:1. Naturally he chose not to reveal the mistake. He also became a Sociology examiner for the Associated Examining Board. The job enabled him to get a mortgage on a miniscule one-bedroom house in West Croydon, opposite the curry house and next door to the delivery yard for Sainsbury's first ever supermarket. Pauline used to phone me regularly to ask how to cook cabbage and similar things. She was an even more inexperienced cook than I was.

Having talked to Diane Williams who had been at Goldsmiths College, I found out it was possible for me to obtain a teaching diploma in drama with only 5 'O'levels as the entry requirement. This would be useful if I wanted to teach – I could not face a course in shorthand and typing which was the other 'fall back' job people were always suggesting. This meant I needed another 'O' level. "What is the easiest 'O' level to take?" I asked Kate Read, Tubs wife, who was an FE lecturer. "British Constitution" she said. No local centre ran such a course, so I signed up for a correspondence course with Wolsey Hall and began to submit weekly essays on a subject I found dry as a bone.

In October my mother organised a first anniversary party for us to compensate for the fact she had not been at the wedding. It should have been called a survivors party given the number of personal traumas we had all worked through that year. Thankfully she knew nothing of mine. The same month Beverley discovered she was pregnant again. She and Rusty began to plan a wedding in the hope they could conceal the pregnancy from her parents till after they were married and then pass the baby off as premature.

Around that time Terry and I attended the Young Socialists conference in Malvern. Two weeks later I missed a period and it was soon confirmed I was pregnant too. It was probably the only thing that was conceived at that conference. It looked as if applying to Goldsmiths would have to be deferred for a few years. We told Bob and Honor. "Well you'll be the first", said Bob. 'Little do you know', I thought. We told my parents at a New Year party they were invited to by Tubs Read.

The hunt was on for a new home now, as there was

no way I wanted a new baby to live in this excessively damp environment. We had made the flat look quite presentable, removing a rotting cupboard in the bedroom and supplying our own bed when the one the landlady supplied collapsed under us, but all our laundry was speckled with black mould and our leather shoes were green with mould. It was a great party flat but it was pretty rubbish to live in, although the location was perfect and ensured a regular stream of visitors. We decided to take the landlady to the rent tribunal and made it a joint case with the Indian family above, in the hope we could get them re-housed by publicising their plight to the local councillors. In this we were aided by the new 1965 Rent Act, which appointed independent rent Officers to set a fair rent.

However before the visit by the Rent officer, we removed the new carpet we had bought and other cosmetic touches, which had made the flat look considerably better, and reduced it back to its original condition. The day of the visit both Terry and I were in bed. I had a suspected miscarriage and Terry had some peculiar condition called crystals on the balls. Rusty and Beverley showed the delegation around with our landlady. She must have thought it was all deliberately stage-managed. The delegation, which included the rent officer and two local councillors were impressed with the evidence of damp we showed them and I heard mutterings of 'disgraceful'. They reduced our rent by one third and also that of our neighbours. The rent was fixed, and the landlady could not increase it until there was evidence of substantial improvements.

My affair with John Palmer had finished quite a few months prior to this, and we had not as yet publicly announced I was pregnant, but Marco deliberately slipped it into the conversation when Palmer was down The Woodman one night. I saw the look of momentary panic cross his face before he did the maths and realised he was not implicated. All around us babies were being born or on the way. Rosemary had Janice. The Gillman's had Seth (I wondered if they would call the second one Rueben). Jack Kearney was shortly to father twins and 10 months later a second set, though only one survived. How they coped with 3 babies under the age of one in a tiny cramped flat beggars belief. It was festooned with nappies.

At a pre-Christmas party Terry heard that a family called the Boxes wanted to rent out their house in Thornton Heath while they spent a year in America. We visited. There was a rowing boat hanging from a beam in the front room, the kitchen was minimal and apart from a front bedroom upstairs, there was a bedsitting room and small kitchen, which could be sublet. There was a decent size garden. They offered to remove the boat and repaint the living room. Terry was keen to take it. I was not. I had enjoyed a full social life while we were living in South Croydon. Thornton Heath was a long bus ride away and none of our friends lived nearby. After the baby was born in August I would be very isolated. But Terry got his way. At the beginning of 1966 we moved to 63 Warwick Road.

# 1966
# I BECOME A MOTHER

We moved in January – the same month as the Palomares accident when a US B52 bomber refuelling mid air over the coast of Spain collided with the tanker, releasing four hydrogen bombs. One fell into the Mediterranean Sea and was recovered intact nearly three months later. Of the remaining three, two detonated on impact, with a non-nuclear explosive, which nonetheless contaminated an area of one square mile with plutonium.

The US government flew much of the contaminated soil back for burial in South Carolina, but 40 years later there were still traces of contamination in the soil of Palomares. The US agreed not to fly over Spain in future with nuclear loaded weapons, but it once again illustrated the dangers of nuclear weapons and the chance of lethal accidents. As someone now incubating a new life, I was in a state of heightened awareness of all the hazards that could affect my unborn baby.

We had moved into a space that needed considerable renovation. The owners had neglected it for years. The windows were so rotten it was hazardous to open them – dotted with pigeon shit they were on the point of falling apart. Flocks of pigeons would collect under the eaves of our bedroom window cooing us awake every morning and driving Terry to murderous thoughts.

He even borrowed an air rifle from Spider to try and despatch them.

The bedroom curtains in the back bedroom, which we hoped to rent out, stank of soot and disintegrated when I tried to wash them, so I needed to make new ones. We pushed an ancient piano out of the back bedroom meaning to take it apart and take it downstairs but the weight of it defeated us. Most serious was the woodworm. The whole house was riddled with it. Piles of dust were evident around each doorframe. We told the agent, who conveyed the problem to the Boxes. They did nothing, but agreed the build up of dust was a nuisance. Given this was their family home, I was amazed at their negligence.

The ever-fastidious Terry took one look inside the oven and decided the cooker was impossible to use – it was filthy. He confined it to the cellar and we got our first household purchase – a New World Gas cooker on HP. Mrs Bedells had presented me with a New World gas cookery book when I got married, and when my pregnancy became noticeable, and I got self conscious about modelling, I gave up work and had time to experiment more with cooking, although the kitchen was so tiny it was difficult to do anything much. – Terry made a spice rack for the kitchen to cope with all the new condiments we were beginning to cook with and we blocked off the side door to give us room for one small working surface. I also doggedly continued with the correspondence course for the 'O' level I was due to take in June, and attended Mothercraft classes which got me into a panic about all the things I needed for the new baby.

Anxious that Terry should finally complete his PhD

before the baby put in an appearance, I tried to chivvy him into completing his research. He had been engaged on this research for 6 years now and seemed to have lost all interest. Friends who had read the draft said that he started off as a liberal and ended as a revolutionary, so there were clearly inconsistencies of style. I even went up to the Institute of Historical Research myself to look at some of the early minutes of the London Corresponding Society in order to try and help with some of the research. Easily side-tracked I found myself reading instead accounts of 'fallen women' who had become a charge on one of the London parishes. In an advanced stage of pregnancy they were frequently bundled onto barges and rowed across the Thames where they could be dumped as a charge on another parish before their child was born. They were then frequently sent back on the same barges by the other parish, also trying to minimise its Poor Law expenses. There were accounts of some of these unfortunate women giving birth mid river.

Terry finally did submit his dissertation and was told to revise some sections and submit more statistical data in order to re-submit for a PhD. As the bulk of the work had already been done and at most they were asking for a couple of months additional revision, I was astounded that after all this time he was prepared to abandon all that research and just accept an M.Litt, especially since an Oxbridge M.Litt was worthless as it could be purchased by any Oxford or Cambridge student with a bachelor degree without further study for an administrative fee of £10. (This peculiar and archaic symbol of privilege would go unchallenged for many years.) But he was adamant and that was the end of the matter. Later

I was to reflect that he was not an innovator, someone who pushed the boat out or accepted challenges, but someone who found a comfortable academic sinecure and then did not step out of his comfort zone. He was academically lazy.

In February Harold Wilson announced a General Election in March, as his tiny majority was proving unworkable. This time he got a clear majority of 96. He announced that decimalisation of the currency would come into force in February 1971. My father said it was a con trick to put up prices, as the old sixpence would become two and a half (p).

We had now a rented TV and therefore were able to enjoy what, in hindsight, were the golden years of television. With a baby on the way, and several miles from most of our friends, I was now spending more time at home. TW3 had ended and so had its successor *Not so much a programme (more a way of life)*, which, although it did not have the same impact as TW3, introduced Eleanor Bron, John Fortune and John Bird to television audiences. 1966 brought *The Frost Reports* written by Graham Chapman and Marty Feldman, which introduced John Cleese and the rest of what would become the Monty Python team, along with Ronnie Barker and Corbett. The reports covered a wide range of subjects, authority, elections, money. One of the funniest was the report on the British Class System, with a classic sketch between the two Ronnie's and John Cleese.

In addition to satire, *Late Night Line up*, a ground-breaking discussion programme, brought Joan Bakewell to prominence as a broadcaster. It was deliberately scheduled as the last programme of the evening before close down to give the participants the opportunity to explore topics at length – they often ran over. In January of that year Ivor Cutler, Joseph Losey and Harold Pinter were among the guests. Losey's film *The Servant*, an intense psychological drama, had a huge impact on me. During the early part of the year we saw an incredible range of new film releases which included *The Battle of Algiers, Alfie, Cul de Sac, Morgan – a suitable case for treatment, A man for all seasons* and '*Who's afraid of Virginia Wolf*' in which Elizabeth Taylor and Richard Burton tore each other apart – very reminiscent of my parents.

But most significant of all, was the Wednesday Play. So significant, that none of the people I knew went out on a Wednesday night so we would not miss it. The Wednesday plays ran for six years from 1964 to 1970. Sidney Newman, the BBC Head of Drama, wanted plays with what he called 'agitational contemporareity'. *The War Game* (withdrawn by the BBC under pressure from the government in 1965) was one of these. Dennis Potter, Jim Allen, David Halliwell, Nell Dunn and Jeremy Sandford, were among the welter of playwrights who had their careers launched by the Wednesday play. Dunn and Sandford's play, *Cathy Come Home* was to have a seminal influence. Produced by Tony Garnett and directed by Ken Loach, it was a play about homelessness and was voted the best single television drama by a Radio Times readers poll in 1998, over thirty years after it was produced. It led to a public outrage at the state of housing in Britain where children could be put into care because there was not enough cheap housing available for their families.

Plays like *The Lump* and *The Big Flame* were to follow which championed working class struggles to unionise and improve conditions in exploitative industries like building and the docks. *The Big Flame* was criticised by Mary Whitehouse as 'a blue print for the communist takeover of the docks'.

Concern about how these dramas could influence the public came from many quarters and in many ways reflected the cultural shift between the 1950's and the rapid social and political changes of the 1960s. From the trial under the 1959 Obscene Publications Act of the unexpurgated version of D H Lawrence's *Lady Chatterley' s Lover* in 1960, in which the judge Mervyn Griffiths Jones famously asked the jury to consider "if this was a book you would wish your servants to read", the old order was being challenged as utterly out of step with the times. As Bob Dylan sang, times were most definitely changing.

One of the most vociferous opponents of change, and of the BBC under Sir Hugh Green in particular, was Mary Whitehouse who founded the *National Viewers and Listeners Association* in 1965, which led to the revivalist *Festivals of Light* backed by Lord Longford, the journalist Malcolm Muggeridge and Cliff Richards. Whitehouse described Green as 'the devil incarnate' presiding over 'the propaganda of disbelief, dissent and dirt, promiscuity infidelity and drinking'.

She also campaigned against *Till Death us do part,* the very successful 10-year series created by Johnny Speight, which started in 1965, in which bigots like Mrs Whitehouse were parodied through the loudmouthed ignorant central character, Alf Garnett.

Mrs Whitehouse also campaigned against the *Little Red School Book*, a manual of children's rights, and *Oz* the alternative underground magazine published in the UK and Australia, which championed gay rights and campaigned against police stitch ups. An indication of what she approved of, is the award made by the NVLA to Jimmy Saville for 'wholesome family entertainment' with *Jim will fix it*.

One way or another, it felt like this was our time, but pregnant and living in a rotting suburban villa in Thornton Heath hardly gave me an opportunity to keep at the pulse of things. The Vietnam war was escalating and drawing the approbation of many, Bob Dylan, Joan Baez, Jane Fonda, John Lennon and Yoko Ono, were vociferous in their opposition, as were the Berkeley students who organised the first mass demonstration of 10,000 people through the streets of Oakland California at the end of the year.

Mohamed Ali stated he would 'not go 10,000 miles to help murder, kill and burn other people simply to help the domination of white slave-masters over other people'. Later in the year Bobby Seale and Huey Newton formed the Black Panther movement, for the self-defence of the black community and on a programme of revolutionary socialism. Despite the support of leading female academics like Angela Davis, a clear vein of sexism dominated the movement. Once asked what the role of women was in the Black Panthers, Huey Newton famously answered 'horizontal'.

On the home front we were engaged in a programme of painting and preparation. I scoured fire salvage sales for towelling nappies and made sheets and blankets for the baby's cot, my mother produced knitted shawls and cardigans and bought me a crib, I found a second hand coach built Silver Cross pram and was proud that my total outlay for the baby came to only £20.

I found I was living in the same road as a former

drama teacher at Grandison who had a toddler. It was odd to think my child would only be a year younger than hers. I also met an old Grandison girl on the bus called Linda Fitt, who when she heard I was married and pregnant decided she would make a call. She did and flirted hard with Terry, offering to massage his shoulders and back. She was later to regret this, as having stayed the night, he made a pass at her and she fled in the morning like a startled rabbit and I never saw her again. I figured this was a quid pro quo on Terry's part for my affair with John.

In June I had to travel to a secondary school to take my British Constitution 'O' Level. The invigilator, an elderly male teacher, kept frowning at me throughout the exam. By then I was in full bloom and had difficulty sitting comfortably at the school desk. When he came to collect in the papers he asked me somewhat aggressively if I was a pupil at the school. He looked mightily relieved when I said I was an external candidate.

Following this, my mother hired a caravan in Brighton and took me down there for a week of sea air and sunshine, figuring I would have little opportunity for a holiday when the baby arrived. I had not spent time with my mother on her own as an adult, and, about to become a mother myself, I realised how re-assuring it was to have her around. We had a new bond now. What I did not know, was that she had taken to going into churches to pray fervently that I had a healthy baby. It was the one and only time I knew my mother to resort to prayer.

Beverley had married in the spring, and had to come clean about the impending birth to her parents. Justin was born on July 5th 1966 and became Honor and Bob's first grandchild. During her labour Beverley, who had the baby in Mayday Hospital, heard one of the (male) doctors saying "this girl's not breathing properly" to which she rejoined "If you can do any better, you can get up here and do it yourself" – I always admired her feistiness.

It was a month and a half later that I got the tell tale signs that my baby was on the way. An ambulance whisked me off at midnight to Purley Maternity Hospital, minus Terry who opted to stay at home; as he wasn't sure how late the buses ran back. He clearly had no intention of staying to support me. I can't say that I minded that much. Most hospitals did not allow fathers into the Labour room anyway and most women felt they would get in the way. The new man had not arrived yet, or so far even galloped over the horizon.

I had thought little about the birth and had only a hazy idea what was to happen to me. The elderly Sister who admitted me, while proving to be extremely competent as a midwife, needed an empathy transplant. The first thing she said to me was "I hope you are not going to make a lot of noise like some of these girls – we have builders in the building and what will they think?' 'Maybe that they are in a Labour ward?' I thought. I was deposited onto a none too comfortable trolley with a thin rubber mattress, my pubes were shaved and I was left alone with a buzzer to press if I needed anything. Every so often I would press the buzzer, just to have sight of another human being and wished I had stayed at home longer in a comfortable bed, (though our bed at home was not that comfortable as Terry had hauled the mattress onto the floor as he said the bed gave him a back ache).

The pains eventually reached a level at which they

decided to give me a Pethidine injection. The staff kept asking me if I felt like pushing. I had been told that women have an overpowering urge to push when the third stage of their labour arrives, but I had no urge to push. Like a generation of women before and after me, I do however remember saying at one point "I've changed my mind" to which the Sister replied, "Yes, you girls don't mind getting yourself into this condition do you? But you don't like the consequences!" She was a right vindictive old cow.

Her third intervention was a classic. Midway through an extremely powerful contraction she decided was a perfect time to fill out my admission form and ask me lots of questions. As she raced through the name, address and next of kin section she reached religion. "Oh none, none", I yelled. "Good God girl", she countered, "Don't you wonder who created the sun, the moon and the stars". Not at the moment I thought, and he must be a fucking sadist if he does exist – putting women through this and then taunting them with this catholic bigot.

Eventually because I was fed up with them asking I said 'Yes, I felt like pushing'. The third stage of labour seemed to last forever – like shitting a cannonball – and I pleaded several times for an episiotomy to speed the birth. The Sister would have none of this and kept applying steaming hot compresses to my skin to make it stretch. I was to be grateful for this later when I saw the discomfort of those women who had stitches. Finally at 10am my baby was delivered. "Look" they said as they held up this tiny creature newly expelled into the world – what a shock – a mini me with a penis! He weighed in at 6lbs 6ozs.

Opening my suitcase to get a new nightdress for me the Sister had one last parting shot. On top of my luggage was a copy of the International Socialism Review and Brendan Behan's *Borstal Boy*. "And that man was no credit to his country" she pronounced.

Within an hour Terry had arrived. I always remember his look when he walked into the delivery room. It was pure love. The baby looked like a little bird. Huge eyes, long eyelashes, a prominent forehead and a little nose dotted with yellow pressure spots, which I was told would soon fade. I could not stop looking at him. I was amazed at the miracle of his existence. I had been sure I was having a girl and had only one name for a boy – Alex. Terry vetoed this, on the grounds that he had been to school with a boy called Alex who wore a hair clip and he didn't want his son called this. We had recently seen Dominic Behan perform in a folk club – what about Dominic I said? And so it was. Dominic Karl entered the world on 19th August 1966. The miserable git of a sister approved. "A saint's name" she said. We did not bother to tell her he was also named after Karl Marx.

Terry departed to give my mother the news and bring her to visit. I was removed to the ward minus the baby. Hospital born babies in the 1960's were kept in a nursery and only delivered to our bedsides at four hourly intervals to be fed. It was a heat wave that day and I had had nothing to drink since 10pm the previous night. I asked for some water and was ignored. I asked several times. It was only when my visitors arrived, that I finally got a jug of water.

My mother was over the moon about her new grandson and greatly relieved it had all gone well. Terry told me it had taken nearly an hour to get her up the road to the bus stop, as she had to stop everyone she met and tell them about the baby. I felt close to my mother in a very special way now, and knew instinctively she would nurture my little son as much as I did.

Right from day one (we were not 'released' for 10 days, or until the baby's cord had dropped off) the hospital felt like prison. Patients were allocated 3 nappies a day – if your baby needed changing more often – tough. (We soon learned to do raids on the laundry cupboard for spares). Small babies who needed feeding more frequently than four hourly were often heard screaming in the nursery before feeds – mine was one of the loudest. We were not allowed to visit them.

If the baby woke and cried before the official feeding time it was ignored on the grounds that the baby would be 'spoiled' by demand feeding. It was poppycock and disadvantaged small babies like mine. We could only pick up our babies to feed them at 6am 10am 2pm 6pm and 10pm and they were then removed for the night. The concept of picking a baby up just to cuddle them was alien to the regime. We had to change them in their cribs – we were not allowed to put them on the beds for risk of soiling the bed linen. No help at all was offered to establish breast-feeding and each feed time a bottle was plonked on the table at the bottom of the bed and we were told to bottle-feed if we had problems breast-feeding.

My baby who had been left to cry for an hour would be brought into me exhausted and fast asleep at the official feed time. 'Tickle his toes to wake him up" I was advised. He would wake with a start, latch on frantically to my engorged nipple, take a few desperate sucks and then vomit it up – his stomach was full of air. At which point I would be advised that maybe my milk did not agree with him. I persevered, determined to breast-feed but in increasing pain, my breasts rock hard from unexpressed milk.

I brought him home after the 10 days in Bob's car. Honor and Sheran, Terry's younger sister, were at the house, which smelled of furniture polish and was as clean as a new pin. They had brought presents for the baby from themselves and from Terry's grandparents. I was very touched. The first night at home I was exceptionally nervous and did not sleep a wink overwhelmed by a sense of responsibility for this new little life. The baby did not adjust well. He cried a lot and worse still, I developed cracked nipples, a by-product of lack of care and support from the hospital in setting up breast-feeding properly. Eventually after three months it was so painful, I gave in and put my son on the bottle. I was never to forget my utterly miserable experience of a hospital birth and resolved that, if possible, any future births would be at home.

After the first few months of sleep deprivation when my whole life seemed to resolve around feeds and washing dirty nappies, I was sunk into the deepest gloom. I felt as if my previous life had ended forever and that I had died and gone to hell. I dragged myself miserably through each day tense and unhappy. Once Dominic finally got the hang of sleeping through from midnight to 6am, I began to regain my optimism and enthusiasm for being a mother. I started visiting the local mother and baby clinic and that is where I contracted chicken pox. Despite being exposed to this numerous times during my childhood I had never caught it. The consequence was that when I did get it as an adult I was seriously ill. Dominic also caught it but very mildly. My mother was wonderful. Visiting daily she nursed us both back to health, but I did not escape a facial scar or two.

During those first few months, I became reclusive and lost an interest in the outside world. Terry was working full time now, but without the benefit of a permanent contract at Balham and Tooting Technical College, and I was on my own for much of the day, apart from pushing the pram to the shops. The local Sainsbury's had a series of counters and you had to queue separately at each one for different goods. Butter came in large blocks and you indicated how much you wanted cut off and it was patted into shape and packed in greaseproof paper, same for cheese. Sugar was packed into blue bags with a scoop. You had to go to a kiosk with your bill to pay.

Supermarkets were a totally new innovation – the first Sainsbury's supermarket had just opened in West Croydon but not in our neck of the woods. Where I lived spices and herbs were difficult to acquire and convenience foods were non-existent. Milk was delivered – after my experience with the rounds-men at Bowyers, I always knew to a penny how much my bill was. Pregnant and nursing mothers were entitled to a free pint a day and we had vouchers for the milkman. My shopping bill was usually about £4 a week. Turkish towelling nappies were boiled in a gas boiler, rinsed and wrung out by hand and on rainy days hung on airers all over the house-we eventually got a Flatley dryer. I had no washing machine and those that did exist – the twin tubs – were so labour intensive they were hardly worth the effort. I bundled our washing up in pillowcases and took it to the launderette.

I had passed my 'O' level, but had no time to open a book or think beyond the next meal or the next pile of washing. Sometime in the autumn term, Terry saw a job advertised for a lecturer in Economic History at Birmingham Polytechnic, applied and was offered the job to start the following term. The Principal of Balham and Tooting Tech concerned at the slippage of part time staff had instituted a rule that all job references had to go through him. It was rumoured his references were so barbed, part-timers often found their job prospects affected. Terry had got round this by getting a reference from the Head of his Department. He was overseeing an A level group and intended to stay till their examinations in June 1967 and transfer to Birmingham in the autumn, which would give us time to organise a move. He planned to keep quiet about the job and just give the standard months notice before the end of the summer term.

I was unhappy because I did not want to go to Birmingham and had not been given a choice. I had no income apart from what Terry brought in so wherever he went I had to go too. I wanted to continue to live close to my mother – she provided me with the only reliable respite from my son and I did not want to lose her support and her company. I still wanted to go to Goldsmiths. Terry started making enquiries about house mortgages. He thought he could afford it. We would be rich – he was going to earn £1,000 per year.

If at times I felt desperate and trapped by my situation, married reluctantly at 18 financially dependent on my husband and a mother by the age of 20, what happened on 21st October that year put everything into perspective. Watching the news on TV we heard of a catastrophic disaster. A coal tip above the little welsh town of Aberfan had slid down a mountain and engulfed a farm, several houses and a school. It took just five minutes to take the lives of 116 primary school children and 28 adults. We watched in stunned disbelief. I suddenly felt a terrible anguish for what those parents were going through. I realised how utterly precious my little son was to me and how I would feel if his life was brutally cut short, as these little children's lives had been.

The National Coal Board blamed the disaster on abnormal rainfall. Lord Robens the chairman, who had briefly served in Atlee's Labour government after the war, told a TV reporter that nothing could have been done to prevent the slide, attributing it to 'natural unknown springs beneath the tip' – a statement challenged by local people who said the NCB had been tipping on known springs clearly marked on maps. Slag heaps littered the coalfields of Wales. The disaster made mining communities wonder who would be next.

The Tribunal of Inquiry found the NCB wholly to blame. Lord Robens closing statement was so inadequate, even the NCB asked for it to be ignored. Robens opposed any more action than was needed to make the remaining tips safe, even after the Prime Minister had promised villagers the tips would have to go and offered additional money towards this, eventually topped up with 10% of the money raised from the disaster fund – a bitterly opposed and much resented contribution.

At the inquest a father demanded that his son's death be recorded, not as asphyxia, but as, 'buried alive by the National Coal Board'. Alex Glasgow the folk singer, also from a mining family in the North East, had recently written one of his most haunting songs '*Close the Coalhouse Door*' about the human price of coal. After the Aberfan disaster, he added a third stanza in memory of the children who lost their lives.

*Close the coalhouse door lads*
*There's bairns inside*
*Bairns that had no time to hide*
*Bairns who saw the blackness slide*
*Bairns beneath the mountainside*
*Close the coalhouse door lads*
*There's bairns inside.*

Coming so soon after my son's birth, it was to be a tragedy I never forgot.

We spent Christmas at Beverley and Rusty's house and Honor and Bob also visited. Beverley was clearly thriving in her domestic arena. She had a well-equipped kitchen and produced wonderful pastry – something I was still unable to master. She was a model of generosity and I envied her the rented house they lived in for its location, so close to our other friends. Rusty clearly supplied her with a more generous allocation of housekeeping money than I had to manage on and seemed relaxed about bank overdrafts. Terry was much less open handed. I had learned thriftiness from my father. It was just as well.

Try as I might I was just not cut out to be an earth mother and although I planned to have another child, not wanting Dominic to be the only one, I figured if I had two as close together as possible I would be free of children by the time I was 40. For Beverley it looked as if she saw mother-hood as her central role in life and it was clear she would not stop at two children. I was already planning what courses I would take in Birmingham since Goldsmiths was clearly out of the question now. I had recognised how much I cherished my role as a mother. But I wanted other things too.

# 1967
# FLOWER POWER, MINI SKIRTS, PSYCHADELIA, AND...BIRMINGHAM

By February Dominic was beginning to talk. Due to Marco's unstinting efforts his first word was 'bugger' Honor suggested Marco should have his mouth washed out with soap, apparently unaware that Keir her youngest, constantly muttered the word when he was angry and this had been Marco's inspiration. Dominic's next words were "Ho Ho Ho Chi Minh" – we had taken him in a pushchair to a number of demos. "You are indoctrinating that child," said my mother. America increased their troops in Vietnam throughout the year to 475,000 and the protests mounted on both sides of the Atlantic. In April Mohamed Ali the boxer was stripped of his boxing title and not allowed to fight for three years when he refused military service.

At the LSE a sit-in was organised against the appointment of Dr Walter Adams due to his links with Ian Smith's racist regime in Rhodesia, and in protest at the subsequent suspension of two student union activists for their part in the demonstrations against Adams. Further eruptions at the LSE were to follow. I recall Pauline Marks smuggling me into the LSE for one such sit in. Students were beginning to question the pedagogical hierarchy of their universities and insist they should have a say in academic appointments.

This was a year of changes. Abortion was legalised in Britain and homosexuality decriminalised. Britain and Ireland applied to join the EEC. De Gaulle, the French premier vetoed British entry. In Bolivia Che Guevara was assassinated, and Israel launched a 6-day war against Egypt, Syria and Jordon which resulted in 20,000 Arab deaths to 1,000 Israeli, and tripled the amount of land annexed by Israel, dramatically de-stabilising the balance of forces in the Middle East.

Barclays introduced the first 'hole in the wall', in South Africa the first successful heart transplant took place, and TV went colour for the first time. Not for us though. We watched in fascinated black and white addiction a new series called *The Prisoner*, in which a former secret agent was abducted and held in captivity in a strange community by the sea from which he was unable to escape. The series was filmed in Port Merrion in Wales, the Italianate village designed by the eccentric architect Clough Ellis. Patrick McGoohan played the agent, No 6. We waited with baited breath to discover who was No.1!

In the cinema *The Graduate, Bonnie and Clyde* and *One flew over the cuckoos nest*, were released, the latter leading to considerable debate about the treatment of mental illness, the manufacture of madness and the use of ECT. It was a year when attitudes to authority were being challenged. This went together with a growth of a drug culture among young people, the emergence of the hippy 'flower people' and the summer of love, which was to inspire the musical *Hair*.

In the spring of 1967 over 100,000 young people converged on Golden Gate Park in San Francisco for a spontaneous peoples festival that combined music and an exploration of alternative life styles. Gender equality, communal living and free love were all concepts being explored and they fascinated and interested me as an alternative to the nuclear style family I was being boxed into. While as serious minded socialists, we rejected the 'turn on, tune in and drop out' philosophy of Timothy Leary, the American psychologist who was encouraging young people to explore the potential of psychedelic drugs, we also recognised that this was also part of a significant anti-authority anti-war social movement.

The Monterey Festival that followed in June convinced me I was on the wrong continent – all the fun and the action was on the West coast of America. Musicians as diverse as Ravi Shankar, Janis Joplin, Jimmy Hendrix and Otis Redding played alongside The Who, Eric Burdon and the Animals, Jefferson Aeroplane, the Mamas and the Papas and The Grateful Dead. The Rolling Stones would have appeared but for the drugs bust of Mike Jagger and Keith Richards. The festival was to inspire Woodstock two years later.

Meanwhile we prepared to depart for Birmingham. Terry's plan to keep his new job secret from the principal of his technical college had backfired. The Principal of Balham and Tooting Tech met the Principal of Birmingham Polytechnic in the spring at an academic meeting and was asked "what's this chap Terry Mandrell like who we are getting next term". The Principal was furious. He came back and sacked Terry on the spot, oblivious to the fact that he had students being prepared for A levels who would now have no tutor for two months before their exams. He did us a favour though, as Terry was able to claim the dole over the summer, money that was badly needed with the move imminent.

We had little of value to move, a couple of chest

of drawers, a double bed and a cooker. Terry's ancient grandparents lived in a tiny cottage in Ampthill. When we visited them there I had been struck by the immensely grand furniture in their little house. It turned out this had been acquired many years previously at an auction in a Hyde Park mansion – I believe Terry's grandmother had been in service and may have been given preference in their acquisition. They had a curved mahogany dinning table, which came down to a central stem on which was the carved head of the first Duke of Wellington. Accompanying this was 6 carved dining chairs with seats covered in blue and gold brocade. They also had a magnificently ornate chaise longue, and a matching button back granddad and grandma armchair.

Early in 1967 both the grandparents died. Knowing of our interest in antique furniture (a minority interest at the time), the family offered us the chaise longue, the armchairs and the dinning room chairs. The deal was that the furniture was a family heirloom and we could have them provided we never sold them. We agreed and invested a fair bit in reupholstering them in gold dralon. The unique table was given to Uncle Arthur, a rogue uncle who promptly sold it and bought some G-plan furniture with the proceeds. Sacrilege! The remaining magnificent furniture stood waiting in our bedroom for the move north.

On July 13th it was my 21st birthday. I got a telegram from my parents and we went to their house for a birthday lunch. I bought myself a new orange mini dress on the way there. Twiggy, was the new 'in vogue' model and the fashions favoured the slim and leggy. Luckily I was both. We left Dominic with my doting mother while we went to see *Little Murders* by Jules Feiffer at the Aldwych, which was a parody on the growing gun culture of America. It was my first theatre visit since Dominic's birth. Terry liked the cinema but could only be lured to the theatre if there was something political on.

Terry had an tenuous link with Stuart Hall, the Jamaican director of the Centre for Contemporary Cultural Studies at Birmingham University, through the New Left Review Group He rather cheekily asked if we could stay one weekend to go house hunting in Brum. Stuart and Catherine his wife were very welcoming, fed us and suggested areas for us to try. My favourite was Moseley, which had a bookshop and a ready supply of capacious Victorian houses on the market. Terry was dubious about their re-sale value.

I went house hunting alone. At one fairly pleasant Edwardian House in Blenheim Road Kings Heath I was shown round with another potential buyer. Discovering I was new to the city, the other viewer was quick to reassure me that this was a 'nice' area as, she dropped her voice, 'there are no coloureds here'. I couldn't resist it. "Oh well there will be when we move in," I said. "My husband's Jamaican". I reckon she went down to the Estate agent like a shot to put in an offer.

Eventually Terry found what he was looking for and bid for it – I was not consulted. It was characterless 1930's semi-detached in Kings Heath, a leafy suburb south of Moseley. The house cost £4,400. The area felt a bit stockbroker belt and did not have the slightly arty feel of Moseley. I felt the people we would be living next door to would be unutterably suburban, and we would have little or nothing in common with them (or I wouldn't). In this I was correct. But Terry was the mortgagee and he was going to have it his way. He even hurried the sale through before my 21st birthday so that my name would not go on the deeds. The house sale did not complete in time for the beginning of the autumn term, so he took a temporary bed-sitter and I came up to Birmingham to see him on occasional weekends. Finally in October we moved to 82 Haunch Lane and my London life came to an end.

The house had three bedrooms – all a decent size, a garage, a kitchen, dining room and small lounge. It had lots of storage space, a 100-foot garden to the rear and a long drive and front garden. It needed lots of renovation. About the time we moved to Haunch Lane, Stuart and Cathy moved from their Selly Oak flat into a Victorian house I had coveted on Prospect Road in Moseley. They were thinking of starting a family too. It was my turn to be cheeky. When we visited I noticed an old Victorian table in the coal shed. "Do you want that?" I asked. Catherine said she didn't, so we arranged to get it collected and at least started life with something to eat off!

Our weekends were now dominated with repairs and improvements – Angela a friend of mine calls it the Nitromor years, as so many of the boomers were engaged in the same occupation. Gradually we began acquiring items like a washing machine, a fridge and a welsh dresser. White, orange and olive green were the fashionable decorating colours of the day and the posters of Toulouse Lautrec were as popular as flying ducks over the mantle-piece were in the 50s. We also had a Brueghel reproduction of *The peasants wedding*, a print of Picasso's *Guernica* and Alfonse Mocha's wall panel reproductions from Athena prints. We planned to knock a load-bearing wall down between the kitchen and dining room in the new year.

The only problem was money. From assuming we would be rich living on £1,000 per year Terry announced that his entire income was now taken up with house costs and bills (he had an expensive endowment mortgage). I would need to work to put food on the table. This meant finding child-care for Dominic. I reviewed the far from satisfactory options, reluctant to leave my one-year-old with any of them. Nursery school places would not be available till he was three.

The only solution was to become a child minder myself. I registered with the local council and put an ad in the local shops. I soon found myself looking after several children – I had four at one stage besides my own, all under five. There was Kevin Brougham, a sickly anaemic looking small boy who came complete with a spotty face and a snotty nose and a mother who related a long list of foods he would not eat. His breakfast was four Black Jacks bought for a penny from the sweet shop en-route to my house. He was one of my successes. We had a battle of wills over food, but by the time he left me two years later to go to school he would eat anything and everything, the spots had cleared up and he had put some flesh on his bones.

The next child I was asked to mind was Mark Shackelton (related I was told to the explorer). He caused me a terrifying half hour when I lost him in Sainsbury's only to find he had climbed the stairs to the staff quarters where he was entertained with cocoa and chocolate biscuits while he wisely kept shtum about whose little boy he was. I also looked after two sisters, Claire and Carol and later, little round Lucy, the youngest of 11 who looked like a Mabel Lucy Attwell illustration and had serious behavioural problems.

My parents were also considering a move now that they had a property to sell. My father was just a few years off retirement and confident he could get a transfer to another tax district. My mother being a nurse could always find work.

She conceived an interest in Minehead in Somerset where she knew a family of farmers. It turned out she had once had a romance with the son of the family. Maybe she was yearning for a past she had not had? But first they had to sell Northway Road and that looked as if it would take some time; such was its state of disrepair.

Encouraged by my good 'O' level result, I registered for an 'A' level evening class in Sociology at Mathew Boulton Technical College and was soon immersed in the studies of Willmott and Young, Bowlby, TB Bottomore and C Wright Mills. This led to a few moments of conflict with Terry when he could not decide if he wanted an intellectual wife or a skivvy. Coming home early one day he found the kids fighting in the garden while I sat immersed in *Childcare and the growth of love*. This worried him less than the fact that I had not swept under the rush matting in the hall. He lifted it up and started to berate me for keeping a dirty house. I laughed. He was not as terrifying as my dad with his vacuum cleaner dramas. I just thought he was being silly. Later, rather shamefaced, he apologised. I had to remind him he had not married a replica of his mother.

I took some time to get used to Birmingham, but living in the leafy southern suburbs there was plenty of parks and attractive places to visit. Cannon Hill Park contained an Arts Centre and it was a favourite of mine. The north of the city was much more bleak and industrial and driving into the city from the north was not a pleasant experience. Birmingham had a road network designed to make it easy to leave the city, which cynics said was one of its greatest assets. We both had bicycles and put a child seat on the back for Dominic, but could not afford a car and neither of us could drive anyway so we did not take advantage of our closeness to Warwickshire and Shropshire.

The neighbour on our right was a builder. He and his wife had a plump son called Stephen and a daughter called Sally, although they always called her 'fairy'. They were clearly aspirant consumers wanting to keep up with the Jones. Unfortunately they were living next door to the uncompetitive Mandrells. The wife told me that they were not much worried about 'Fairy's" education because she was a girl and would only marry when she got older.

The neighbour on the other side was Miss Mildenhall who was a member of the ladies section of the Primrose League, an organisation set up by Disraeli to further Conservative principles. She liked us initially because Terry worked on the garden and her own garden was her pride and joy. Our relationship was to deteriorate over time – rather like the garden.

The most interesting people on the street were the Alexiou's. Margaret was a lecturer in the centre for Byzantine Ottoman and Modern Greek Studies at Birmingham University and her father was the head of the centre. Her husband was a left wing publisher who had fled Greece after the military coup. They were to have twin boys, both with varying degrees of autism due to birth complications. Margaret was in my baby-sitting group, which allowed us an occasional night off, provided we reciprocated baby-sitting hours.

Some of our friends from London visited us that first cold winter when we had yet to sort out our heating. Marco and Pauline sat in coats complaining of the cold and telling us that Birmingham was the pits of a place to live in. Sue and Henry Miller came up with their two children and Pat and Rose Fortune visited with their two. I still missed my friends but I was about to gain a whole new social group.

Politically we were in an area ripe for development. Roger Rosewell who was working as a trade union organiser for ASTMS soon visited us. Nattily dressed in a suit and sporting the obligatory Groucho Marx moustache he was keen that we helped build a Birmingham IS group. Michael Rice a student at Aston University who was currently staying in Rosewell's flat in Harborne (and being treated like a minion) was also keen.

Over the next few years the group was to swell although initially students and teachers dominated it. The group included Godfrey Webster, who looked about 12 and was one of the most dangerous drivers I ever travelled with, Ray Osborne with matinee idol good looks, who was doing a medical degree, Colin Falconer, Mary Pearson, Bob Whitehead, Hestor Bolton, Chris and Margaret George, followed – they were all teachers. John Hutchinson who sported a small goatee beard was doing a degree in architecture. He had joined IS in London in '67, came up to do a year working with Reddish development Corporation in 1969 and recruited Mike and Lynn Pedley in 1971 who both worked at Tractors and Transmissions factory. James Douglas and James Youngman, were students with upper middle class parents, (James Douglas's father was a diplomat while Youngman's father had a vast farm in Suffolk and used to send him up a brace of pheasants from time to time.) Then there was Roger Clipsham who had set up the Claimants Union. He knitted and was learning tap dancing.

More significantly were our first industrial recruits, Geoff Johnson and Vic Collard, who worked as a checker at Lucas Chester Street factory and was on the Birmingham East District committee of the AUEW. Victor, a hard drinking, hard smoking working class intellectual had a florid complexion, a very prominent hooknose, and a style of speaking reminiscent of Mr Punch. He joined IS because, he said, that unlike the Communist Party, they had a sense of humour (though he had a strong friendship with one humorous CP member, Sarah Cummings, a college lecturer and a feisty single mum who was a joint friend to us both). IS also offered intellectual stimulation and had a strategy to fight productivity deals. Vic and Geoff sold the IS pamphlet *Employers Offensive: Productivity Deals and how to fight them* extensively in the factory and this helped to bring in new industrial members. Larry Blewitt, Roger Griffiths, Larry Connolly followed. The upstairs room of The White Lion on the Bristol Road became our meeting place, and Haunch Lane the unofficial centre of operations.

Into this assorted and disparate community came our friend Henry Miller, who had accepted a post at Aston University and bought a huge old Victorian house on Grove Avenue in Moseley in anticipation of his family joining him. The day he moved in his wife dropped the bombshell that she was leaving him. She sent him a long letter elucidating all the ways he had irritated her over the past five years, which seemed to boil down to the fact that he was hopelessly impractical and loved to party. She wanted a divorce. Henry was devastated. He had not seen this coming. He pointed out he had just bought a large family house for them all, to which Sue replied – well you can fill it with students and have a lot of parties. Which was more or less what he did do. I remember us taking him to the pictures to see the Beatles *A Hard Days night* in an attempt to cheer him up.

I cannot remember where we spent Christmas that year, possibly back in Croydon with Beverley and Rusty. Beverley was pregnant again, but despite my best efforts I was not joining her into maternity this time round.

# 1968
# INTERNATIONAL PROTEST YEAR

On January 5th Alexander Dubcek was elected first secretary of the Communist Party in Czechoslovakia on a programme of reforms, which did not sit well with the Soviet Union. The Prague Spring was to mark months of popular resistance, even in the wake of invasion by Warsaw Pact troops in August. It was to usher in a year of extreme protest.

In Vietnam the New Year TET offensive by the Viet Cong, launched major military attacks against the South Vietnamese and US troops and sparked off terrible reprisals by the Americans, notably the May Li massacre of civilians, one of the most shocking US war crimes. Eddie Adams iconic photograph of a Viet Cong Officer being shot circulated the headlines of the world and won him the Pulitzer Prize. It heightened criticism of the war in the US. Eugene McCarthy challenged Lyndon Johnson for leadership of the Democratic Party on an anti-war ticket and the poll was so close LBJ decided not to stand for re-election. In March, a demonstration outside the American Embassy in Grosvenor Square London, was met with extreme violence from the police. 91 people were injured and there were 200 arrests.

In April, Martin Luther King Jr. was assassinated. His murder triggered race riots throughout America. In England Enoch Powell made a scurrilous attack on immigrants in his infamous 'rivers of blood' speech, ironic since as Minister of Health in a former Tory government he had encouraged immigration by advertising for nursing staff in the West Indies. Ted Heath removed him from the Shadow Cabinet.

But the events that were to lead the closest to civil war or revolution occurred in France. In February the French communist and socialist parties had formed an alliance to try and defeat the government of George Pompidou and the presidency of Charles De Gaulle. In March students including the anarchist Daniel Cohn Bendit (later known as Danny the Red) occupied the administrative offices of the University of Nanterre in Paris, protesting against the traditional values of the university that refused communal student residencies and the political bureaucracy that controlled university funding. Cohn Bendit, who held a German passport, was threatened with expulsion (there were later calls for his extradition as a 'dangerous alien').

Further protests followed and on May 2nd the authorities shut down the university. The following day a demonstration by students from the Sorbonne against the closure was broken up by the police. Hundreds were arrested and dozens injured. On 6 May 20,000 students marched in protest against the police invasion of the Sorbonne. This led to a violent confrontation with police wielding batons and the students building barricades and prising up cobblestones to hurl at the police. Tear gas broke up the demo.* Hundreds were arrested.

The next day High school student teachers and young

---

* Years indeed decades later the Stone Roses were to adopt a lemon slice as their logo, a well known antidote to the effects of tear gas and in direct homage to the near revolution of May '68 . Veterans of the battles were to become known as 'soixante-huitard' – sixty eighters.

workers gathered at the Arc de Triomphe demanding all charges against the students be dropped and the two universities reopened. When these demands were not met, a huge further demonstration was called on the Rive Gauche, where again there was a violent confrontation between both sides, which went on until dawn. Many of the demonstrators were later to claim agent provocateurs infiltrated the ranks and threw Molotov cocktails and set fire to cars to discredit them.

The heavy handed tactics of the governments evoked a wave of sympathy for the demonstrators and many eminent writers singers and poets came out against the government. We watched the conflicts in excitement on our TV and got used to seeing protestors in helmets with visors and battle fatigues on our screens – not the usual demonstrators day wear at all. This was serious stuff.

On May 13th two of the major unions came out on a one-day strike in support of the students and over a million people marched through Paris. Pompidou reopened the Sorbonne and dropped the charges against the students, but these concession did not quell the unrest, fuelled by De Gaulle's derogatory remarks " *La réforme oui, la chien lit non*. It inspired a famous cartoon poster of De Gaulle with the words *'la chien lit est vous'*. Chien en lit – to shit in bed is a French metaphor for chaos but for years we interpreted it as dog shit.

Students took over the newly opened Sorbonne and declared it a people's university, and occupations spread to the factories throughout France. At the height of the conflict 11 million workers went on strike for two continuous weeks, which represented 22% of the entire French population. On May 24th there was an attempt to burn down the Paris Stock Exchange. Then on May

29, De Gaulle, the President, left France for an unknown destination. We thought revolution was imminent. Many of the IS comrades decided they needed to be out there in the thick of things and made off for Paris, including Roger Rosewell.

Unlike the revolution two hundred years earlier, this uprising was as much cultural as it was economic. It had started with students wanting the right to sleep together. It was about establishing a more permissive society on all levels. The factory strikes were not organised by the CGT unions but were more wildcat and radical in their demands. Even when the unions wrested substantial economic improvements in pay and conditions, this was no longer enough. The workers did not want a loaf – they wanted the whole bloody bakery. Fearing that the anarchists and the Trotskyites would outnumber them in any future government, the Communists now pulled out of the alliance. Francois Mitterrand of the Federation of the Democratic and Socialist Left, seeing an opportunity for the Socialists to act as a compromise between De Gaulle and the Communists, stated he was ready to form a government. So did Mendes France, out of retirement, who had the backing of the Communists.

De Gaulle had retired to Baden Baden to ensure he had the support of the French military HQ in Germany. Grimaud the Head of the French police now boxed clever and negotiated with the revolutionaries marching through Paris shouting "Adieu De Gaulle" and suggesting the communists were plotting an armed uprising. Pompidou persuaded De Gaulle to dissolve the National Assembly on 30 May and call a new election for mid June, threatening a state of emergency if the workers did not return to work. The government had leaked to the media that the army was waiting outside Paris, and immediately after the announcement 800,000 Gaullists marched through the capital waving the national flag – a counter demonstration orchestrated by De Gaulle. The Communists agreed to the election, and the possibility of revolution, which had come tantalisingly close, receded. Workers gradually returned to work, students called off street demonstrations and in the aftermath many left organisations were banned.

There were to be many revolts after May '68, but nowhere else did something that started as a student revolt against traditionalism nearly bring down a government. Rosewell returned with a cache of French posters and tales of all night debates in the Odeon cinema. Many years later I had one framed. Its says

*Je participate*
*Tu participates*
*Il participe*
*Nous participons*
*Vous participez*
*Ils profitent*

Much of the excitement of international politics left me feeling a voyeur, unable to participate – I watched Lindsay Anderson's subversive surreal masterpiece *If* on a rare cinema visit, where a revolution at Eton ends with pupils mowing down their own upperclass, and reflected that my chance of changing the world or fighting the ruling class was hampered by a severe shortage of baby sitters. Instead I found myself the endless purveyor of cups of tea and meals for the comrades who were a regular presence in the house. I had no sooner cleared up the chaos from a day of child-care, than they would be arriving to print off stencils on the duplicator, now housed in our garage. One day I made a coffee cake and they consumed the lot before it had even cooled down from the oven.

In industry, women were feeling sidelined too. In June the Ford women's machinists went on strike at the Dagenham factory over a re-grading issue. Their job was categorised as Grade B less skilled, rather than Grade C skilled, and on top of this, they were paid 15% less than the men on Grade B. Their three-week strike was successful when Fords ran out of a backlog of seat covers and production ground to a halt. Many of the male trade unionists were not as sympathetic as they might have been.

However the strike got the support of Barbara Castle, the Secretary of State for Employment and resulted in an immediate increase of 8% in their wages and full Grade B pay the following year. It would take a further six-week strike in 1984 before they were re-categorised as Grade C workers. The strike of the Dagenham women led to the setting up of the National Joint Action Campaign Committee for Equal Rights NJACCWER which led an Equal Pay demonstration the following year which in turn led to the Equal Pay Act of 1970. But there were to be a fair few changes for women by then.

Rosewell was a queer bird. He had been recruited to IS early in the 1960s in Kingston by John Palmer (to his huge later regret) and had been in the Young Communist League and the Labour Party young Socialists. Jim Higgins in *More Years for the Locust* written in 1997, describes him as 'a toy Bolshevik, full of conceit, and strutting around as if he was a cross between Robert Redford and Arnold Schwarzenegger'.

Hindsight is a wonderful thing. At the time it seemed to me he was merely over-compensating for a sense of chronic inadequacy. He seemed to live in a fantasy world most of the time and I think saw himself more of a Jimmy Hoffa trade union leader than a Will Thorne. Hoffa, leader of the American Teamsters union was effective at building the union, but was also a corrupt gangster. We should have been warned. Hoffa was to cross swords with Robert Kennedy the US Attorney General, who was ruthless in his pursuit of corruption in the Teamsters Union. Kennedy had made other enemies due to his pro Israel policies. He was shot dead by a Palestinian in June 68 just days after winning the Presidential primaries in California. It might not have been a Hoffa designed murder, but I am sure he shed few tears.

Roger took to giving me trips out in his ASTMS supplied Ford Cortina. These soon ended up at his flat and in his bed. It is something I look back on now with great regret given what a renegade the man turned into. But at the time he was flavour of the month. Much admired by Tony Cliff, and on the IS National Committee. All I can say in my defence was my life was unutterably boring and a bit of vicarious pleasure from time to time was badly needed. Terry was a creature of habit, with few interests outside politics and history. He gardened and was self-taught on the piano – that was it. He was regular in his habits and used to go out at the same time every night to get a cider refill from the off licence on the corner. Later he brewed his own beer. He was never someone who was going to startle me by his impulsiveness or his imagination. He didn't believe in fantasy worlds.

I still had my quota of Socialist Worker to sell and on

Sundays used to set forth with the pram to sell them in the council estate at the end of Haunch Lane – 10 was the average. Every week I took the lift to the top floor of a block of flat to sell a single paper. Each week the son of the household would come to the door and shout back to his mother "Ma, it's the Social Worker". I doubt they ever opened the paper.

One weekend I delivered them by bicycle. Terry had used my bike when his had a puncture and had got it stolen. I had to use his. He had fixed a bracket to the front wheel frame to hold a front light, but like many things Terry did, he hadn't finished the job properly. Coming down a steep incline at speed I saw the bracket wobbling and before I was able to brake, the bracket had swung into the wheel frame and I was flung forward over the handlebars with my face slamming into the very sharp loose chippings on the road. I sustained a very deep v shape cut under my nose and above my lip and my face swelled up to double its size. Terry summoned by a concerned householder, got Roger to drive me to the hospital where they put several stitches in the cut without anaesthetic, which was acutely painful. For weeks I stayed out of sight till the swelling subsided, so embarrassed was I by my appearance. I still have the V shaped scar to remind me.

June also saw me sitting my Sociology A Level. Marco had been able to provide me with a lot of useful background material now he was examining for the Associated Examining Board. He read some of my essays and coached me into adapting my style from enthusiastic proponent of C Wright Mills and Marxist Sociology to a more objective academic style acceptable to the examiners. He must have done a good job because despite taking the exam after only 9 months of a two hourly weekly evening class, I got a Grade B. I was well pleased and so was Terry. Rita was shaping up.

I still wanted that second child. Dominic was now two years old but despite our best attempts there was no sign of a second baby. Beverley now had a daughter Tanya and I was sure there would be another before long. I went to the fertility clinic and was put on a regime of temperature taking daily to find out when I was most likely to ovulate. Still nothing, so an appointment was made for me at Showell Green Women's Hospital, where, in front of 13 medical students, they pumped gas through my fallopian tubes to see if there was a blockage.

It was painful, but not so painful as the sequel a few weeks later when I started to get acute pains in the same place together with a greenish discharge. My GP confused me by informing me I had dysentery (though with none of the normal symptoms). I was told that I had to stop minding other children, as it was highly infectious, so my mothers had to make alternative arrangements.

The pain was so acute one night, a locum had to be summoned. After examining me he said I most definitely did not have dysentery but I did have a septic infection, as the instruments used on me "may not have been as sterile as they might have been". An early morning visit from the younger female GP in our practice confirmed this, and I was bundled off as an in-patient to Showell Green where they proceeded to give me tetracycline injections every four hours in alternate legs.

Luckily it was the school holidays, so Terry was home to look after Dominic. While in the hospital I noted that

*The Halladay Clan: From left to right, my gran, me aged two, my Aunt Elsie (the religious one) and my mother*

*The Roy Clan: My father on the left, with his anxious younger brother Harold and Auntie Elsie (the sweary one) overdressed and put on a pedestal – rather as she was in life*

*First Holiday in Wales with my mother aged around two*

*Aunty Joan's Dance school Fancy dress party: Front row I am second from the right dressed as Red Riding Hood. Taken shortly after my first favourable theatre review aged three in an otherwise scathing attack on the dance school display*

*64 Northway Road: My home for the first sixteen years of my life. A less than 'des res' Hitler knocked about a bit*

*Aged around nine – A very serious student of the Sylvia Bryant Stage School*

*1956: First holiday abroad My Mum and I on the ferry home from France*

*On holiday in Italy aged eleven (below and opposite top)*

*My mum my gran and me aged fourteen out on a day trip with Uncle Eddie*

*Demo against Gaitskell 1962 I am on the front row far right with my DIY fringe! Photo Croydon Advertiser*

*Me on the left with Elaine Bramley in Great Yarmouth as dancers in Roundabout the show at the Britannia Pier theatre. The press photo of the show is missing – this one was taken by a Russian sailor who lured me on board his boat*

*One of a number of photos taken for Spotlight magazine when I was seventeen: I remember the second session was cancelled as it was scheduled on 22 November 1963 the day of President Kennedy's assassination*

Photo: Peter Gillman

*From the left: Pauline Hibberd in the foreground, me, Terry and Jack Kearney in the doorway of The Woodman pub, where all the left activists in Croydon hung out*

*Paul Palowski a peace activist from Poland asked us to pose with these placards in Croydon High Street. From left to right: Me, Terry, Pauline Hibberd, Carol Northcott and Pat? The slogans from left to right read*

*How many bombs are necessary to bury Poland underground?*
*Polish movement for disarmament*
*Poland! Leave the Warsaw Pact*
*Poles! Help us disarm Poland*
*We'll be stronger without weapons*

*Dominic at nine months when we were living in Thornton Heath and with his dad*

*Me on my twenty-first birthday feeding Dominic aged one*

*Minehead Somerset: Dominic aged two with me on the right: The cornet was a distraction after he fell in some nettles.*

*Minehead Somerset My mother with Dominic and Terry*

*Dominic aged four at nursery school*

*1971 Dominic with baby sister Anna in our garden in Birmingham*

*Anna at nine months in her pram*

*Anna aged two – last one at the table at her nursery school Christmas party*

*1977 Anna and Dominic in our Springfield Road garden Birmingham*

*My father Fred showing off his pin board with travel trophies, Edwardian nudes and other memorabilia. Photographed by the Torquay Times after he did some talks on his experience as a tramp in the 1930s. He also stood for the local Labour Party – despite not being in the party.*

a number of other women were being treated with antibiotics for surgical incisions that did not seem to be healing.

After a week my knee swelled up. The consultant visiting me informed me cheerfully that they only dealt with the area from the waist to the pubes and since my knee was lower it came outside their jurisdiction, so they were removing me to Selly Oak Hospital. Here they bandaged me up with a metal splint, told me to keep my leg up till the swelling went down and discharged me home. Re-occurring infections in the fallopian tubes were to become a regular feature of my life for some years.

Sitting with relief in my back garden that August, glad to be home, I heard the news that France had exploded her first thermo nuclear Bomb in French Polynesia. De Gaulle had said it would help the weak Polynesian economy. The news of his death from natural causes two years later was perhaps fortuitous. Frederick Forsyth's fictional *Day of the Jackal* produced in 1971 might have inspired quite a few potential assassins if nature had not got there first.

Late summer I visited Somerset with my mother and we looked at various houses in Minehead as the sale of Northway Road was finally imminent. One was a chocolate box cottage, with tiny rooms. I loved it, but we vetoed it on the grounds of size. My mother wanted to make sure she had a home we would visit regularly on our holidays, as she was anxious to spend the maximum amount of time with her grandson whom she loved dearly. She and my father had already visited us several times at Haunch Lane. Dominic suffered from eczema and I was advised that he should not wear wool next to his skin, but this did not deter my mother. Almost weekly a small package would flop through our letter box and inside would be a pair of knitted tights, a hat, a duffle coat all produced at break neck speed while she was on night duty. She even made me a sweater dress, knitted so well it is still in my possession 50 years after its production. It's the warmest garment I own.

Eventually we located a 3 bedroomed semi-detached on Poundfield Road half way up a steep hill with a good sized garden full of plum trees and a substantial vegetable patch, It had a kitchen twice the size my parents were used to and a more modern bathroom. Despite Northway Road being a wreck, you got more for your money in Somerset. This was considered a sensible buy and well before Christmas my parents moved. My mother got herself a job in the local cottage hospital and my father a transfer to the tax office in Taunton, which as there was a good train connection, was not difficult.

My mother already knew the Darts, Elsie and Lydon. Hardly my father's types – Lydon went stag hunting and they were deeply conservative. Indeed my dad might have gone mad in this semi-feudal environment of the calloused forelock (acquired by the local peasants tugging them reverentially to the local squire) if it was not for the happy accident of discovering an old friend from his youth Ern Bendall living in the town. Ern brewed very powerful homemade wine. Fred was to join him in this new hobby and we spent many a happy inebriated evening in the company of Ern and his wife. The Bendall's lived up a steep hill. We floated down it after each visit. We joined my parents for a Christmas in Somerset. My mother acquired a second hand cot for Dominic and a small chair for him to sit in when he came to visit.

# 1969
# IRELAND PRAGUE CAMBODIA– MOON LANDING–I GO TO COLLEGE

Barbara Castle may have had a hand in securing re-grading for the Dagenham women strikers, but she and Wilson had plans to constrain the unions-the year opened with the presentation of a White Paper *In Place of Strife* which, among other things proposed that a ballot should be called before strike action. The paper caused a major split in the Labour party and was quietly shelved. January also saw Rupert Murdoch purchase the *News of the World*, and marked the beginning of the troubles in Northern Ireland.

In October 1968 a civil rights march in Derry had been broken up quite violently by the Royal Ulster Constabulary – a subsequent protest march of 1,300 a week later, was blocked by Ian Paisley and his supporters. Peoples Democracy had then announced they would start the New Year, with a march from Belfast to Derry, inspired by the Selma – Montgomery American Civil Rights March. The March began on January 1st but was continuously attacked by Loyalists with no intervention by the RUC. The tally of 100 injured confirmed to the Catholic population that the RUC could not be trusted with impartial policing. The march brought Bernadette Devlin to prominence. Within a few months, at the age of 21, she was to become the youngest MP to date in the UK Parliament, representing the Mid-Ulster constituency for five years as a socialist republican.

The wave of student protests across Europe reached the University of Madrid. Franco's response was to declare Martial Law in Spain. In Prague, Jan Palach, a Czech student, chose self-immolation in Wenceslas Square as an act of protest at the crushing of the Prague Spring by Warsaw Pact troops. An estimate of 500,000 people attended his funeral on January 24th to protest the Soviet occupation of their country.

The US was now bombing Cambodia to 'flush out' the Viet Cong and the Sino Soviet conflict was gathering pace. The Beatles gave their last public performance on the roof of the Apple building and in March John Lennon celebrated his wedding to Yoko Ono with a 'bed-in' for a week in a hotel in Amsterdam, where they were interviewed by the press on their views on world peace. During a subsequent Montreal bed-in, Lennon composed *Give Peace a chance.* Back in the UK, the voting age was lowered to 18 and Concord 'old droopy' was given its first air test.

The pregnancy tests had left me with a re-occurring infection in the fallopian tubes and there seemed no prospect of another baby. I decided that I needed a plan B. I was finding child minding a thankless and demanding way to earn very little and I figured if I could acquire one 'A' level I could acquire three and could then look to taking a University degree and getting myself some decent employment. In the meantime there was plenty of extra mural activity to engage with in the International Socialists and this included a few brief affairs.

I was not a natural mother and often found myself utterly lacking in patience to deal with children. I was a strict disciplinarian. I think the problem was that I had come to motherhood too young, before I had matured enough to take on the responsibilities it involved. I smacked children I thought were naughty – it wasn't frowned on the way it is today, felt guilty (I had also read my Doctor Spock), redoubled my efforts and ended up shouting at them. What I resented most was having no free time to pursue my own interests. I loved Dominic passionately but it did not stop me being a tough mother much of the time. A friend once heard me shouting at the kids in the garden. "It was bloody terrifying", she said. On the flip side, some children of progressive left parents who were never subject to any constraints seemed obnoxious out of control brats. I counted Justin, Beverley's son among them. Jim Higgins had what he called a 'nause rating' for the worst. Donny Gluckstein, Cliff's son scored a straight 10.

I was getting involved in a lot of house improvement having developed a real interest in interior design and was finding I had a good instinct for colour and design. The previous year Rusty and Beverley had come to stay and we had knocked down a supporting wall between our kitchen and the dinning room. This meant putting in a reinforced concrete lintel. Terry had insisted that he and Rusty could do the work themselves and then nearly ruptured himself turning the lintel when they found they had put it in upside down. We had to learn a lot about house improvements in a very short time, as we couldn't afford workmen.

This room was now painted white with an orange ceiling. We had a low light over the table and I made lampshades for table lamps and converted twill sheeting into curtains. It was an era for converting old furniture and creating dramatic interiors, and I enjoyed this, though I sometimes needed to compromise on my ideas, as Terry was forever frugal on cost, even though we did everything on a budget. We had installed a solid fuel fire with a back boiler, which was supposed to fuel our central heating. It was very ineffectual and required a lot of work getting the fire going in the morning. In the end we converted the system to gas. Gradually we worked through the house painting and furnishing and now into our second year, it was considerably improved. We used a lot of chip paper, which went over lumps and bumps well and was very cheap. Future generations would curse us for this.

At Easter we visited our friends Jennifer and Spider, who had been left a dilapidated Victorian house by an elderly relative at the end of a rough track in a place called Stanford Le Hope in Essex. (They used to call it Stanford Le Hopeless) The house had an elegance and grace missing from our Birmingham semi, but needed extensive repairs and improvements. They had acquired a mortgage to pay for this, and their first major acquisition was a light green Aga. Jennifer produced wonderful meals on this, often very late in the evening, as preparation was extensive and interspersed with a lot of wine, talk and cigarettes.

We went for walks in the marshes around their house, clad in wellies as the long grass contained adders – their cat brought one through the cat flap one day. They had also acquired a sheep dog called Sally. Jennifer was expecting a baby in the summer. She cut Dominic's hair for me, for which I was grateful, as I had not made a very satisfactory job of it myself. Terry insisted I cut his hair too (why waste money on barbers?) As it was curly and grew upwards it was easy, a bit like cutting privet. Dominic's was another matter.

We also visited Minehead to see my parents. My mother was settling into a job in the cottage hospital but finding the private patients a trial. They treated the staff like servants, and my mother had already refused to fetch and carry for one elderly dowager earning her the title 'Red Roy'.

My father was clearly missing the London cultural nightlife and had found no convivial work mates in Taunton. I think it was unlikely he could take the same liberties he had enjoyed in Croydon taxes. There was one cinema in the town and this closed down during the winter months when Butlins shut. He was also very conscious of the parochialism and small town mentality of rural, deeply conservative England where outsiders were dubbed 'grockles' – the slightly derogatory term applied to tourists and new arrivals.

We were also to experience this rural prejudice. One very wet day out of season, we took shelter from the rain in a lean-to next to a shuttered teashop on the end of a jetty. We had some friends with us, and my small son in a pushchair. Suddenly the shutter flew up and we were confronted with a furious woman who told us we were on private property "Get out," she screamed – "or I will call the police". Terry, trying to appease her, said that he didn't know she was open and perhaps we could buy a cup of tea as there was no shelter near at hand and we had a small child with us. "I don't want your kind of people here," she said. "No" I said "but you don't mind making money out of us during the season do you? Try and move us". "Go away" she shrieked to Terry "and take that hussy with you". Welcome to Somerset!

Ern Bendall made up for a lot. He was great fun. A talented artist, he was semi-retired and had a small light repair business, which supplemented his pension. Both he and my father grew huge plums – the biggest I have ever seen – they were more like melons. Many were converted into wine. The soil was very fertile in this part of England and my father was getting enormous pleasure out of his substantial kitchen garden.

I remember long walks in the wonderful surrounding countryside, Dunkery Beacon and the Quantock Hills – the setting for *Lorna Doone*, one of my mother's favourite novels. We visited Watersmeet, Dunster, Lynton and Lynmouth with its quaint little funicular railway and Nether Stowey where Samuel Coleridge Taylor lived when he was famously interrupted by the man from Porlock while writing *Kubla Khan*.

There was a sandy beach in Minehead where we would take our little son. One day he fell into some nettles near the back of the beach and we rushed to get him an ice cream to take his mind off it. I have always been amused at how small children can stop mid cry at the sight of a chocolate or an ice cream. I still have the photo of him sucking the cone with his smart new haircut, and me beaming at him, the crisis averted. My mother was next to me and perhaps at her happiest. In my mind's eye I can picture her now, what she was wearing, the wind in her hair. I almost feel I could reach out and connect with her. I wasn't to know then how little time we would share together.

We returned home to the news of British troops being sent to Ireland. Originally seen by the Republicans as a peace – keeping force, this view was soon to be modified. In France De Gaulle stepped down from the presidency and was replaced by George Pompidou. In June the Stonewall riots in the US heralded the beginning of the gay rights movement, and the first American women's liberation conference was held. July saw the start of withdrawal of troops from Vietnam as part of Nixon's 'Vietnamization' policy of transferring the burden of fighting the resilient Viet Cong, to the South Vietnamese army. The war was costing America more than it could afford, not only morally and financially, but in the GI death toll which reflected the growing opposition.

July brought news of two deaths. Brian Jones of the Rolling Stones was found drowned in his swimming pool, helped on by copious quantities of booze and drugs. Another drowning involved the doomed Kennedy family. Senator Edward Kennedy had driven his car off a jetty on Chappaquiddick Island late at night, which resulted in the drowning of his young female companion Mary Jo Kopechne. Inexplicably Kennedy did not report the accident to the authorities till the following morning and later evidence suggested that if he had, she might have survived. I was reminded of Marilyn Monroe's suicide in 1962. Monroe was known to have had affairs with both Robert and Jack Kennedy. The whole dynasty seemed dogged by scandal and disaster and it was clear, much was hidden from the public.

July 20th gave the Americans something to boast about for a change. Everyone was glued to their TV screens to watch Apollo 5 land on the moon. Somehow it seemed so unreal and unlikely. I thought of the money energy and effort that had gone into the space race and somehow I could not feel the thrill many did when Neil

Armstrong announced "one small step for man, one giant leap for mankind". After seeing Kubrick's *2001,* the previous year the reality had far less impact. For many Americans their focus was more earth bound. In November 500,000 were to march in Washington against the war. Combined with the cost of the space race, the war was crippling the American economy – a retreat from both seemed inevitable.

My life was still dominated by domesticity, punctuated with time off at IS conferences and schools. Quite often I found myself confined to a gloomy room reserved for the crèche. In the summer I went to Keele for an IS event and propositioned the beautiful James Douglas, a young IS member. I was the first woman he had slept with. Returning from a trip to Europe shortly after, he brought round a magnum of cheap Spanish brandy and the three of us managed to polish it off in a night. James collapsed on the front room sofa.

I was woken the next morning by insistent knocking at my front door and realised that I had overslept and Lucy's mum was at the front door waiting to drop her off. I rushed down in my dressing gown, my head hammering, and let her mother in, only to recoil in embarrassment when I opened the kitchen door to see a trail of vomit that snaked across the floor and erupted in the sink. The empty brandy bottle was on the table as incriminating evidence, next to an overflowing ashtray.

To say the kitchen smelt none too sweet is an understatement. If I had been Lucy's mother I would have scooped up my child and retreated in horror, but this mother of eleven was made of sterner stuff. She waved aside my apologies, dumped Lucy down and fled. James regretfully but predictably, soon moved on to students younger than me. He reminded me of Steve McQueen – quite irresistible.

John Hutchinson, the young zealous architecture student often drove me around to sell papers – we were now selling regularly at the car factory at Longbridge to the early morning shift. He drove a death defying Austin with a hole in the chassis so big the front seat passenger could see the road going by. I do not understand how it could possibly have been deemed road worthy, as MOT tests did exist then. John drove like a maniac taking corners on two wheels and had a number of eccentricities like sticking a piece of paper over his petrol gauge because he said it distracted him from the road watching his fuel go down.

He was a powerful raconteur (though his jokes were never shorter than half an hour in length – they still aren't) and he loved the arts, theatre and Tudor architecture as well as having a thirst for revolutionary politics. Together we visited the Birmingham Arts Lab, opened the previous year, which was to help launch the careers of cartoonists like Steve Bell and Hunt Emerson, playwrights like David Edgar and David Hare and singers like Ruby Turner.

For a short time John and I were more than friends, and the friendship endures to this day. I offered to cook for him if he contributed his share of the costs as he always had a lean and hungry look when he visited us and I was aware of the inadequacy of the cooking arrangements in his bedsit. After a week of supplying substantial meals which he hoovered down with relish, I asked him for a couple of £s. He was taken back. "But that is more than I spend in a week" he said. I asked him what he lived on. The answer was tinned pilchards and a 1lb of apples. I did not continue the offer.

Undeterred John was to join us when we visited Jennifer's parents for a summer holiday in Carbis Bay near St Ives in Cornwall that August. The Fry's had a small visitor's flat under their capacious house and John turned up there in his Austin. Terry said that Jennifer's mother, whose family had made a fortune from the Cornish tin mines and later the diamond mines in South Africa, tolerated us revolutionaries living in the flat under her, because if there was a revolution she could use us as collateral. Jennifer's father was a retired BOAC pilot and a prominent local Liberal and flew Jeremy Thorpe the party leader back and forth from the Scilly Isles.

About this time Roger Rosewell was learning karate and progressing slowly through his belts. John was learning Taekwondo. Rosewell decided to teach some of us Karate in my back garden. He illustrated basic moves and then showed us a flying kick. Given my ballet training I mastered this easily. We were then invited to do our worst and aim a flying kick at what he regarded as his steel hard midriff. I did so, only to see him crumple in pain. The moral being, six months of Karate training is no match for 14 years ballet training. John meantime aimed his bamboo sword at a hedge at the bottom of my garden and with a blood curdling yell, which nearly gave the old dear next door a heart attack, he charged forward and rent the bush in half.

I had seen many of Roman Polanski's films, *Knife in the Water, Repulsion* and *Rosemary's baby* with their bleak dark themes. Polanski had spent much of his early life evading capture in wartime Poland, while his mother perished in Auschwitz. His adult life was to contain nightmares too. In August 1969 his wife Sharon Tait was brutally murdered by Charles Manson and his gang, while Polanski was away working in London. She was two weeks away from giving birth to her first child. It seemed beyond belief.

September came, Dominic started nursery school and I went back to college to do 'A' Levels in Economics and English. The Economics lasted 3 weeks before I got bored. I told my father. "Well Carlisle called it the dismal science," he said. I dropped Economics. The English course I loved. I was in a class of women returners and I absorbed *Hamlet* one of our set texts like a sponge and delighted in Orwell's essays on the English language. Unrelated to the course, I read *The French Lieutenants Woman* by John Fowles and was fascinated with the connections he made between the plight of Victorian as opposed to contemporary women and *The Children of Albion: Poetry of the Underground.* My life seemed to be opening up at last.

November saw the launch of *Monty Python*. It was more surreal than satiric, zany in the way the Goon shows had been zany – but better. It was a wholly new kind of television comedy, aided by Terry Gilliam's weird and grotesque animation. It launched the Python team, particularly John Cleese, Michael Palin and Graham Chapman and spawned a new word for comic absurdity, 'pythonesque'. It was another programme we tried hard never to miss.

Rosewell had become the Industrial IS organiser and had to give up his flat. I needed a replacement income for the loss of the childminding. We decided to take him as a lodger and he moved in before Christmas. I was now living in an unacknowledged ménage a trois, though Rosewell had plenty of partners elsewhere – so for that matter did I – making up for all that experience I should have had before I got married. Once when asked how he managed to get so many attractive women into bed with him, Roger said it was all a matter of statistics. If you asked virtually every woman you met to sleep with you, a small proportion would always say yes.

# 1970
# LIFE, FEMINISM AND DEATH

Living with Rosewell as a lodger was a weird experience. He often preferred egg and chips at a greasy spoon café near where we lived, to eating a proper meal with us. Maybe he saw this as engaging with the working class. It seemed to me that he tried on different personalities for size all the time – he always seemed to be playing a part. He was addicted to *The Untouchables* series on TV, though it wasn't always clear whether he saw himself as govt agent Eliot Ness or Al Capone. I thought the series was shit and the acting execrable.

Early in the year we were invited to a wedding in Brighton. Tubs Read and Kate had divorced and he was marrying again. We travelled down to the wedding with Robin Parker, a railway man, and his wife Beryl (on the way back the fan belt broke and both Beryl and I had to use our tights as temporary substitutes to get us back to South London).

During the rather dull wedding reception, I noticed a queue forming for a jumble sale over the road in the church hall. I had become an enthusiast for jumble sales as so many good clothes could be acquired for next to nothing, and although I resisted the urge for an hour, in the end asked if anyone would mind if I slipped over to the sale. By then everything was running down and all remaining items were reduced to one penny. It was then I spotted an Eliot Ness replica pin strip suit complete with waistcoat and, to add to its authenticity, inside was an American garment workers union label dated 1932. What an amazing find! I bought it on the spot for one penny and brought it home.

I hadn't immediately marked it out as a garment for Roger, but he took one look at it and immediately claimed it. It fitted like a glove. The following day he arrived home with a black shirt, a white kipper tie and a grey trilby. He had given Dominic a toy gun, a replica luger, for a present prior to this, (though I did not approve of militaristic toys and much to my son's displeasure, vetoed an Action Man a few years later). Rosewell now reclaimed the gun and took to swaggering about wearing the 'bulge' under his suit. I thought the whole thing ridiculous but essentially harmless, a bit like the enthusiasm some men have for model trains. Terry's increasing addiction to soft porn magazines bothered me more.

For years I had been feeling sidelined by my lack of education, inability to earn a decent living commensurate with the men in my life and therefore being forced into a dependency which irked and frustrated me. I always felt I was a square peg rammed into a round hole, my main role servicing the men in my life in one way or another. So it was with great pleasure I joined Irene Breugel and Margaret George to attend the first Women's Liberation Conference on February 27–1st March at Ruskin College Oxford.

I admired Irene. She was in IS, but clearly had a mind of her own. She was still legally married to Pete Binns but was to revert to her maiden name of Breugel soon afterwards. She had a flat in Moseley and a job in the Centre for Urban and Regional Studies. We travelled down in her Volkswagen and her friends in Oxford put us both up along with Dominic my son. Neither she nor Margaret George had children, and both were financially independent. For me, the sense of liberation I got from attending was probably the greatest.

It started with the provision of the crèche. My experience of crèches organised at political conferences were dire. This one was different. Children had a suite of rooms and were divided into age groups. Cribs and a quiet room was organised for babies. Older children had an outside play area and entertainment laid on and lots of toys and equipment to keep them happy. Parents were asked about food fads and allergies and each child was fed lunch in the crèche. Amazingly, men ran the crèche throughout the three days. I felt I had died and gone to heaven. This was the first time I had been able to attend a conference confident in the knowledge my son was having a good time elsewhere – so good that at the end of the three days he was reluctant to leave.

The conference attracted leading women academics like Bea Campbell, Selma James, wife of CLR James and Catherine Hall, wife of Stuart Hall. There were about 500 of us there. The conference set up local networks, analysed women's roles and relationships and defined sets of demands for social and economic equality for women. These were:-

*Equal Pay*
*Equal education and Job opportunities*
*Free 24hr nurseries*
*Free contraception and abortion on demand*

There was also a lively discussion on wages for housework introduced by Selma James, and the establishment of a women's history group with people like Dorothy Thompson, Catherine Hall and Sheila Rowbotham involved. There was a call for women to donate their wedding rings. I only had a second hand one I had bought in an antique shop, but at least it was 21 carat, so I cheerfully chucked it into the bucket. The buzz at the conference was exciting – for the first time since I had got active in CND when I was 16, I felt I belonged. I remember driving through Oxford with Irene and seeing the slogan painted on a wall *'a woman needs a man like a fish needs a bicycle.'*

In the aftermath of the conference, 4,000 women marched through London in March and handed a petition to the Prime Minister at Downing Street with our demands. Over the next few years there was a huge upsurge of academic research on gender, from *The sociology of housework* (Anne Oakley) to Sheila Rowbotham's *Hidden from History*.

I had already read Hannah Gavron's book *The Captive wife,* a pioneering study of the loneliness and frustration of housebound mothers, as part of my Sociology course. I had not appreciated at the time that Gavron's death by suicide in 1965 mirrored that of Sylvia Plath's two years earlier. Both were mothers of small children and both of them gassed themselves in houses a few minutes walk from each other.

There were parallels with my life too. Gavron had gone to RADA at 16 (I had attempted to do so) she had married at 18 to an academic six years older than her. So had I. I had also made a half-hearted attempt on my own life, but I had no intention of solving my problems this way again. While their children had not deterred Gavron and Plath from taking their own life, I knew I could never pass this legacy on to my children, though I knew my mother had made attempts to end her life. I felt invigorated by the women's movement and for the first time felt connected to other women engaged in the feminist struggle.

Later in the year, feminists were to disrupt the Miss World competition, which led to the mythical stories of bra burning and a comment from Bob Hope that "pretty women didn't have these problems". It reminded me how the suffragette's decades before had been depicted as ugly spinsters who could not get a man. *Shrew*, was a new kind of women's magazine which now gave us a voice, so different from the bland and inane commercial women's magazines, it was followed by *Spare Rib* and then *Women's Voice*, produced by IS women and only grudgingly acknowledged, if at all, by the leadership of the group.

Most IS males seem to think feminism was a diversion from the 'class struggle' and unless the women in question were trade unionists out on strike they did not warrant the same attention. I felt that Anne Oakley summed things up well *"Clearly society has a tremendous stake in insisting on a woman's natural fitness for the career of motherhood – the alternatives are all too expensive"*. I wanted housebound mothers to be taken as seriously as women trade unionists by our male comrades, who paid lip service to equality but rarely changed a nappy or took time out to look after their children.

Students also felt the pressure to convert from academia to manual workers as they thought that only there could they play a full part in the 'class struggle'. Michael Rice had made the move to the factories and Dave Adshead also moved seamlessly from graduate to (bad) building worker, but I was concerned to hear that John Hutchinson was considering chucking in his five year architectural course to do likewise, a month prior to graduating. Realising that John was not cut out for this kind of transition, I took him to task, saying it was crazy to chuck in 5 years work so close to graduating. Even if he only regarded this as a meal ticket he should complete, but didn't he think we would need architects too in any future socialist society? I persuaded him to take the degree-something he later told me he was eternally grateful for, because it was to provide a meal ticket rather more effectively than Lucas Electrical might have done. 1972–4 he worked in London where he met his lifetime partner Siri Lowe, before returning to work for Telford Development Corporation. John's final career post was to be architectural advisor to the Palace of Westminster.

1970 was election year, and for the first time 18-year-olds would be able to vote due to a change in the law on January 1st which lowered the age of majority. All the opinion polls predicted a Labour victory, so it was a real shock when the Tories won by 30 seats and Edward Heath ousted Wilson as Prime Minister. Wilson blamed it on complacency engendered by the polls, others thought that Powellite working class Tories had swung the vote. The Liberals also had lost their seats to the Tories. The election had been fixed early because Wilson predicted that decimalisation, which was due to be introduced in February 1971, would be unpopular. Ian Paisley the Northern Ireland unionist bigot gained a seat. So did Bernadette Devlin standing as an Independent, which ensured there would be some lively debates in store.

In June I was to take my 'A' levels – I had expected only to be entered for English as I had only attended three Economics lectures all year. With some consternation I found in May that by accident I had been entered for both. Terry offered to take Dominic down to my mother's in Somerset during the Whitsun holidays to give me some uninterrupted revision time.

I remember watching them go off down the road with Dominic pedalling like the clappers on a three-wheeler tricycle he had recently acquired, leaving me on my own with Roger the lodger. The inevitable happened and we slept together, but I also put in a good amount of preparation for my English exam, though I remember I only had time to read a couple of pamphlets on Value Added Tax and the Common Market and rely on some background knowledge of the car industry before I took my Economics papers.

The following month I sat both exams and felt very satisfied with the English papers. I did not expect to pass the Economics. The exams were in late June and by then I had begun to wonder if I might by some ironic chance be pregnant. We had tried so hard for four years to have another baby. Now when I had decided to give up trying and had planned a University course instead, it looked as if fate had intervened again. I went to the doctors for tests in July and my pregnancy was confirmed.

I told Terry and I can remember him saying, "Is it mine?" I had been anticipating this and calculating the probabilities. Terry and I had made love on the day most likely for me to conceive. The other probability was more remote, enough for me to say "Yes", but it was a close call nonetheless. Not only was I sure it was his, I had no wish for there to be any other father and certainly felt Rosewell would be a very unsuitable alternative. He was about to move out to take over the post of the Liverpool organiser and I found I was looking forward to him leaving with a considerable sense of relief. I had taken too many risks not thinking I could get pregnant, I did not want to be reminded.

We had made arrangements to go down to see my parents in early August with Tubs and Jill (I spent part of July working in an office to try and earn enough to pay back to my parents the £100 deposit on the house they had lent us – I figured if I didn't do this it might never be paid back-Terry didn't seem in a hurry to do so). I had not yet told my mother about the baby but I knew she had been hoping for a second grandchild for some time and as the day for us to go to Somerset got closer I experienced a tremendous sense of urgency I could not quite fathom.

The Reads had moved to Market Deeping, a small town near Peterborough the previous year and had a garden that was more like a smallholding that backed onto the River Welland. They had a virtual orchard at the rear of their house and two crazy boxer dogs called Victoria and Albert. They assured us that they would be putting the dogs into kennels before they came down to my parents. Jill, also pregnant, said she needed a break from them too.

The day before we were all due to travel down to Somerset, the Reads arrived complete with dogs. They had obviously made no effort to put them in kennels. They seemed to take the attitude 'love me, love my dogs'. Our garden was virtually uncultivated, but watching the boxer's race crazily around my garden I knew there would be problems and I was in a state of acute anxiety when Terry put the phone call through to explain we had the dogs with us as well.

My father was emphatic. There was absolutely no way we were going to come to stay with these dogs. He said they would wreck his carefully cultivated garden. He was almost certainly right. They would have done. An even stronger argument against the dogs was that my parents had an elderly cat that would freak out if two large dogs invaded the house.

I wanted to scream. I felt utterly desperate. I had been experiencing an uncanny and disproportionate sense of urgency about going down to see my mother and I could not bear the thought that at the last moment I was going to be prevented from doing so. Terry, a dog lover suggested, with a total lack of diplomacy, that maybe my parents could put the cat in a cattery for a week. My father exploded. He told Terry in no uncertain terms what he could do with his barefaced cheek. Our visit was abandoned. I was in utter despair. I asked to speak to my mother who was also bitterly disappointed. She had got food in for our visit and was looking forward to it so much. Very reluctantly and feeling I had been robbed of something very precious, I told her over the phone about the baby. Then being unable to control myself I went upstairs and sobbed hysterically and uncontrollably for a very long time.

Terry could not understand why I was so upset. He reasoned we could go back with the Reads, spend a week with them and then go on to my parent's house. What difference would a week make? I did not know except that something told me that it would make all the difference in the world. Call it a premonition. I have had three such premonitions in my life. I learned after this one to never ignore them. Not that they have ever enabled me to change the course of events.

We went to Market Deeping. Because my mother was so upset at us not going down that week she and my father arranged to go and visit her brother Edward who was living in the New Forest for a few days. On the way back from there, my mother took a fall in the coach station café in Taunton where they changed buses. Apparently the floor was greasy. She fell awkwardly and was in considerable pain. She should have gone directly to the A&E dept at the hospital in Taunton. She would not. She later told us she was pretty certain she had broken her leg and would be kept in, but she did not want to be admitted to Taunton Hospital because she thought my father would not come to visit her that far away and because we were due the following week.

The bus journey over bumpy rural roads from Taunton to Minehead cannot have helped her condition. When she got to Minehead and was taken to the cottage hospital, they told her they had no facilities for fractures and promptly returned her back in an ambulance to Taunton. Here her leg was set in plaster and she was kept in overnight. She should have stayed longer but she would not and discharged herself anxious to be home for our arrival. My father could hardly contain his anger. He had planned a week's holiday for himself in Austria and was due to leave at the weekend. My mother's accident meant that he had to cancel his holiday to look after her. Compounded with the cancellation of our earlier arrangements he was in the foulest of moods.

This was the atmosphere that greeted us on our arrival. My mother her leg in plaster was trying to get up and down stairs on her behind. I immediately took over and insisted she rest in bed and saw to the cooking and shopping. Dominic was happy to play with his grandma while she was in bed. My mother fished out an old leather bag and they had a protracted game of buses with Dominic playing the conductor and giving her tickets out of the bag. Terry managed to upset my mother announcing the fur rug in our bedroom had fleas, but by and large my father provided most of the acrimony. I acted, as I had done so many times as a child, as a cipher between my parents.

I spent much of my time with my mother in her bedroom. I felt an uncanny and urgent need to spend as much time as possible with her – every minute seemed precious. I began to get more and more alarmed, because on her journeys up and down stairs she started to get seriously out of breath and mentioned a shooting pain in her right arm. I consulted with Terry. We were both concerned, fearing a possible stroke and being the sensitive type, Terry said he had had a terrible thought that if anything were to happen to my mother we would be lumbered with my father. I insisted a doctor was called. My father told me I was making a fuss about nothing but I put the call through anyway.

While we were waiting for the doctor to arrive, my mother sent me out to do some shopping. While I was out, the locum called – her regular doctor was on holiday. My father was digging in the front garden when he arrived. "I don't know why my daughter has called you out" he said, "It's quite unnecessary. She's just a bit breathless – it's secondary shock that's all. I've seen cases like this in Civil Defence in the war." Such was his vehemence, the young doctor clearly felt somewhat intimidated. He looked at my mother's notes, noted she had a history of nervous breakdowns and prescribed tranquillisers.

I was totally unconvinced, but this was 1970. No one questioned doctors then. Reluctantly we prepared to depart. The following day my 'A' Level results arrived. I had gained a Grade 'A' in English. I had even managed a scrape pass in Economics. On the way back from the office that evening I nearly stopped to ring my mother and tell her the results, but I deferred doing so, thinking I would do it the following day.

Next morning a call was put through to me at the office. It was Terry. "I thought I would bring Dominic into town to do some shopping" he said. "Can I meet you at lunchtime?" I was very surprised. I was not used to this kind of spontaneity. I arranged to meet him in a church square nearby. As if in a dream I saw a taxi approach and Dominic standing in the taxi door as it stopped by me. I got in. "Your mother is dead" said Terry.

The cause of death was an embolism, something not uncommon when a limb is broken, more common still when the person concerned has diabetes. My mother had mild diabetes. It was in her notes. The doctor either had not spotted that or had been too intimidated to look properly. My mother had sustained a complicated fracture to her knee and a blood clot had formed round the break. It had travelled up through the body to the artery leading to the lung, which had been the cause of her breathlessness and eventual death. My parents had a lodger who was an ambulance driver. My father had called him in a panic that morning. He took one look at my mother and said "Get an ambulance now".

My mother suffocated to death on the way to the hospital. It was an eminently preventable death. An

X-ray would have picked up the blood clot and Warfarin and a week in intensive care would have dispersed it. My mother was 58. She had never had the chance to retire and have a proper break. She was robbed of her second grandchild and the chance to see all her grandchildren grow up. I was robbed of a mother I loved dearly at the age of 24 and at the time when you need your mother most, when you are pregnant yourself. We were just beginning to bond as adults. Her death left me utterly bereft, but I could not cry. Something had warned me of the disaster pending and I had already wept copiously. I just felt numb.

Terry fearing I would have a miscarriage if I had to deal with the aftermath, said he would go down to Somerset to be with my father and to oversee my mother's funeral and I could come down on the day. He asked Godfrey Webster and Ray Osborne if they would move in and look after me while he was away.

I went through the next couple of weeks in a daze. Ern Bendall met me at the station and took me back to his house the night before the funeral. He and his wife were both deeply upset. The funeral was in Taunton. I remember nothing of it except seeing my uncle Edward there. He had always been very close to his sister and he looked devastated. I tried to talk to him but he could not or would not speak to me. I could not bear to go near my father. My anger at his treatment of my mother was too raw.

Back at the house I handed him an envelope containing £100. It represented five weeks work and their loan returned. I did not want to be beholden to him for anything. He burst into tears. I did not comfort him. I was left in my mother's bedroom to pack up all her clothes, but before I did so Terry had something to give me. "This is a letter from your mother" he said. She had been writing it to me the night before she died. In the letter she asked me to give the enclosed bag to Dominic since he had enjoyed playing conductors with it. She then apologised for my father's terrible behaviour during the week we had spent there. She went on to say that if she had her time over again she would have divorced him, but now she felt she was too old to start again. I made a silent vow then that I would never write a posthumous letter like that for my own children to discover.

Packing up her clothes was an ordeal. There were hairs on the jackets and dresses – she had been wearing some of these clothes just days ago. In her work-basket I found a pair of bootees – she had already started to knit for the new baby.

It was decided my father could not stay there alone, and would need to come back with us. He was lachrymose in his grief. I could offer him no comfort. I could do dutiful things, find him a bed make him a meal, but any warmth I felt for him had vanished. A week after my mother's death my Uncle Eddie died. We were not invited to the funeral and after that I never heard anything from his family again.

Eventually my father left. He said he was going to sell the house. He had never been happy in Minehead and was going to move elsewhere. Later in the autumn we heard he had a sale and had decided to move to St Marychurch in Torquay.

We spent some time decorating and preparing the back bedroom as I had opted for a home birth this time. I decided to attend National Childbirth Trust classes – I was going to make a better job of the birth this time. Attendance of partners was expected – things were changing. I felt seriously adrift, Terry was my only anchor now and it did not seem a very solid one. I asked the comrades to find another home for the IS duplicator – they did but only a day before the birth. Dominic asked if he could have a baby and a puppy for Christmas. All I wanted was my mother back again.

# 1971
# A BIRTH. I MEET THE LOVE OF MY LIFE. I APPLY TO UNIVERSITY

Various things happened in January. The Open University began and Terry registered as a summer school tutor. Rolls Royce went bankrupt and was nationalised. On the world stage Idi Amin deposed Obote in Uganda and began a reign of terror, which was to lead to a mass expulsion of Ugandan Asians, many of whom would settle in Britain. Appollo 14 landed on the moon.

On Friday 5th February I looked at my near completed bedroom and decided I hated the 1930s fireplace and that it had to go. I got a chisel and a hammer and set to work. By lunchtime I had it out and had walked the reinforced concrete fireplace down the stairs and out in the back yard in a pair of flip-flops. Sheer madness – the baby was due in a week! I returned to take the plaster off the chimneybreast wall and to score the brickwork ready for it to be whitewashed – exposed brickwork was very fashionable then.

Terry returned at teatime and was flabbergasted at what I had done. We spent the evening whitewashing the wall and boarding in the cavity where the fireplace had been. I had been told that a birth is imminent when a woman gets a sudden rush of energy and suddenly want to take on mammoth projects. It's called the nesting instinct. Either way I was satisfied the room was finished, but the effort was too much for Terry who retired to the spare room feigning flu and had to be fetched and carried for over the weekend.

Lying alone in the bedroom on Sunday night my contractions started. Not wishing to wake Dominic I called out softly to Terry. No answer. He was dead to the world. I timed the gap between contractions and went next door to wake him up and tell him my labour had started. It took a long time to wake him and make him understand. He went to phone the midwife and then helped me clear things up in the bedroom ready for her arrival, wearing a mask, as he did not want to pass on his germs.

The midwives arrived at 2am. They examined me and announced that I still had a way to go. They stayed with me for a companionable hour knitting, chatting and occasionally examining me to check on progress. At 3am they decided I was still a long way from the second stage of labour and that we should all try and get some sleep and left. Terry returned to the spare room.

At 5am I got a desperate urge to push. I called Terry. Again, no response, I had to go and shake him awake again. This time walking was very difficult. Ignoring my requests that we needed the midwife now, he asked if I could hold on for another half an hour? He explained that in half an hour he would be able to summon the daytime midwife who came on duty at 6am. If he called the nighttime midwives, by the time they had delivered the baby they would be working overtime and he was in principle against overtime working. I was too euphoric and confused to consider how peculiar and detached his response was.

For half an hour I practised the breathing exercises we

had been taught to minimise the urge to push because it had been explained that we must not push till a midwife had examined us and confirmed the cervix was properly dilated or we could sustain an internal tear. At 5.30 the daytime midwife was called. She arrived with a student midwife at 6am. Can I push I asked? "Good God girl you could have pushed hours ago" she said. In three pushes the head crowned but the baby looked blue – the cord was round its neck. I was told to stop pushing immediately while the chord was cut from round the neck. Two more pushes and I was delivered of a baby daughter. She weighed in at 7lbs 8ozs.

The midwife put her in my arms and gradually I watched as the colour came back into her small face. I had managed the birth without drugs cuts or tears and she was a good weight. The midwife and her student were impressed. What will you call her they asked? The name Ann or Annie had been in my family for years. It was my mother's middle name and my grandmother's name. I wanted to keep a link with my mother. "Anna" I said. The student smiled "Why that's my name" she said "and this is my first home birth". We were delighted with the coincidence and Anna became not just a midwife, more a special friend. We corresponded for some time afterwards.

Dominic had been taken to school that morning in ignorance of his sister's birth. We figured if we told him he wouldn't want to go to school and we needed a few hours of peace and quiet to recover. When Terry collected him at 3pm and told him the news he was tremendously excited and set off at a sprint up the road. Bursting into the bedroom he demanded to see the baby.

I hushed him and told him she was sleeping in the

crib and to not disturb her. He stared in. "But she's got no hair" he said disappointingly. "It will grow," I said. "Wake her up, I want to play with her" he said. I explained little babies needed a lot of sleep and she would not be ready to play with him for quite a few months. "I will save her some of my baked beans from tea," he said. I explained that new babies just drank milk for the first few months of their lives and she would not be ready for beans for a very long time. He absorbed all this information. A bald sister, who you couldn't eat with or play with, who wasn't even able to wake up and say hallo. He kicked the crib in disgust. "Can I have a puppy instead," he said.

My father was telephoned with the news and burst into tears. Later in the day Gilda, a girl who had gone out with Roger phoned about something entirely unrelated. "Did you tell her about the baby?" I asked Terry. "I didn't think she would be interested" came the reply.

Despite this rather detached response, my second experience of childbirth was immensely better than the first. I was able to eat what I liked and get up when I liked. I established breast-feeding with absolutely no problems and got a lot of support from the midwives. I avoided cracked nipples this time with the advice of an old midwife who had worked in the 1930s. She told me to paint my nipples with Friars Balsam and leave it to dry and it would then provide a protective layer over the nipple. I followed her advice and it worked! Indeed I produced so much milk I was able to donate breast milk to the premature baby unit in Birmingham. I was provided with a breast shield which collected the milk which leaked from one breast while you were feeding the baby on the other and I produced several ounces a day which were frozen in small sterilised bottles supplied by the hospital. The milk unit collected twice a week and even paid me so much an ounce and that 'milk money' was my only income for six months.

Anna the student midwife was especially attentive of her small namesake and I bounced back fast. Two days after the baby was born I went down the pub for a drink with Victor Collard and some of the IS engineering workers. It was Wednesday and they had last seen me heavily pregnant at the branch meeting the previous Thursday. Victor was flabbergasted at my rapid transformation as I was back wearing my pre-pregnancy clothes.

It took time for Terry to bond with the baby but I noticed him gradually spending longer watching her and getting involved with her. Roger had come over and viewed the baby and told me I should have called her Jane. He liked the name "Lady Jane Gray". He bought a matinee jacket his mother had knitted. It was so large I used it as a bolero. I cut the visit short. I did not want to add to Terry's insecurities. We needed time to bond as a family and we did not need the presence of someone who had came too close to comfort to fathering my child.

Seven days after Anna was born, Britain went decimal on February 15th. It was a couple of weeks later before I ventured out to shop with my new daughter, only to find everyone had adjusted to the new currency, while I was still struggling to make sense of it.

Terry was anxious for his sleep not to be disturbed because he had to teach during the day, so we put the baby in the spare room and when she woke in the night I went into the other bedroom to feed her. It was very unpleasant on a cold winter night to have to get out of a warm bed and to transfer to another cold uninviting one. There was a fashion for Bri-nylon sheets at the times and they were slippery and cold next to the skin. Still I obliged.

I don't know whether it was my hormones being all over the place, or something more sinister surfacing in my subconscious but for several months while I made those night time trips to feed the baby I would slip into the same re-occurring nightmare as I dozed off with the baby still feeding at my breast. The nightmare would start with a black hearse slowly creeping round the corner of a side road onto our local High street. I knew the mafia were in the car and they were looking for me. I would squeeze myself back into the doorway of Woolworths, which had a cigarette kiosk protruding into the road. In the kiosk was a naked man with a manacle round his neck, which chained him to the floor. In the kiosk with him was a huge black gorilla and I knew he was going to tear the man limb from limb. I knew I would be next if I uttered a sound. The terror this nightmare invoked would wake me with a start. It ensured I kept awake, because as soon as I drifted into sleep and saw that hearse I would force myself awake again. Thankfully when Anna cut out night feeds, the nightmare faded.

Birth control was now an issue. I had two children and wanted no more. The birth pill had by this time become widely available, but as there was a history of thrombosis in my family, it was not seen as the best contraceptive for me, especially given the concerns associated with the early high oestrogen pills. The family planning clinic recommended an IUD called a Dalkon Shield. I had one fitted. Within weeks I was doubled up with pain similar in type to the septic infection I had contracted from Showell Green Hospital. I was fitted with a second IUD of a different type – apparently it was more expensive so they did not offer it initially.

What I did not know at the time was that 200,000 women made claims against the Dalkon Shield manufacturer A H Robins, for pelvic inflammatory disease and loss of fertility derived from its use. Robins filed for bankruptcy shortly afterwards. At the time medical information was not freely available – we had no internet and patients were deprived of access to their medical records. Health professionals kept their cards close to their chest – patients rarely heard the bad news. It was only researching for this book 45 years later I discovered this.

While I had been off the scene and not following the news, Enoch Powell had been up to his old tricks warning of an immigration explosion and demanding a mass repatriation scheme for immigrants. The Home secretary Reginald Maudling announced an Immigration Bill, which would strip citizens of the Commonwealth of their right to remain in the UK. Commonwealth citizenship has been part of a sop offered to the citizens of Asia and Africa historically when we were still busy plundering their countries to add to the wealth of the British Empire. It was offered when it was assumed few of the 'natives' would wish to settle in Britain. The Windrush generation had been useful to us when we needed our health service propped up with additional nurses and our transport system needed drivers. The Asian community had found work in our mills and our foundries. They had enriched the British economy with their taxes and their labour power, now, with rising unemployment, the government wanted them all to just go away.

The government were also in the process of trying to introduce a draconian new Industrial Relations Bill. This would concentrate power in the leadership of unions, make no-strike agreements easier to implement and introduce punitive fines or the sequestration of union assets as a penalty. The whole trade union movement was up in arms. A 'Kill the Bill' campaign was launched and in March 250,000 trade unionists marched in protest against its implementation. 1,500,000 members of the Amalgamated Engineering Union staged a one-day strike on 1st March. On 18th March a further strike brought out 3 million trade unionists. The next few years were to see unprecedented action among the union rank and file, often against their own Trade Union leadership.

The leadership of the IS group were keen to acquire another Birmingham organiser at this time of increased strife, as it was seen as a key city for the development of an industrial cadre. Granville Williams from Exeter was a new protégé of Tony Cliff's and he persuaded Granville to take the post. Terry and I were asked to put him up temporarily until he could establish a base. I imagined him to be Jamaican with a name like Granville, so I was rather surprised when he arrived in August, to find a tall slim white man with glasses, a long drooping moustache (which was the obligatory fashion for IS male militants at the time), and a very broad smile standing on my doorstep. He had a striking resemblance to Hank Marvin and a chunk missing from a front tooth.

He proved himself an amenable and thoughtful lodger. I discovered he was separated from his wife who was at present back in Exeter doing a degree and that he had one daughter, Joanne, six months younger than Dominic. He had been a teacher and was a great help when we organised Dominic's birthday party, coming up with all kinds of games and activities for the kids. His easy going and modest style went down well with our engineering workers too and he could put away the pints with the best of them. For a time he went around with Hilary Luce a dark haired introspective student of Italian, who was a talented amateur artist.

However we did not want a lodger for the long term. Anna could still be an erratic sleeper and it was useful to have that spare room to put her in, so Chris and Margaret George who had recently bought a new house in Handsworth offered to put him up – in an act of extraordinary generosity they also gave him unlimited use of their car. How generous this was soon became apparent, as we discovered his reputation for writing off cars.

Some time early that year we had acquired a Morris Traveller, and I started to take driving lessons. To save money, Terry said that since what I really needed was practice, he would go out with me in the car with the L-plates on and I could practice with him. Having never had a driving lesson in his life Terry nevertheless felt it was incumbent on him to play the part of a driving instructor, so when I approached a roundabout and changed down to second he informed me I was in the wrong gear. "Well what gear am I supposed to be in" I asked. "Fourth" he said authoritatively. After that I decided to go out with the more patient and knowledgeable Chris George who had the advantage of a licence.

Still not ready to take my test, my father was anxious for us to visit him in his new home. We had the car but no driver. Joe Quigley another IS member offered to drive us down to Devon. My father had acquired an old

Georgian house built on a slope. The front door was straight off the road but the back living room was on the first floor and below was a studio flat which he let out from time to time even though the kitchen in the damp cellar section of the house was far from perfect. Irene expressed an interest in coming too, so we approached my father about putting them both up in the studio flat, which would mean we could all go. He agreed. We drove down in the Whitsun Holidays. We had seen little of my dad for a few months and during that time he had been hard at work painting and renovating the house, which was a potentially elegant end terrace on Western Road (potentially, as it was clear my father would never spend the money to improve it in the way it needed).

Not wishing to impose on him by the import of 4 adults and two children, even if two were to be tucked away out of sight in the studio flat, I bought the food for us all and cooked for everyone including my father. He was initially pleased to see us but it didn't take long for his irritation to rise to the surface. He had a hot water tank for the bathroom but would not let us turn it on for more than an hour a day. He told us we could boil a kettle to wash with, but Anna was still in towelling nappies and that was a tall order. He soon started to mutter about 'mess' even though I scurried around picking up, washing up and in many cases cleaning rather more thoroughly than my father. Everything had to be done to his rules, from what we ate to what saucepans we cooked with, and after a few days he let rip with one of his legendary temper tantrums which went on for hours, in which we were all roundly abused including our two friends.

"This is crazy," said Terry. "We are supposed to be on

holiday". We searched around and found a caravan for rent in Maidencombe, packed up and departed.

The following morning my father sought us out and begrudgingly suggested we return. He wasn't going to apologise, but suggested we were doing something utterly unfeeling by moving out and not giving him the chance to use us as a punch-bag for his bullying. I had kept my lip buttoned since my mother died and dutifully put my father up for months before he sold the house and moved. Now I had had enough. I turned to him and said, "you made my mother's life a misery, you are not going to make mine one too". His face drained white. It was the only time I ever confronted him about my mother and I would not do it again. I recognised he was carrying around a huge burden of guilt. He was just incapable of self-control and like a child had to lash out whenever he was in pain.

The caravan holiday turned into something of an adventure in the end. Terry propositioned and slept with Irene and I slept with Joe. On one occasion I slept with both Joe and Terry when Irene departed*. It was very erotic. Anna disturbed by all the changes would wake in the middle of the night and wail, and then the only way to get her to sleep was to drive her round the country lanes at three in the morning, with Joe driving us both in his Y fronts. As we coasted back into the site and cut the motor hoping we had got her off to sleep, a little cry would reach us from the back of the car and

---

* Terry later decided this entitled him to a night of partner swapping with Joe Quigley's girl friend. They were invited over and after much food drink and talk Terry announced he was taking Joes girlfriend to bed – she looked surprised but complied without demur. Joe spent the night in my bed, suddenly stricken with a fever brought on, I have no doubt, by a consequence he had not anticipated.

we would have to turn round and drive away again. It was certainly challenging.

On my return I took my driving test. I was told I would be borderline if the examiner asked me a lot of questions. I badly wanted to pass. Not only because it would give me an independence I had not had till now, but also because if I didn't pass first time and Terry did, I would never live it down. I was asked a lot of questions and tried to throw a surreptitious glance at the examiner after the test to see which colour form I was being given, as there was a different colour for passes and fails. Much to my relief I passed. I got out, untied the L-plates and threw them into the back of the car. I was just driving off when the driving instructor tapped on my window. "I just had a thought," he said. "How were you going to get back if you hadn't passed your test". "But I did" I said. I drove back ecstatic and called in to tell Belinda my NCT teacher the good news. She was delighted for me.

The car made a big difference to my life. Suddenly I could escape and when things got too oppressive I would do just that. Once I drove to Peterborough and asked Tubs and Jill to put me up. Terry tracked me down after a few days.

One night I drove a very drunk Granville back to Handsworth in my car. He wanted to stop to walk in the park, and began to kiss and fondle me. 'You know I will love you and leave you" he said, which was rather presumptuous of him because at the time I had not given any indication I was interested in him – indeed I was not sure that I was. I changed my mind half an hour later when we consummated our relationship in a Handsworth car park with the windows of the car steaming up around us.

Sex with Granville was the most passionate and fulfilling I had ever experienced. His stamina was extraordinary. We made love for hours, and on the rare occasion we could spend the night together we would make love all night. He brought me to a level of ecstasy I had never experienced before. He said it was the same for him; I was the most exciting woman he had ever made love to. We got into a pattern of meeting every Thursday morning at my house and I looked forward to these few hours more than anything else in the week.

Not only that, he was a man of many parts, interested in literature, the theatre, visual arts, films and music as well as politics. He had a thirst for new ideas, he wrote poetry and was so unlike other sectarian socialists who lived for politics and nothing else. Having said that, he had started life in the Socialist Labour League so he had political stamina, but it was leavened by a well-developed sense of humour and a sense of proportion. He had a relaxed and infectious charm and a real sense of style. He was the first man I knew to buy a pair of loons – he was a dedicated follower of fashion – and he had a great body to show them off. It was a dancer's body, slim and well proportioned. It was not long before I was seriously in love with him.

But like much else in Granville's life there were a lot of things unresolved including his marriage to Kitty. He had not entirely abandoned the relationship, nor could he, given they had a child. I was in the same position. My marriage offered me little physical satisfaction and it was clear that the more education I received the more we were growing apart. In truth we had always had little in common outside politics, but now I had more confidence to exert my own tastes and preferences. Terry also recognised this tendency among his mature women students at the Open University, who were beginning to challenge their husband's opinions and fallibility on many issues. "I think I have been responsible for a number of divorces", he said after the annual summer school.

For some of the Birmingham comrades, Mike and Lynn Pedley, John Brown and John Hutchinson, the summer offered an opportunity to attend the *Lutte Ouvriere* annual festival in France. Since the May '68 events, the International Socialists had developed a fraternal link with this French Trotskyist group. Terry's only notion of holidays was to go and stay with friends in England. Something like the *Lutte Ouvriere* summer festival was a bridge too far. Holidays invariably involved trips to Torquay, or to one of our friends, but wanting to give my father a wide berth this summer, we had made no plans for a holiday. Granville suggested we travel down to Exeter when he went down collect Kitty and Joanne. He was taking them up north to visit her mother and said we could stay in the small terrace house she was renting in Exeter in her absence, and feed Joanne's pet rabbit. We agreed. Exeter was a good touring base for a holiday.

The night we arrived Granville took Kitty out for the evening, and we stayed in to babysit the three children. Kitty was an attractive woman with long curly auburn hair, considerable style and charisma, a fierce intelligence and a caustic wit. I liked her but also found her a tad intimidating.

Checking on Joanne I found a small moon-faced girl sitting up on a mattress on the floor, which had been pulled off her bed. She was soaked in urine, which was cold. She had obviously wet herself some time ago but seemed quite unphased by this as if it was a regular occurrence (I later found it was). I had not been warned or offered any guidelines and searched futilely in the small cluttered bedroom for more bedding. In the end I took off her soaked pyjamas and wrapped her in a blanket. She took this all very calmly as if she was used to lots of different people looking after her. She had a way of looking at you that was very knowing and adult. I found it unnerving in a four-year-old.

The house was exceptionally basic. There was no bathroom – Kitty and Jo took baths in the University on Gandy Street. We would have to manage with the sink in the kitchen. The toilet was outside in the yard, along with the rabbit. He seemed to have the run of the space.

The following day I went into Exeter with Granville and the two oldest kids and he showed me around. The electricity between us was palpable and from time to time he would brush my hand as we walked through one of the gardens in the town. We took the kids to Exmouth where Granville lit a fire on the beach – I found he loved lighting fires. He had brought a tin of baked beans with him; a penknife and a couple of spoons so we ceremoniously heated the beans and ate spoonfuls sitting round the fire. The kids loved it. The following day Kitty and Granville departed. I had tried to keep my feelings under wraps but Kitty had sharp eyes. On the journey north she told him that I was clearly in love with him

With Kitty and Granville out of the way the sexual tension lifted and I thought we could enjoy a family holiday. I counted without Mr Fastidious. Terry was appalled with the dirt in the place and proceeded to spring clean the house deaf to my pleas that we were only here for a week and did it matter? He flung out various straw mats, which he announced were too filthy to clean and I thought he was going to have a seizure when he saw the state of the cooker and the grill pan. We chiselled off fossilised sausage stuck to the back of the cooker in black grease with Terry muttering continuously.

But his greatest ire was reserved for the rabbit that understandably preferred the relative comfort of indoors to the dubious pleasures of a dark yard. Being a black rabbit he knew was to his advantage, so at night he would position himself by the back door and as soon as we opened it to go to the loo, he would shoot in and make straight for the boxed-in studio couch where squeezing through a small hole he knew he would be safe from all pursuers. Terry would lie full length on the floor doing an eyeball to eyeball with the Bunny. "I know what you are doing in there you bastard" he yelled, "you're shitting aren't you?" This was almost certainly the case given the evidence of many small black pellets visible through the hole, which indicated this was a regular port of call.

If we did go to the beach I cannot remember. I remember visiting Topsham but that is all. We certainly didn't build beach fires and I went home leaving behind a very clean terraced house stripped of its mats and a cryptic note from Terry "We cleaned up – have thrown away rotting mats".

My romantic fantasies about Granville needed a reality check and it was not long in coming. It was the glimpse of his jacket in Sue Thomas's wardrobe that made me put two and two together and realise he was living with her. I did sometimes wonder if she left the wardrobe open deliberately when she invited us back for some food. Not only this but it was soon clear he was paying attention to many other women. It made me confused, especially when he came out with really naff statements like "Sex with you is so good – the very best – I wanted to see if it could be that good with someone else" to justify his herculean efforts as the local IS Casanova.

I resolved to try and put him out of my mind and focus on what I had always planned, to apply to Birmingham University for the following year when I hoped to get a nursery place for Anna. It would be a more productive use of my time than mooning over some man. I applied to read Combined Honours in Drama and Sociology. I was summoned for a non-interview as most of the time was spent giving me directions for a faster route home; they had clearly decided they wanted me. But not it seemed on the Drama/Sociology course. Apparently I had "too much experience" and this, I was told, could divert less mature student from their academic studies (I never fathomed out the rationale behind that or why I had to be responsible for other students motivation). They would however, be happy to offer me a place on the English / Sociology course. I did not argue, I accepted, figuring it might be possible to swap options when I was in situ.

Meantime Granville was talking of moving to Wolverhampton and sharing a house with Paul and Jenny Holborow. I visited them there and met Kitty and Joanne again who were up from Exeter on a visit. Sue Thomas was there too and seemed to have moved in. There was some talk of Kitty moving up to Wolverhampton too in the near future. Granville sure had a complex emotional life – worse than mine. It made my head spin.

Granville was very focused on the political work of building the branch. He had a considerably greater rapport with industrial workers than Rosewell (not difficult – though Roger had to his credit brought us Geoff Johnson and Victor Collard, a formidable industrial militant with an astounding intellect). Granville was soon adding to the recruits at Austin Longbridge, Tractors and Transmissions, including Roger Griffiths, Larry Connolly, Malachy Doyle, Larry Blewitt and John Strong. We sold the papers regularly at the factory gates at 7am taking it in turn to pick up those without cars. We started producing a handout called *The Austin Worker* (the duplicator had returned to live in the garage, alongside some of Terry's exploding home made beer – a product of too much yeast). Fed regular information from inside the factories, the bulletin gained an increasing following.

But it wasn't all hard work. We partied hard and the men, mainly, drank heavily. The Rolling Stones produced *Sticky Fingers* that year and *Brown Sugar* was a popular number to bop to – Granville liked it particularly and would always seek me out to dance with him when this came on. Mike and Lynn Pedley had a house on an estate in Erdington and would often host parties. The mood was one of optimism and growth – we were on a high politically – the Heath Government were no match for the unions.

Dominic started 'proper school' in September at Wheeler Lane Primary, a conventional but not very inspiring local primary. Despite the fact that his vocabulary was impressive for a five-year-old and he was producing many wonderful pictures, he was slow to pick up reading. Many of us on the Left were interested in progressive education and the free school movement and friends like Mark Abrahams and Rusty had taught at AS Neill's school, Summerhill where children were given the freedom to self regulate their attendance at classes. I found the competitive atmosphere of the mothers asking what number reading book their child was on, as a sort of one-up manship, distasteful. Ivan Illyich's newly published book *De-schooling Society* suggested school operated like an advertising agency, regulating pupils to accept conventional society. As revolutionaries we wanted more for our kids.

Dominic seemed to be picking up as much from television as he was from school and was an avid watcher of *Star Trek*. I loved watching *Magic Roundabout*, with him, not just because characters like Dylan were clearly designed to amuse adult viewers, but because of the magic words of Zebedee at the end of each programme "Time for Bed"! Dominic had learned better than to confront me head on in battles like bedtime, but at the same time he had a mind and will of his own. One night I was startled to hear heavy breathing when I sat down to watch TV late in the evening, only to find Dominic watching TV through my legs from under the chaise longue!

My only consumer luxury at the time was a Kenwood Major, which had all sorts of attachments for liquidising, mincing shredding and grinding coffee beans as by now my cooking range was expanding. It cost an arm and a leg at £20 – (though given it is still going forty five years later maybe it wasn't such an extravagance). I had it by virtue of back payments when my child allowance was delayed after Anna's birth. Apart from that we ran a basic household. "Fairy" the girl next door suspected as much and I overheard this conversation between her and

Dominic over the garden fence with great amusement. "We've got a freezer" she said, "have you got a freezer?" No said Dominic unconcerned. "We've got a tumble dryer. Have you got a tumble dryer?", "no" said Dominic just as detached. The conversation continued with the 'fairy' trying to invoke consumer envy in my small boy. Having run through a catalogue of possessions No 84 possessed and we didn't she reached the pièce de résistance. "We've got a colour TV" she began – "Great," said Dominic-"I'll come over!"

Internationally a number of events were noteworthy before the end of the year. The Indo-Pakistan war ended in December with the creation of the independent state of Bangladesh. Migrants from Bangladesh were to become the largest group of immigrants to the UK from the Indian sub-continent in the course of the 1970s. By January 1972 Pakistan had withdrawn from the Commonwealth and announced they intended to develop a nuclear weapons programme.

In Canada a boat called Greenpeace set out on its first protest voyage to Amchitka in Alaska to protest US nuclear tests. It was to grow into the leading international environmental campaigning organisation. The Grammy Award song of the year was Don McClain's *American Pie.* It presented a rather bleak morality play about American society, though at the time McLain joked that its only meaning was that he would not have to work again.

In Northern Ireland the conflict was growing, and the attitudes of the republicans to the British troops becoming increasingly hostile. When 300 Irish nationalists were rounded up and held in indefinite internment without trial following a new law passed by Stormont in August, it was denounced as a clear breach of the UN

Human Rights convention by the Catholic community. In October Ian Paisley formed the Democratic Unionist Party and just before Christmas the UVF (Ulster Volunteer Force) killed fifteen and injured seventeen more in a bomb attack in a pub in Belfast frequented by Irish Catholics and nationalists. It was the deadliest attack in Belfast during the troubles.

Despite the evidence to the contrary, the British security forces asserted the bomb had exploded prematurely while being handled by members of the IRA in the pub, implying the victims themselves were partly to blame. The RUC was biased towards this view and spread the disinformation to discredit the IRA. The bombing sparked a campaign of tit for tat bombings and shootings, which were to make 1972 the bloodiest year of the conflict. Many Irish IS members were to prioritise Irish politics in 1972, and for a short time Bernadette Devlin was to draw crowds to IS organised meetings.

# 1972
# BOMBS, STRIKES, SALTLEY GATE AND A SEPARATION

'*One measure of the class struggle is the number of days lost in strike action*' wrote Tony Cliff early in 1973 looking back at the momentous year behind him. Certainly by that analysis 1972 was a tremendous year for the working class as there were more large scale and prolonged strikes than in the previous ten years. Between January and October 22,202,000 days were lost through strike action.

Unemployment had risen to one million – double the figure at the start of Heath's premiership.

On January 30th in Northern Ireland an event that would forever be known as *Bloody Sunday* occurred when British soldiers shot 26 unarmed civilians during a National Civil Rights demonstration against internment. 14 were killed, while rubber bullets and batons injured others. Two marchers were run over by army vehicles. The subsequent Widgery enquiry was a complete whitewash. While describing the soldier's actions as 'bordering on reckless' it accepted their claims that they had been shot at. * Bloody Sunday dramatically increased the hostility to the British army among Catholics and

---

* It took 38 years for the truth to be officially acknowledged, that all civilians were unarmed that day, and for the British Government to formally apologise for the murders.

Irish Nationalists and led to a surge in recruitment to the provisional IRA.

Bernadette Devlin who had been an eyewitness at the Bogside massacre was furious when denied the opportunity to speak on the incident in the British Parliament, in defiance of all normal procedures. When Reginald Maudling the Home Secretary claimed the paratroopers had fired in self-defence, she crossed the house and famously slapped him round the face. Later she said she wished she had got him by the throat. She instantly became our folk hero. In the course of the year she spoke on several I.S. platforms – 4,000 turned up to hear her in Dagenham and a meeting in Wimbledon Town Hall was stuffed to the gunwales. Rosewell spoke alongside her once or twice but it is clear who was drawing the crowds, it was not the IS apparatchik, but this reserved and passionate young woman who had already gone to prison for her believes and was to be nearly murdered for them a few years later.

On 22 February a retaliatory attack on an army HQ in Aldershot killed 6 and injured 19. The IRA warned of future attacks against British regiments serving in Northern Ireland but the dead were not military personnel. They were five female kitchen staff and an army priest. I thought with despair how the violence unleashed could ever be resolved. It went back centuries. I supported unquestionably the republicans demand for a united Ireland free of British rule, but the way to such a resolution seemed impossibly mired with the blood of the innocent as well as the guilty-how many more had to die – the bombings seemed like the politics of despair – a resort for those who have exhausted every other avenue. In March Heath suspended the Northern

Ireland parliament – they would be ruled from Britain for a time at least.

January also brought the first official miners strike since 1926 (there had been a short two week unofficial strike in '69 over surface workers hours). The issue in 1972 was one of pay differentials as miner's pay had been dropping down the wage league tables continuously through the 1960's, set against a background of inflation and pit closures. This strike was the first to use flying pickets where miners visited groups of related workforces and asked for the support of railwaymen and power workers not to handle coal during the dispute.

The death of a Doncaster miner killed by a non-Union driver mounting the pavement in an attempt to break the picket line at Hatfield colliery, led to bitter confrontations with NACODS the colliery deputies and under managers union (often referred to derisorily by NUM militants as the "National Association of can-carriers, obedient dopes and suckers) and led one Labour MP to warn that this could be another Ulster in the coal field. The government called a State of Emergency on February 9th when power cuts resulted from combined action by the power workers and the miners. I can remember we were advised to turn on lights and flush the toilets at the same time to intensify the power surges.

The West Midland Coking plant in Saltley Birmingham had escaped the attention of the Midlands NUM for the first two weeks of the strike. When it became clear there were at least 100,000 tons at the depot the gas board were willing to sell in breach of the guidelines agreed between the government and the NUM, which were to supply only priority customers such as hospitals and old peoples homes, it became clear to Scargill and others that it was critical to close it. Two hundred miners from outside the area were brought in to provide a round the clock picket, but more needed to be done to stem the tide of lorries getting through. I can remember an IS meeting on 9th February when Henry Miller proposed that we should all go down to the depot the following day to support the picket. I was not able to go, with a small baby and a child to take to school, but Granville and many others were resolved to be there.

At first the police appeared to have the upper hand and there were a number of unjustifiable arrests, but then, like military reinforcements, Arthur Harper, District president of the AUEW and convenor of Tractors and Transmissions appeared beneath a huge AUEW banner accompanied by hundreds of workers from the engineering factories, who had down-tooled and marched to Saltley to support the miners. Their presence was decisive and the gates were closed.

Granville rang me full of elation and excitement and came straight over to celebrate this victory, and we made love for hours with great passion and pleasure. He was so happy. Much as I was cheered by this victory I was conscious that once more, I had experienced events vicariously through someone else, and while I could do nothing about this, there was a feeling of missing out on something momentous that others would long remember. Granville later wrote about it as an experience that was out of this world, an experience you could not erase. He of course did not mention how he celebrated after the event.

There were things I could change on the home front though. A chance meeting with an acquaintance just finishing teaching practice introduced Terry and

I to a primary school called Grendon Rd. She raved about it. The Head, Mr Chew, sounded innovatory and non-doctrinaire, and the structure of the school very progressive. We decided to check it out. Grendon Road was in a district called Hollywood about a mile from our house. The school was in the process of acquiring a new open plan building, which suited their freer child centred approach. They offered Dominic a place and we transferred him early in the year.

By happy accident he was put in Mr Fairfoul's class, an inspiring teacher, with a quirky sense of humour and an anarchic sense of irreverence for authority and red tape. He introduced us to the Dr Seuss books when Dominic still failed to make reading progress with the Janet and John reading scheme. "He's bored with them" he said. We bought him *One fish two fish red fish blue fish*. It struck a chord. He loved the zany cartoons and within a week was reading. He was already drawing cartoons and was developing a sophisticated sense of humour.

Dominic kept Mr Fairfoul as a teacher for most of his Primary education. Every time he went up a year Mr Fairfoul went up with him. They both shared the same jokes. He invited Dominic into the staff room one playtime to hear a recording of the Goon show. No one objected – at least not while Mr Chew was the head. Later a more traditional head took over but this did not blunt Mr Fairfoul's style, though it did mar any subsequent promotion.

I have a strong recollection of one particular evening early in the year. I had been at a political event in town. Granville was there and so was Sue Thomas. She was clearly expecting him to give her a lift back to Wolverhampton at the end of the night, but he showed no inclination to do so and she left, running to catch the last train. I realised I was experiencing a final rift between them (within a week or two she was partnered up with a post grad student called Dick Pratt). Granville asked me if we could go somewhere quiet to talk. There was an area called the Gas Street Basin by the canal and we spent a couple of hours there – taking pleasure in each other's company. He had always been cautious to express his feelings, but now he told me how much he loved me and how he wished we could be together properly. We had never had more than a snatched few hours together. We resolved to go away for a week at Easter and I said I would arrange something. This year CND was organising a one day Peace festival at Aldermaston in April with John Peel but it never occurred to me to go. The mood that had taken us on the marches had dissipated into other types of campaigning.

Driving home, for the first time since the John Palmer affair 8 years ago, I contemplated leaving Terry. It seemed such an act of betrayal to even think this way and I felt a complicated mixture of guilt and a responsibility for his happiness even though I knew in my heart I did not love him, had never loved him in the same way I loved Granville. But we had now been together for ten years, had children and had built a home together. I did not see a route through. I felt I was clutching at straws but I was resolved that if nothing else, Granville and I should have a holiday together. I booked a tiny cottage near Stackpole Quay in Pembrokeshire. I told Terry I needed a break. I did not say why. He did not ask. I am sure he knew.

My first act of independence was to buy an ancient Swedish Volkswagen for £60. Terry had now passed his test and would need the family car. The car was ancient with a split front window and sounded like an old bus with TB. A few days before we were due to go to Pembroke I was asked to drive Tony Cliff up from Birmingham to Stoke for a branch meeting. I was nervous about the car and even more nervous about accompanying Tony Cliff.

I had seen more of Chanie Rosenberg his wife than Cliff. She had stayed with us a couple of times and I can remember her eating through a whole bowl of home made coleslaw designed for four people. I was told that Chanie was a disastrous cook and that if you got sausages burnt on one side in her house to be grateful as they would undoubtedly be raw on the other side. The consequence was that when she ever stayed with anyone who had acquired even basic cooking skills she ate like a gannet. I felt relaxed with Chanie, but Cliff seemed a bit intimidating despite being about 5′2 in his stockinged feet. I just could not see any point of reference outside politics and I did not feel I knew sufficient politically to keep up my side of a conversation during the hour it would take us to get to the meeting.

Also even with zero mechanical skills, the noise the car was making as we proceeded up the motorway sounded increasingly worrying. Then just as we came off the slip road the car gave a jolt and there was an awful grinding noise. I restarted the engine – it coughed and spluttered and took us in a series of jerks and jumps to our destination. I dared not stop, so determined was I to get Cliff to his meeting on time. Cliff was totally unperturbed. All through the meeting I waited with some anxiety worrying whether the car would get us back to Brum. We set off back about 11pm – the car choked and spluttered but eventually got going, but we had only gone a short distance back on the motorway when the car emitted a dreadful grinding noise and ground to a halt. I lifted the boot to find oil dripping all over the rear of the car. I had managed to steer it onto the slip road leading to Keele service station, so we were able to walk up to the motorway café where I could phone Terry. He told us to wait where we were and that he would come and get us as soon as possible.

I tried to entice Cliff into the café explaining that we would have a good hour to wait but I could not get him to come indoors. He just paced about outside before he came up with an even more alarming suggestion about how we could pass the time. "Let's slip over there into the trees" he said making a lunge for me. I side-stepped him and declined. He tried some heavy persuasion trying to lock me into a bear hug. I was acutely embarrassed. The guy was a good 30 years older than me – old enough to be my father – almost my grandfather – he was no Adonis and he really expected me to respond? I had looked on him with some awe as something of a guru. I had not expected to have to repel these insistent and unwelcome advances. Is that really what he expected?

It was the longest hour of my life. It had nearly stretched to two by the time Terry arrived. "What took you so long?" I asked with relief. The answer was that he had driven over to pick up another comrade who he thought had the appropriate mechanical skills to repair the car. I laughed – clearly neither of them had seen what I had seen, but it did not take long for them to realise that the vehicle was in a terminal state and that we would have to go back with them.

Two days later Mike Pedley towed the Volkswagen

back and dumped it on our drive. I now had no car to visit Pembroke but Terry lent me the Traveller. I went to collect Granville (now back in Handsworth with the George's). It took ages for him to organise himself and there was an awkward moment when he had to phone Terry about paper sales and slip in that he would be away for a few days. We drove down stopping for a picnic. I was a bit subdued thinking there would be a showdown with Terry when I returned. I had made a beautiful picnic and prepared food for our arrival as I knew how much Granville appreciated good food, often having snatched and inadequate meals. This was the first time we were to be together for a whole week and I wanted it to be good in every way.

We went to bed early to make love and it was then that I got the pains – violent pains in my stomach and inside me and we had to stop. The pain was so bad, that robbed of sleep all night, Granville had to drive me to the local cottage hospital the following day. There the sister examined me and listened to my history. She said I had an infection in the Fallopian tubes and that the new coil I had been fitted with had probably exacerbated the infection. She asked if I had children. I said I had two. That's good she said because you have so much scar tissue on your tubes with all these infections that it has almost certainly made you infertile. I was prescribed antibiotics and was discharged having been told that I was to have no sex for a week or until the pain went away.

I was devastated. We rode back in silence and I felt Granville detaching from me. I could not make love, I was doubled up and could hardly walk, and I had a temperature. Each day I would join him at Stackpole

Quay where he made a campfire on the headland and then he would disappear to run, do athletics, swim or go for walks leaving me in miserable isolation next to his smoky fire. When the week had run its course we hardly spoke on the way back apart from him saying that if the coil was causing me all these problems and had led to my infertility why not have it removed if there was no longer a risk of pregnancy.

A few weeks later I travelled up to see him in Wolverhampton – Kitty was there. The visit confused me – all around me people were sleeping around and having affairs – there was no certainty – but I wanted a future with Granville and I did not know if it was possible. Spaghetti Junction the confusing tangled road interchange just outside the city had been finally completed and I speed across the M6 interchange missing my turn off, and then worried about the car conking out for lack of petrol as I couldn't get off the damned motorway until I had nearly reached Coventry. Worse still I had Anna in a car seat in the rear. Losing my bearings seemed like a metaphor for my life.

July brought the threat of another general strike over the imprisonment of five dockers (the Pentonville 5) for being in breach of an injunction imposed by the National Industrial relations board against picketing a cold storage company, as part of a national campaign against containerisation which threatened their jobs. The strike threat brought about a government climb down and the dockers were released after a week although it did not prevent a subsequent dock strike.

This year Terry and I holidayed somewhere independent of friends for the first and, as it turned out, the last time. We had visited Stanford le Hope earlier in the year only to find our friends had fled – the house was abandoned. Jennifer and Spider were also breaking up and separation was in the air. We rented an idyllic coastguards cottage at Prawle Point in Devon, the southern most point in Devon – the sunsets were magnificent and Henry and Erica, a new girl friend, plus Bessie Marks joined us for the first week. It should have been a great holiday. I know Terry was trying hard to close the rift between us, but I could not stop myself being irritated by everything he did, to such an extent that Bessie commented to him "you don't seem to be able to do anything right do you?" Terry had always watched every penny like a hawk. Now suddenly he wanted to buy me a dress in the local shop perhaps reflecting on how most of my clothes came from jumble sales. I declined but accepted a much cheaper Tee shirt.

Looking back on that holiday now I feel so guilty – I had known heartache myself and on this holiday I was inflicting it. During the second week I visited Totnes for an assignation with Granville. We had booked a B&B for one night. We met earlier than intended, walked through cornfields, made love in the middle of one and I came back to the cottage in the morning more firmly convinced than ever that I could not go on with this marriage.

When we got back I took off to visit Jennifer – I discovered she was buying a house in York near her sister in law who was also splitting up with Jennifer's brother. There were a lot of women there – most going through break-ups and we all slept in the small front room where the walls and the ceiling had been painted a rich Biba inspired chocolate brown. I remember we listened to a new release, Rob Stewarts *Maggie May* on the juke box in the local pub and the words *'all you did was wreck my bed, and in the morning kicked me in the head',* seemed to express a common disillusion we were all feeling with relationships.

On the way back from York, Roger Rosewell pleaded with me to come over to Liverpool for a quick visit to see the commune he was living in. It was a vast mansion near the centre of the city which had been bought ridiculously cheaply by two moneyed IS members, because the area was 'going down' in estate agents parlance and no-one wanted to take on a mansion with about 16 bedrooms – unless you wanted to live collectively. It seemed to be housing most of Liverpool IS. Someone's child who was living there gave me a tour. There were three levels of cellars. Extraordinary place. Commune living seemed to have a lot to recommend it, but Roger failed to revive my interest although he certainly tried.

I had received an extensive book lists and was preparing for my degree, which I was due to start in October, so I embarked on some reading. Granville who had an English degree lent me some books. *Moll Flanders* was on the reading list and I enjoyed this, but Richardson's *Pamela* struck me as one of the dullest books I had ever read. A whole book devoted to a woman protecting her virginity from all marauders. By the end I just wanted her to give in and get it over with.

I also read Virginia Woolf's *A room of my own* and Doris Lessing's *The Golden Notebook.* Both had a profound influence on me. With my new grant I created a new image for myself. Long Indian print skirts were coming in, cheesecloth shirts and full-length tapestry coats. I acquired all these plus a wonderful full length tiered dress from Laura Ashley and some new LPs, Carole

Kings *Tapestry* being the one I remember playing the most as many of the lyrics struck a chord. I realised I had skipped a stage in my development, from adolescent to married woman without passing through a stage of independence and development and I yearned to go backwards and recreate this – even artificially.

Looking at postcards in shop windows near Moseley I saw a spare room offered in a house in Balsall Heath. I went to see it. It was in a garret and there was a padlock on the door. The landlord was Pakistani and a strong smell of curry permeated the house. It was a small dirty room with a bed, a table a gas fire and not much else. It felt cold and very damp. I rented it. I moved in a table lamp a bookcase and my books. I painted the whole place brown and orange and threw an Indian bedspread over the bed. I had a student room at last! A place where I could study, a room of my own away from my family, an independent place I could invite Granville to.

I knew I was fostering an illusion though. Terry and I sat down and faced facts. I told him that I could not go on as we were. That I did not want to stay together out of habit and that if we separated now we were young enough to rebuild a different life with partners we were more compatible with. I said that I did not want to be writing a letter to my children as my mother had to me in her fifties, looking back with huge regrets and wishing she had left my father for a better life years earlier. He accepted much of what I said, but he kept asking me why, if that was the case, I had wanted a second child. I said that I had not wanted Dominic to be an only child.

We worked out a plan. I was due to go to university and would not be able to afford an independent mortgage and support the children till I finished in three years time and got a job. Terry said he would continue to pay the mortgage while I was a student, and we could look to get a divorce in a couple of years. The Divorce Law Reform Act, which had come into force only the previous year had made life much easier for people like us. It had abolished the concept of guilty and innocent parties and had enabled couples to get a divorce on the grounds of 'irretrievable breakdown' and evidence of two years separation. We agreed the house would be put on the market when I graduated and any profit split 50–50, which could be used as a down payment on separate homes, though obviously we would need to buy smaller and cheaper houses. We would divide the house contents down the middle with the exception of the Mandrell heirloom furniture, which would obviously go to Terry. I agreed to joint custody of the children with care and control vested with me.

I had been allocated only a married woman's grant but the existence of the room of my own enabled me to re-apply as a separated student. Someone came to check it out, and I was allocated a single students grant (I abandoned the room when Terry moved out of Haunch Lane). My separated status also entitled me to an automatic nursery place for Anna in September. The Day nursery was in Stirchley, equidistant between Kings Heath and the university, but I would need a car as Terry was taking the Morris Traveller. I had tried to get the Volkswagen back on the road, even installed a new engine, but there were so many other faults it was clear I was throwing good money after bad. I reluctantly sold it to the scrap man and Chris George helped me locate a Ford Anglia that fitted my needs. It cost me £125 and proved the most reliable of cars although there was a knack to starting it, which few people other than me could master.

Henry Miller offered Terry a room in his capacious Grove Road home. He moved in September. I was relieved to hear that within weeks he had started an affair with Henry's sister Helen as this reduced my guilt enormously, especially as Granville had moved in with me. My father exploded when I told him we had separated, accusing me of being a "bloody fool". I didn't mention how influenced I had been by my mother's posthumous letter, nor did I mention Granville.

I was soon far too taken up with starting University to dwell on my problems. I was 26 when I started my first year, eight years older than the youngest students, but in terms of life experience decades ahead. There were only two mature married students in my intake year. We had been told that only the brightest students were offered places on the Combined Honours Course as in truth we would be completing 75% of each of the Single Honours courses in each subject so the workload was very demanding. What made it worse was that because my subjects were in different faculties, one in Arts and one in Humanities, neither faculty seemed to want to take responsibility for the cross-faculty combined honours students and frequently there would be clashes in timetabling or incompatible work loads.

Early on I checked out the Drama course as I had not given up the idea of transferring and I was aware that Clive Barker was on the drama staff and had a background in Joan Littlewoods Theatre Workshop. However what looked set to defeat me were the hours that drama students needed to be on the campus for productions. I needed to be out of the university by

3pm every day to collect Anna and Dominic and could not expect Terry who had his own work schedule to pick them up and look after them as often as would be needed if I was to transfer to Drama – even assuming the university let me.

Reluctantly I accepted that I would have to stay put and work my way instead through the English literary canon – it looked like the 25% I could drop could include Beowulf-but I would have to study Samuel Richardson's *Pamela* – or as she was known by her detractors – Shamela. However there were some delights on the way I was sure, including a second year course with the Centre for Contemporary Cultural Studies, which seemed the only bridge between my two subject areas.

The Sociology first year course was designed for students who were new to Social Sciences, so I found I was going over a lot of familiar ground I had already covered in my Sociology 'A' level. The Head of the Dept was Professor Baldamus who specialised in Industrial Sociology, two friends from Croydon days were also on the staff Peter Lassman a friend of Marco's and Julie Hiscox, who had been in Croydon CND and followed me to the Actors Workshop.

Having personal friends among the lecturers some of whom were a similar age, did mean I identified more with the staff than the students. The latter all seemed terribly young and a bit facile, so I was delighted when I discovered John Strong a Longbridge car worker who had joined IS was also doing an undergraduate degree in Political Sciences and we had some lectures in common. John was married with a couple of kids and lived up the road from me. He was in culture shock having given up the rigours of life on the shop floor for the relaxed pace of a University student, and could not get used to the fact that no penalties were imposed when he was late with essays because his youngest child had kept them awake nights. He kept saying to me "Bloody hell Hazel this is all right isn't it?" Having spent years cocooned in domesticity, I agreed. Looking up one day from a volume of Wordsworth's poems I was reading in the university library, it struck me how enormously privileged I was, to be subsidised by the State to read the Romantic poets while someone else looked after my baby daughter.

I had little time to socialise and enjoy the extra mural side of university life, (I would have particularly like to have joined the film society), so I made few friends among the students, though in my second year I did discover a ballet class I could attend. My life was regulated by the University clock and whatever activities, whether they were academic or social, ceased for me at 3pm. I raced home collected my kids and spent the time between 3.30pm and 7.30pm when they went to bed seeing to their needs, feeding them and sorting out the washing ironing shopping and everything else that needed doing. I started my college work at 8pm after the washing up. It was hard but the structure gave me a discipline younger students did not possess.

My first Sociology assignment had a word limitation. I wrote an essay double the length because I could not say what I wanted to say in less. I expected to get penalised. Instead I got over 72%, which I was told was unheard of for a first essay. A second essay got 78%. My tutor told me that Baldamus had been asking who was this new brilliant Sociology student.

Granville was out almost nightly at meetings so I would often only see him when he staggered home usually with

10 pints or so under his belt. He seemed to think it was pretty macho to drive drunk. I remember him saying to me once "you know I nearly killed myself getting over here to you". Beer did not seem to have the effect on his body it did on many men. With him it seemed to act as an aphrodisiac. For the first time I felt I was on the right track with my life though I never felt totally secure in my relationship with Granville. He was easy company, good humoured, passionate in bed, but somehow unfocused and sometimes quite detached. I put it down to the demands of the job rather than a quicksilver personality. I should have paid more attention.

Outside university there was still a lot of demands politically, especially since Haunch Lane had become the official address of the IS organiser. We had regular visits from the Industrial comrades who often extended their evening at the pub with a 'carry out' at our house, from Jim Higgins – usually accompanied by Ruth Nelson his lover, and from comrades typing up factory bulletins or broadsheets at all hours of the day or night. One of the comrades was a telecom engineer. He told us what code to put in to check if our phone was being intercepted. It seemed that it was. Once I picked up the phone and a voice at the other end said Birmingham Police station.

Fund raising became an area I took on board when it was discovered I had a good ability to put events together. At this time a print shop had recently been acquired at 6 Cotton Gardens and money was needed for the new administrative and print centre. I remember organising a concert with Jake Thackeray a wonderfully droll singer in the George Brassens tradition and Alex Glasgow. We supplied a buffet as well and the event raised a record amount for one evening.

I also was encouraged to draw up a list of progressive staff at the University and I travelled round from department to department, collecting cheques from radical lecturers and professors. Stuart Hall anticipating what was behind my request to see him had his chequebook open when I arrived. "What's it for this time" he would say – I tapped him more than once.

Lectures in the English dept were quite formal. Professor Spencer headed the Shakespeare Institute. He arrived on the dot and would leave mid sentence if the University clock tolled while he was speaking. David Lodge who was to make a fortune from writing novels about 'Rummidge' University was also a lecturer. I found both of them detached and uninteresting. I began to skip lectures.

One thing I never skipped was the weekly seminars with my tutor Tony Davies. They were the highlight of my week. I meet him at a party some years after graduating and mentioned how I prioritised his seminars. "That's interesting" he said, "Because you were the main reason I came to them!" I remember discussing Lessing's *The Golden Notebook* in his tutorial. I had underlined many page references – the book seemed uncannily close to many of my life experiences. There were three 18-year-olds in the group with me, only one of them female. They did not connect with the book at all. The girl was in my sociology group too. Attending a lecture with her, addressed by Professor Baldamus, with his heavily accented Germanic English, I was amused to note that she had scribbled something down about the philosopher Cunt. I corrected her spelling.

Christmas 1972 brought Hanoi the heaviest single US bombing raid of the Vietnam War – the heaviest since

WWII. Nixon and Kissinger were trying to conclude a treaty, given the mass public outcry against the war both in the US and internationally, but Kissinger's ineptitude as a negotiator had exacerbated rather than concluded a treaty acceptable to both North and South. The raid was justified by Nixon as 'bombing the Viet Cong back to the negotiating table'. On Christmas Eve, Olaf Palme the Swedish Prime Minister compared the bombing of North Vietnam to Nazi massacres. The US responded by cutting off diplomatic contact with Sweden. *

Granville spent Christmas with Kitty and Joanne. I do not recall how we spent ours. Just before the New Year I found a draft of a letter he had been writing to Kitty to say how awkward he had found the visit (she was living with someone else) and that although the situation with me was still 'fluid', they had to wind up their relationship for good. "So it goes," he had written. Very Vonnegut.

* Palme was assassinated in 1986. To this day his assassin has not been identified though there has been many theories about who might have been involved. His radical politics made him enemies in both South Africa and the US.

# 1973
# A YEAR OF CONFLICTS: POLITICAL AND PERSONAL

The troubles continued and intensified in Ireland with casualties from bombings or assassinations on both sides being reported on a distressingly regular basis. Kids threw stones and rocks at soldiers, women in Derry clattered dustbin lids on the cobbles to warn of the approach of the British army and in March the first bombs claimed casualties in England when two car bombs, one detonated at the Old Bailey, injured 200. The Heath Government was still in power – just – but clinging to the wreckage. Early in the year 'Grocer Heath' negotiated the country into joining the EEC alongside the Republic of Ireland and Denmark.

In the US the Watergate scandal was beginning to break. The conviction early in January of members of the Nixon Committee who burgled the Democratic Committee National Headquarters in 1972 to bug phones and steal top secret documents, was leading a trail direct to Nixon the president. 'Tricky Dicky' as he became known had attempted to arrange the intervention of the CIA to impede the FBI enquiry into the burglary and arranged hush money for the burglars. Bob Woodward and Carl Bernstein's investigation for the Washington Post, thanks to an inside informer known as 'Deep Throat' blew the gaff on much of the cover-up and revealed the existence of secret tapes which Nixon refused to hand over. It was 1974 before Nixon finally was forced to resign as President. Demonstrators throughout the year outside the White House encouraged passing motorists to 'honk if you think he is guilty'. Another slogan of the time was a picture of Nixon looking particularly seedy with the slogan 'would you buy a used car from this man?'

Anna now two, had settled well into nursery school, had been toilet trained with little or no problem and was turning into a beautiful little girl, though she was a persistent thumb sucker. Dominic had learned to ride a two-wheeler bike and had a new superman cloak and Tee shirt, which Henry's girl friend and I had made him for Christmas, plus a toy sword made by his dad. My father came to stay and filmed them both for posterity on his super 8 cine camera.

Terry and Helen were no long together. He languished after another very beautiful IS teacher called Janet Rowe, but she eluded him. He was now being pursued by one of his students Margaret Cross. Margaret had baby-sat for us a few times when Terry and I were together and clearly had a bit of a pash on him. She was from an upper-middle class family in North Manchester, her father was a barrister, she was an Anglican churchgoer and her accent was plumy.

While Terry had no problem using her for unpaid babysitting he used to ask me to drop her home at the end of the night because he 'could not stand her bloody posh accent'. I thought this excessively rude as I had to make excuses for him and it was clear she was only babysitting as a favour to him. Rather a large woman with small inverted eyes she had rather attractive shoulder length hair but she was no beauty.

However she was the possessor of a shrewd business brain. She had already acquired her first house in Moseley, no doubt with the help of mummy and daddy and she filled it with freezers and bought whole animal carcasses divided up into various cuts to save money. The house was full of giant size containers of various commodities bought on the same economy of scale idea. She also used her entire grant for the term buying a Lowry etching and then asked the gallery to store it and re-sell it when she instructed them, no doubt figuring its value would double if not triple with his death*. (she was right). She filled her house with lodgers and language students to make money and fed them on cheap freezer food. She was clearly going to be a venture capitalist.

To say I was surprised that Terry ended up in her bed considering the differences in their outlooks is an understatement but having been handed this young woman on a plate so to speak, he obviously decided it was a too good an opportunity to turn down and saved him paying rent to Henry. During the year he moved into her house on Hillcrest Road, – she was still his student at college which should have proved awkward, but didn't appear to lead to any repercussions. There were a few repercussions from Grove Avenue though when Terry unscrewed every shelf in the upstairs kitchen and took the shelves with him. When it was pointed out that the five people who shared the kitchen had contributed equally to the cost of the shelves, he was reported to have said, "I don't care, I'm having them". Helen was furious. What an acquisitive little charmer I had married.

Margaret's attitude to me now underwent a sea

* Lowry died in 1976

change. Adrian Davies, the kindly university solicitor who had agreed to act for me pro bono in organising maintenance for the children and for my subsequent divorce observed dryly that I was suffering from 'second wife syndrome'. What he meant was that a second wife will work hard to undermine the reputation and influence of the first wife in order to reinforce her own position. I found this amusing initially since I was hardly challenging her role in Terry's life. It was perplexing, but that was his business. If it made it easier for him to accept the separation I was pleased.

Mr Davies also pointed out that the amount I was to get in the divorce settlement (£30monthly per child) for maintenance was only half what it should be, given Terry's salary. I told him not to pursue this. The new divorce law might have abolished the concept of innocent and guilty parties but I still felt guilty. Besides, I knew how parsimonious Terry could be and recalled him telling he was not my 'meal ticket for life', which was grossly unjust given I was claiming minimal maintenance for the children, nothing for myself and had scrimped saved and earned through most of our married life. I did not want a further cause for resentment though and knew anything involving money would exacerbate this.

Margaret was now effectively in the role of stepmother to my children. Terry probably found that very useful. He had not found it easy to manage the children on his own. One Monday morning when he was supposed to deliver the children to school after they had stayed with him, he arrived on my doorstep with Anna in a pair of underpants and nothing else. "She won't put her clothes on," he said. "For heavens sake" I said, "how old are you and how old is she?" I had her dressed and out of the house in five minutes.

I later learned that he had taken her to see a Disney film and that she had taken all her clothes off and sat naked in the aisle sucking her thumb, while various members of the audience ran round gathering up her discarded clothes. "Why didn't you redress her," I said. "Because she seemed to prefer sitting like that," he said. I did not recall having the same problem when we took Dominic to see the Beatles film *Yellow Submarine* back in 1968 when he was not yet two. I had fond memories of him being transfixed by the screen and how we played hiding from the 'Blue Meanies' for months after. Clearly our children had very different personalities, as I was to discover, in so many other ways.

One morning, I called for the children at Hillcrest Road early in the morning, so early that I arrived at the same time as the milkman. Looking through the letterbox when I knocked on the door I saw my small daughter running down the hall towards me. "It's my mummy" she called. Then I heard Margaret's voice behind her "Don't be silly dear, it's only the milkman – I'm your mummy" – said as she opened the door and confronted me. "So who am I?" I asked. I later discovered she insisted Anna called her "mummy" whenever they were out in public. It was to be the start of a rather nasty game of one-up -man-ship with my little daughter in the middle of it all and indicated how insecure Margaret felt within her relationship with Terry.

Not that I did not experience the challenges Margaret was facing as I was occasionally pressed into step-mother duties too, as Joanne, Granville and Kitty's daughter now occasionally stayed with us and her father, busy as ever building the revolution would often hand over her care to me. She was six months younger than Dominic so there was another child for her to play with – or so he figured, in reality they hardly bonded.

Joanne still showed signs of occasional neglect like when I found a large oozing sore behind her ear stuck to her hair, which had been neither discovered nor cleaned. She seemed to be given carte blanche to dress herself and often arrived in a bizarre concoction of clothing, which looked like layers of a dressing up box. I tried my best to engage with her but found it hard. Joanne seemed to have constructed an impenetrable wall around herself and seemed difficult to reach though I worked hard trying. And then there was that knowing look…

Kitty had moved back to Town Tenement Farm in Cullompton near Exeter when she graduated and was living in an (apparently) settled relationship with a guy called Bob Merritt. She invited me down to stay for a break and I went, curious about her relationship (which I had every reason to hope was secure) and because I wanted us to be friends given that I was occasionally looking after Joanne. I certainly did not want to play 'second wife syndrome' – indeed I could not imagine ever wanting to be a 'wife' again.

The whole while I was there I felt Kitty was playing mind games with me. She appeared suddenly at my bedroom door, naked – with some comment of no particular import. She teased me hugely as a 'townie' because I could not sleep for the overpowering smell of silage under my window. Always I felt as if I was being vetted. Bob seemed pleasant if a little distant. I noted he seemed to have a firm but very caring attitude towards

Joanne, which she seemed to respond to well. Granville's attitude to Jo seemed more than a little flaky by contrast. I did not stay long. I was not at ease.

Later on the way back from visiting my dad, I met up with Granville in Newton Abbot and was introduced to Bill Groves who produced a newssheet for IS called *The West Country Worker*. Bill was in his 50s and had recently been made redundant from the local Power station. He lived with his mother, his daughter and his granddaughter in a rambling old Victorian house. His wife had left when their daughter had an illegitimate child, blaming Bill's dissolute radical influence on her. He was helping to bring up Lara the grand daughter (named after the heroine in Dr Zhivago) who called him 'dad'.

He was a multi-talented man. He had a small printing press in his cellar, which earned him some money from small print jobs and resigned to the likelihood of no further employment, he survived on his wit and skill. He had sign-painted his van and set up a small house maintenance business and was almost self sufficient in fruit and vegetables from his allotment. In his cellar was a still in which he produced hooch, next to a boiler in which he cured his allotment grown tobacco. He had spent his redundancy money on tinned food – enough to last the rest of his lifetime – it was stacked in serried ranks in the cellar, which made it feel like a wartime bunker. He was also a sculptor and a gifted cartoonist.

A few months after our first meeting he promised to visit my father when he was holed up in Newton Abbot Hospital with back problems and wrote me a re-assuring card telling me "Don't worry about your dad, he's full of beans, which if I know the diet in Newton

Abbot Hospital is almost literally true". Fred and Bill were to become the best of friends and discovered a shared taste in blue movies – something which Bill kept from the feisty young feminists in the local IS group, who already regarded some of his cartoons as sexist. I would have forgiven him that. He was the gentlest and kindest of men. On my first visit with Granville he played us a tribute LP to Woody Guthrie recorded in 1968 the year after Guthrie's death, with Joan Baez, Pete Seeger, Judy Collins, Tom Paxton and many others. There was a narration of Woody's adapted by Pete Fonda, which we listened to together. It expressed erotic intimacy in such a direct and powerful way it was as if our own thoughts were being laid bare.

*My body is naked and it was born naked*
*No matter how I dress or undress I am naked*
*The best and juiciest of humanly truths are naked truths*
*I feel the same way you feel about my naked places*
*None of my places feel their real best until I get them uncovered, unhid,*
*Stripped down naked*
*And my most naked thoughts have always laid flat on my back on the beds of leading leaves and grass,*
*Counting the tree buds with my hands and the night stars with my toes*
*Go ahead huh – you use ribbon and lace to pull me toward you*
*And I'll use every trick of shadow and shading to pull you closer toward me*

*Your face is already lifted to the sky, and its light makes me wild and crazy for the taste of you*
*Your hips can't make a motion which I can say 'I hate"*
*Your blood can't run in a way which I can stop and send back*
*Your legs can't open in a way that I want to rest*
*Your thighs can't move in a way that I would lock up behind bars*
*I love to see you wiggle your patch of hairs*
*In every kind of design pattern roll sway and twitch*
*I see and taste no sweat more honest*
*Than the drops you have enjoyed between your thighs*
*Your face looks it's proudest it's finest and gladdest this minute*
*As you do roll here like I roll*
*This look, this half-smile across your face,*
*This very minute your hair shaking above my eyes*
*Makes me feel like a lost man getting found!*

*Last Tango in Paris*, Bertolucci's powerful and controversial erotic masterpiece was newly released at the cinema that spring. I went and watched it and was in tears much of the time. The intense sexual relationship between Brando and Maria Shneider in the film, two lovers who remain anonymous within the confines of the apartment they first met in, seemed to resonate with the emotional turmoil I was experiencing in my own life.

In Torquay the film was banned no doubt due to the famous butter and sodomy scene. My father attacked the '*dog-eared parish pump by-law which probably dates from those good old clean permissive days when genteel public executions were a popular uplifting entertainment*'

Fred had found his feet in Torquay. Less parochial than Minehead it was a favourite retirement spot for Londoners so he was not the only 'grockle'. Once more the vitriol dripped of his pen as he wrote furious, witty and deeply sarcastic letters to the *Torquay Times* of the kind which had earned him tributes from *The Croydon Advertiser* and *The South London Press* when he moved from Croydon. He castigated the petty puritans for their attitudes towards mini skirts, wrote furious letters about dog shit and dog owners, decried censorship and the cultural philistinism of Torquay and thundered against the Tories and Sir Frederick Bennett the local Tory MP in particular, hoping he could induce a heart attack in the latter through the power of the pen.

He also wrote detailed and intelligent pieces on the real causes of inflation, pointing out it was price not wage increases which were at the root of the problem and that the stock market was recording record profits while wages remained frozen and labour was cut back by 7%. Not surprisingly since St Marychurch was hardly a cradle of radicalism, he was soon approached by the local Labour Party, who being rather short on numbers and charismatic characters, asked him if he would stand in the local Council elections.

Never one to turn down free publicity, my father did not object but pointed out one small obstacle, he was not in the Labour Party. No one seemed to think this was a major impediment so in due course I received through the post an election leaflet with a picture of my father on the front sporting a grey beard and looking like an ageing lecher. Recalling the Watergate slogan about Nixon 'would you buy a used car from this man?' a friend quipped that the text underneath my dad's election flier should read 'would you leave your daughter alone in the same room as this man?' As well as having a whale of a time giving inflammatory speeches which would never have been allowed in a safe Labour seat my father enjoyed giving talks on his time as a tramp in the 1930's which were vastly exaggerated in both content and accuracy.

During the day Granville was swept up in the huge surge in industrial militancy in local factories and busy building the IS group. With food and house prices still outstripping wage increases – union leaders like Jack Jones of the TGWU warned the government that they would be foolish to ignore working people who were sick of the decline in their standard of living. May Day 1973 brought 1.6 million workers out on strike at the behest of the TUC, mines transport and the docks were particularly affected. There seemed a real possibility of a revolution at that time.

The government having been forced to climb down with the miners and dockers, had not expected the building industry to be able to organise an effective national strike, because many worked on the 'lump', meaning they were effectively self employed, which allowed the big building firms to cut corners on health and safety and blacklist 'trouble makers'. The use of flying pickets however had unified the industry sufficiently to achieve a national strike and the building employers were forced to concede a pay increase in September 1972.

Then the stitch up started, five months after the end of the strike, building workers who had picketed the Shrewsbury area were charged with intimidation and conspiracy and six were thrown in prison. They included Des Warren and Ricky Tomlinson who later became an actor (they were all blacklisted from the building industry after they came out of prison). Their trial on conspiracy charges was yet another attempt by the government to destroy trade union rights. Over 40 years later the campaign to clear their names is still being fought, though one of the six, Des Warren has since died. It is believed the tranquilizers routinely administered to him throughout his three-year prison sentence exacerbated his ill health. Meanwhile McAlpines, the firm behind the stitch up (a major contributor to Tory party funds, who sort much of their profits into the Cayman Islands) boast today of their integrity and high standards

My role since the successful Thackeray / Glasgow concert was to collect subs and money. As well as sending money to the families of the imprisoned Shrewsbury building workers I still have two thank you letters from John Worth the deputy AUEW convenor of Chrysler Coventry thanking the Birmingham IS branch for our whip round for him and his wife when he had his dole suspended for alleged 'industrial misconduct'. John had been victimised and sacked by Chryslers – he was a thorn in the management's side over the implementation of Measured Day Work. A successful divide and rule tactic, which isolated the militant shop stewards from the bulk of the work force, resulted in his dismissal.

A growing urgency was developing led by Tony Cliff to harness this unwarranted industrial upsurge and forge a mass recruiting drive of industrial workers, forming them into factory branches. IS had already accepted the Leninist concept of democratic centralism, which allowed for debate and discussion but unity to the majority once a vote was taken. This sounded OK but Cliff who could make impetuous decisions would brook no opposition and had the energy and time to impose his view on the majority. This was to cause major problems when some of his ideas proved unrealistic and damaging.

We had already set up a Lucas factory branch and there was a substantial teachers group. Mary Pearson a recently recruited teacher was allocated to the Lucas Group in a 'servicing role' – an expression I viewed wryly since Mary was more than prodigious with her sexual favours. Her house in Sparkhill was the centre of many parties – she reckoned she could recycle the carpet to Ansells Brewery. Before too long she had embarked on a passionate affair with Larry Connolly who left his Catholic wife and large family to move in with her.

There were also parties at the George's in Handsworth and I remember the room rocking to The Strawbs version of *You don't get me I'm part of the union.*

Things could get out of hand though, not just in terms of the sexual liaisons that often resulted from these parties, but by the prodigious quantities of booze that were sunk. We occasionally hosted comrades from out of the area. The worst were the Glasgow comrades who had a fearsome reputation for drinking everyone under the table. Having put away 10 pints or more down the pub they would turn up at whatever household was hosting the post pub party with what they described as "a wee carryout" which was not measured in bottles but in crates. One weekend when four of them slept over at the Georges, Margaret found urine dripping through her ceiling into the downstairs room. The Glasgow lads had woken in the night and too incapable of making the bathroom had pissed all over the bedroom floor. She refused to accommodate them after this. "They're animals" she said

It was also in 1973 that we acquired premises to turn into an IS bookshop and meeting room. This was a run down shop in Digbeth near the coach station, which had not been used for years. When we first went to check it out I explored through the back yard and into the shop next door which in its heyday had been a Victorian photographers. It had been derelict for years and I discovered among the dust and rubbish, numerous daguerreotypes and old sepia portraits.

John Murphy who had recently graduated and Bill Carson who was a caretaker at the University took on the refurbishment of the shop. We had little or no money and not a lot of stock but gradually we acquired and filled a couple of shelving units with books and stocked a number of IS pamphlets as well as the IS Journal, Socialist Worker and Women's Voice, the magazine for IS women. John worked unstintingly to repair and make habitable an upstairs room for meetings, and the following year he took on the Herculean task of clearing the cellar and making it habitable for a printing press. I cannot remember there being any heating in the building or for that matter a lavatory.

In September there was terrible news of a bloody right wing coup in Chile. It was a watershed event in the history of the Cold War. The socialist government of Allende had been violently overthrown and Allende was dead. American involvement through the CIA was very evident. Nixon and Kissinger had been trying to find ways to undermine and remove Allende since 1970 and were particularly alarmed by his friendship with Fidel Castro.

The junta elected General Pinochet to power after months of bloody massacres and disappearances of left wing opponents, some of whom, like young US journalist Charles Horman were eventually discovered walled up in the stadium where they had all been herded after the coup, some trussed up like chickens others with eyes gouged out and horribly tortured. Horman's story was to be re-told in the 1982 film *Missing* which illustrated how naive many Americans were about the duplicity of their own government. The US had wasted no time recognising the Pinochet regime.

The reaction to the coup was strongest in France where there were strong fraternal links between the left groups in both countries. They were active in organising solidarity groups to help and 15,000 Chilean exiles were eventually resettled in France – more than any other European country except Sweden.

There are 300 streets and parks in France now named after Allende, the first and much lamented Marxist president of a Latin American country since Castro.

The Heath Government, through the Foreign Office did its best to undermine the solidarity campaign, infiltrating the movement and guiding the BBC Panorama programme through the British Embassy, who in turn secured the co-operation of the junta to set up interviews with Anglo-Chilean business communities speaking approvingly of the coup. A British embassy official wrote, "the balance of the programme should be

60–70% favourable of the new regime".[*] More of concern to them was the Granada *World in Action* team who went out specifically to cover the tortures and murders. The junta press secretary reported "they were seeing things they should not have seen."

The left in Britain was united in their condemnation of Pinochet. The ship builders union urged the government not to sell warships to the regime even though losing those contracts could threaten their own jobs. The government's response was to send spies to shipyards across Britain to check workers were not sabotaging vessels destined for Chile. In Scotland miners raised funds to help 500 Chileans resettle in Scotland.

Labour who was to return to power in 74 would cut off arms sales aid and credit to Pinochet and withdraw the British ambassador in 1977, but existing arms contracts were to be honoured, till Scottish engineers took the matter into their own hands and refused to fix bomber-plane engines destined for Chile, forcing Rolls Royce to break its contract with the Chilean air force.

Unsurprisingly under Margaret Thatcher a prominent defender of Pinochet, diplomatic relations were restored in 1979, along with resumption of arms and warship sales, thus ending any attempt at an ethical foreign policy. During Pinochet's ignominious regime of terror about 40,000 people were murdered and over 1,200 disappeared. 200,000 became exiles. Pablo Neruda the eminent poet was almost certainly murdered under the orders of Pinochet, and the tales of torture, rape and abuse, which were later amassed by Human

---

* Discovered in the declassified documents 40 years after the coup. See *Uncovering Britains secret role in protecting Chile's coup*: Grace Livingston Guardian 7/2/2016

Rights Commissioners, were horrendous. Ariel Dorfman cultural advisor to Allende who managed to escape was to later deal with issues of torture and exile as part of the experience of the Chilean diaspora in his play *Death and the Maiden*.

David Edgar, a local radical playwright who lived in Moseley (a few doors down from Henry Miller on Grove Avenue) contacted us in the autumn. He was interested in the recent sit-in by the work force at the Triumph Meridan Factory, which was facing closure and transfer of its operation to Small Heath Birmingham.* He wanted to talk to some Birmingham engineers and so Granville and I invited him and a number of the Lucas Workers, Vic Collard, Larry Blewitt and Roger Griffiths over for a meal at my house. David, used to middle class dinner parties arrived in good time bringing a bottle of wine and we waited for the arrival of the Lucas workers. Finally the doorbell rang revealing a rather agitated Victor Collard. "Hi Hazel", he said "is the grub ready yet, we're wasting good drinking time". Poor David was rushed through his meal by the Lucas contingent and then led down to an overcrowded smoky central Moseley pub where it was standing room only and he was plied with pints and offers of Park Drive cigarettes. He was a very tall man. I looked up at him-he looked profoundly miserable.

David was later to write *Destiny* about the historical growth of the far right. In West Bromwich in May 73 the National Front had polled 11% of the vote-four years later

* The sit in lasted two years, the Meriden factory eventually bailed out in 1975 by Tony Benn the Minister of Trade & Industry in the new Labour Govt, the workforce forming a co-operative. Edgar was to write *Events following the closure of a Motorcycle factory* about the conflict.

they were to win almost 120,000 votes in local elections in London. He did not shy from difficult subjects.

Late September I started the second year of my Combined Honours course. I had enjoyed my part Ones and got the equivalent of a first in my end of year marks. I had taken courses in 18th and 19th Century Literature and poetry, in Economic History and written two dissertations, one on the impact of shift work on health (concluding that the Continental shift system was injurious to health) and one on the Music Hall strike led by Marie Lloyd against the management of Sir Oswald Stoll in 1926 which led to the formation of the Variety Artists Federation. Alan Plater, who had written a play about the strike, sent me lots of supporting material. It was going to be a challenging year, as unlike single honours students 50% of our Sociology finals had to be taken at the end of Year Two. I chose courses in Economic History, Industrial Sociology and European Sociology specialising in Nazi Propaganda during WW2 and a course in Contemporary Cultural Studies, which was under the auspices of Stuart Hall.

However my ability to study was also wrapped up with my emotional equanimity and this was given a hard knock by Granville remarking casually that he had decided to try a trial reconciliation with Kitty. I asked him if he had not made a decision to finalise their separation months ago and it turned out that the letter I had seen had never been sent, so despite both he and Kitty being in other relationships, it seemed they wanted to put both Bob and I on a shelf while they tried out for size whether there was enough left of their marriage for them to resume it. I was conscious that there was Jo to consider, but also that my own children were no longer living with their father as a result of my relationship with Granville. It was an unholy mess and I was desperately unhappy.

I eventually wrote to Kitty to say that I had not realised that they were considering this, that I had been living with Granville for nine months now and was very much in love with him. I said that I appreciated they had to resolve this one way or another, especially because of their child, but I had not seen this coming and needed her to know I was not casually attached to him either. The word he had used in the letter came back to haunt me – that things were more 'fluid' with me, but that had been before we started living together.

Kitty wrote back. She said she appreciated me writing because she had a lot more time for me than she had for many women but that she had to resolve things with Granville once and for all, and the only way to do this was put their relationship to the test. She said she was concerned to provide some stability for Joanne and she thought Granville could help provide this. She ended by saying that there was so much shit and people living with horrific problems throughout the world (no argument – we had Chile as an example) – that she did not want to dwell on her own, that she did not want to 'own' Granville so that he and I could continue to have a meaningful relationship (whatever that meant). Lastly she said that although it would not be easy to meet me, she hoped that us writing to each other had made it a better prospect.

I could of course have played dirty and written another kind of letter dropping in some additional information which might have undermined her resolve, but I was not prepared to stoop this low as I had a lot of time for Kitty. I had found out about a month prior to this that Granville had started an affair with Margaret George. I felt so angry with the way he felt he could casually slide in and out of bed with any woman that took his fancy while living with me and simultaneously planning to resume his marriage with Kitty.

Margaret was not the most obvious candidate for his lust. She was an exceptionally prim bony bespectacled woman, a Primary school teacher with a very conformist dress sense and a rather severe brisk manner. She would not have been out of place arranging the floral decorations in the local church or pouring tea at the WI. She was the last person I would have associated with passionate desires, but still waters run deep.

She had written a torrid and very explicit response to their love making and posted it to him. I had found it crumpled up in a cardigan pocket I was about to put in the washing machine. Granville was away at the time and I wrote to him saying that just as I thought we were on a solid ground, I suddenly found myself wondering what the hell I meant to him. I asked him to explain about Margaret George. He was dismissive – gave me a 'just one of those things' – kind of answer but it was clear the relationship was still ongoing, as while selling papers with Margaret in town I had to endure her gushing on effusively about how wonderful he was, and how much he knew about literature and how they had wonderful talks about Alan Sillitoe. I wondered if these talks took place before or after he fucked her and whether *The Loneliness of the Long distant runner* had become an essential part of their foreplay, but I played it cool and refused to rise to the bait. It hurt plenty though. As it must have done for her husband Chris-if he knew.

The timescale for Kitty to descend on Birmingham had never been made clear to me, but I also now wanted to know where he intended to live with her and Jo. I urged him to address this problem, as it was obvious, to me at least, that they could not stay at Haunch Lane. Granville sidestepped the issue – he was busy. He gave me little opportunity to discuss the question of accommodation for his family and seemed to have little time to think about it himself. I did not push it because part of me did not want to face the proposed reconciliation and the longer he took to defer plans the better I liked it. Perhaps I thought that in the interim the problem would go away or they would decide against it

In October Granville said he was going down to spend the weekend with Len and Marion Holden in Bedford. They were old friends of his, and Kitty would be there too. He gave me no indication of what was coming. On the Saturday night he rang from the Holden's. "I know this is a big thing to ask and I would not be surprised if you said no, but do you think Kitty could come up and stay for a couple of days – it is so we can look at houses. I told her that you were such a good woman that maybe you wouldn't mind?" With these weasel words he wrung from me a very reluctant agreement – for a two day stay. I was not expecting what came next.

Within a few hours I heard the front door open. Into the room bounded a crossbreed golden retriever (Rooster – a dog rescued from the farm) followed by Kitty laden with a pile of boxes, followed by Joanne similarly laden. They had brought all this for a two-day stay??? Kitty retreated to Granville's recently acquired Morris Traveller for more. I followed her out. The car was loaded to the gunnels with a chest of drawers, angle lamps, boxes of books, records, children's toys, bedding – they had even bought Bob's wine making flagons – the entire worldly goods of Kitty and Jo it seemed. It was obvious they had not just come for two days – they had come to move in. I was in such deep shock I could say nothing, especially after Kitty made a little speech to the effect that she did not want to 'own' Granville and therefore did not expect to share his bed while she was here.

I tried to get Granville on his own out of earshot because I wanted to know what he had told Kitty, but he ran for cover. Telling me he had some urgent IS business to attend to he shot off, leaving Kitty and I to sort out the problems, allocate some space for all their stuff, rustle up some tea for all the kids and billet Joanne into the bunk beds in Dominic's room. For my kids it was all a bit of an adventure so I could hardly say anything when they were around, but after tea with Granville still absent, Kitty and I talked the talk over a bottle of wine. I did not mention I had agreed only to a two-day visit. It was not her fault if she had also been misled and despite all the problems her arrival had brought me I liked her.

I also did not mention Margaret George. But if I was exceptionally reticent, still in a state of shock, Kitty was in a 'tell all' mood. Later on I reflected she did this deliberately to remove any illusions I might still have about Granville's character.

She recounted how she and Granville had spilt up in the first place. It seemed he had a very public affair with Yana Mintoff. Yana was a member of Exeter IS. Her father was Don Mintoff, the president of Malta. Yana flaunted the relationship. Kitty found she was being passed over socially while Yana was invited to parties and events with Granville in Kitty's absence. Kitty arranged to go along to one of these events with a friend of hers for moral support, when she suspected this was happening, and had it out with him. She then decided that if he wanted an open marriage what was sauce for the goose, was sauce for the gander and she began an affair with Roger Protz, the editor of Socialist Worker.

This did not go down well with GW. He had recently been approached by Cliff to come to Birmingham so he took off, leaving her to cope the best she could. Being Granville though he had left a lot of unresolved issues. He had not, for example, even two years down the line told his parents or his mother in law they were separated. He had visited his mother when he was going out with Hilary Luce, and had her waiting in the car while he made the visit. His mother had seen Hilary in the car when she looked out of the bedroom window, but had not challenged him. Perhaps she was used to this sort of behaviour because his father had numerous affairs Kitty said.

Granville's father was a mining engineer. His mother was a cook who cooked for the Directors of the mining company. When they were young, Granville and his sister and brother were moved round frequently, as during the war his father was billeted in many different places. They settled in Eastbourne for a time because the sea air was deemed good for Wyndham, Granville's brother who only had one lung, due to contracting pleurisy as a child.

Throughout his working life Granville's father had lived the good life, but put nothing aside. He had driven expensive cars and had his suits hand made at Saville Row and apparently indulged himself with a succession of secretaries, who, it would seem, did far more than take dictation. For his wife, working for the same company, this must have been the source of some humiliation. The mother and father were now living in a rented house in Sheffield, but it was doubtful how long his father could keep working and then they would have insufficient for the rent on the house, as it was not a controlled tenancy.

Seemed like disloyalty and an inability to plan ahead were characteristics Granville had inherited. Not that words like loyalty had much value in the 1970's – jealousy was officially 'un-cool' and no one admitted to it. We were a new generation experimenting with different ways of living and there must have been many casualties, Lessing had written about a similar tortured relationship in *The Golden Notebook*. I felt as if I was living in a chapter of the book.

Granville returned late and crept into bed. I was locked in misery and said nothing. I was conscious of his wife only a few feet away on the other side of the wall. I was already feeling warmer towards her than I was to him. We slept apart on the far edges of the bed. After a week I decided it was no longer possible to go on with this farce so I told him to move into the spare room with Kitty. I had no-one to talk to about the turmoil going on in my head. I kept the agony to myself. I felt I was doing a penance for breaking up my own marriage.

What was also very difficult was facing all the comrades. I think they were embarrassed because no one asked and no one was told anything, although I suspect Mary Pearson who was especially chummy with Kitty got to find out some of the details. Kitty was a very visible and vocal presence in the local branch and had soon acquired herself a job at one of the Lucas factories, so her worker status elevated her in the eyes of the branch. Joanne acquired a place at Grendon Road School and this made life a little easier as Granville felt duty bound to do his share of school deliveries and collections for her and Dominic.

Granville started the process of applying for a mortgage, Cotton Gardens were prepared to provide back up information on his earnings (even if that meant elevating his salary on paper). The process of house hunting seemed painfully slow. The problem was that there seemed no other comrade prepared to take on a couple, a child and a dog in the interim, so I was the default mode. Terry meantime took to letting himself in, reading through any letters he could find trying to piece together what was going on. He also took to conducting raids on the place. As the person still paying the mortgage he obviously felt he had a right.

I came back one day to see Margaret sitting on the front wall acting as 'look out' while Terry hurriedly filled the back of our Traveller with things he had decided were his. These included all Bob's wine making flagons, which we had stored in the garage. I pointed out these were not his, but he was undeterred. They were in his house and he was having them. He also liberated a yellow plastic dustbin for beer making, which raised a wry smile from me. I had used it for soaking nappies in. I wished him botulism or the equivalent.

With the house bursting at the seams I had further refugees billeted on me. Geoff Johnson had got himself a white-collar job off the engineering shop floor. He had left his wife and was having an affair with a 19-year-old called Lucy. They had nowhere to live. They moved in, sleeping on an airbed in the living room. Geoff and

Dominic got on like a house on fire. Hearing that I had vetoed the purchase of an Action Man, Geoff raided his own son's discarded toys and brought back not one but three Action Men, one complete with a deep-sea diving suit. I came back one day to find them giving the Action Man circuits of the bathtub.

With so many people to feed and get out of the house every morning, I had found Dominic exceptionally slow and disorganised. One day I came down to find he was sitting down for breakfast fully dressed, right down to a school tie and blazer and on time for once. I thought that at last all my pleas for him to hurry up had paid off. I was impressed. Later Geoff confided in me. Dominic had told him "she makes too much fuss, all this take your clothes off, put your clothes on – I've got the perfect solution, don't take them off in the first place!" He had gone to bed fully clothed in a full school uniform, which meant he only had to roll out of bed in the morning to be ready for school.

Rooster was a sweet dog and caused the least trouble in the household despite having a wet dream one night on the fireside mat. I never knew dogs had those. Granville we barely saw. I later realised there was a pattern here. He always worked flat out politically when his personal life was in crisis and it seemed there was crises aplenty developing in the IS group which would lead us to develop an IS Opposition faction. This would take a whole book to explain and since Jim Higgins was to write a fulsome account of this time* I do not intend to duplicate it except to say that plans were afoot to remove both Higgins and Protz from their leading

* *More Years for the Locust: A History of the SWP:* Jim Higgins

positions in the group and there were manoeuvrings going on which were to have implications for many of us. Certainly they required all Granville's energy and time as well as the developing industrial base.

This was why he was not at home when Kitty picked up and opened a typed brown envelope addressed to Granville. Because it looked 'official' she thought it was from the mortgage company as they had found a terrace house in Grisethorpe Road they were planning to buy. Instead she found herself reading a torrid love letter from Margaret George, prefaced with the information that she had sent it in plain brown typed envelope to avoid the 'spy' – (she meant me), which means Granville must have told her I had seen one of her letters. Kitty asked me if I knew about Margaret George. I confessed I did. It clearly had taken her by surprise. She said, "I know about you, and that is different, we have been straight with each other and I like you, but I did not expect this."

I do not know what she said to Granville but she settled down to persecute Margaret George in all kinds of subtle ways. Margaret had a hamster called Serge, Kitty told the Lucas guys it should be called Surge and they started puffing their cheeks out and gobbling whenever they saw Margaret and tittering in her presence. You didn't mess with Kitty. I might have been straightforward with her. She preferred to play things differently.

All this time I was attempting to keep myself from cracking up. The strain of living with Granville, his wife, his child, their dog, two other adults, my two young children and Terry raiding the place periodically was putting me under enormous pressure. I did not know how the Margaret incident had affected Kitty, but the letters to her from Bob poured in regularly to Haunch

Lane. I wanted desperately to know what was going on. So desperate that I steamed open one of them sent in November. I felt utterly confused by the contents. It appeared as if they were planning to live back together again, or at least Bob had been given to understand that they were. He talked about this happening in 2–4months or as soon as he had found somewhere for them, but even he was uncertain because he said "I had begun to think you'd decided to stay in the house you are moving into with Granville, but I take it that's all in my mind" There was also talk of them arranging a summer holiday with Kitty's mother. What the hell was going on? It seemed as if Kitty was manipulating all of us.

At the height of my misery and uncertainty, and feeling I could endure no more I went to the university health centre for some anti-depressants. When the doctor asked me to tell her what I thought was causing my depression she was incredulous. "My God" she said "and other students think they have problems". I remember Bill Carson the University caretaker coming back to the house for coffee one night. He had become involved with IS through an ex-student John Murphy who now ran the Digbeth bookshop. I had an Albinoni LP, and I played him the adagio because he said he liked classical music. I found myself dissolving in tears as I listened. Bit by bit he got out of me the cause of my distress. He had not appreciated what was going on, I had camouflaged everything so well. After this, Bill adopted me as his 'good cause', which translated into supplies of any surplus items in the stores, which he thought I could make use of. One was a huge length of green baize from a billiard table. I covered an old desk top with it.

At Christmas there was a huge present opening before Kitty and Granville disappeared off to visit their families. I wondered how much of it had been acquired legitimately as Kitty was a brazen shop lifter and plastic alarm tabs had yet to be affixed to clothes and expensive goods. I was amazed at how many presents they gave Joanne, which seemed disproportionate to the time they spent with her and smacked of over-compensation. Kitty had been given some presents from women at work and was indignant when one of them turned out to be a plastic flower container called The Pedestal. She decided the woman had given this to her deliberately as a snub because she was so active in the union. If so, I did not know how to take her 'present' to me. A novel by Strindberg called *The Scapegoat*. It was hardly as if I liked Strindberg either.

That Christmas I drove the children down to Torquay to see their grandfather. Terry and Margaret had gone down to the South West for Christmas too. They were staying with Beverley and Rusty who were now living in Somerset with their three children. Rusty had a job at a local staff college. Terry rang me at Fred's to say he would like to drive down and see the children during the holiday and bring them some presents. I knew the children would like this and Fred seemed pleased to see him – he had never approved of our split anyway. We had a really good day together and Terry bought me some presents too, a pair of Levi jeans and a double Jazz Album. This was an immensely thoughtful present for him and it occurred to me, that knowing of Granville's defection back to his wife, he harboured the hope of a similar reconciliation. It got late and he asked if he could stay over night. The kids wanted this too so I said yes. He said that he had told Margaret he might stop over.

Back in Somerset Margaret woke in the middle of the night to feel the bedclothes slid off her and assumed Terry had returned. It was only when an arm went round her waist and she felt a beard prickle her neck that she realised that it was not Terry's arm, and that the body pressing insistently next to hers was Rusty, while Beverley slept in a room a few feet away. I guess that was the end of Christmas visits to Somerset for them both.

I had enjoyed Terry's brief visit but I could not rekindle a flame for him, which for me had never burned that brightly in the first place. I could only hope we could maintain this level of friendship, but friendship after love is difficult to achieve, especially when jealousy plays a part.

# 1974
# THE THREE DAY WEEK, MANY MORE MOVES AND CHANGES

From 1st January to 7th March due to more industrial action by the coalminers, the government introduced a three-day week, reducing the energy supply to Commercial users to three days in every seven. Many of my friends greeted the reduced working week with enthusiasm. Mike Pedley, who had recently acquired a camper van made good use of the extra two days to organise a series of trips out for the comrades. In March Heath stepped down and was replaced by a hung Labour government once again lead by Harold Wilson. In April a new group of Swedish singers called ABBA shot to Eurovision prominence with their song 'Waterloo'. Heath had certainly met his.

Granville and Kitty finally moved in the New Year – I cannot remember when exactly. The pain of the separation was less than the relief of them vacating the house, but Bill Carson obviously thought I needed someone to keep an eye on me. He suggested a student called Sue Pattison as a lodger. She was in the IMG (International Marxist Group) and was doing a PGCE at Birmingham University. I liked her from day one. Suddenly the mood in the house lightened. She had a cheerful and positive outlook and got on well with the kids.

Due to Sue, Dominic discovered morning children's TV. I had been rationing the time he watched the box and had never turned it on except in the evening but one morning having failed to get me out of bed to make him his early morning cup of tea, he tried instead to raise Sue. We must have both had a very late night because she was resistant too. I heard her say "Oh Dominic, piss off will you and watch Blue Peter on the tele". There was a short pause while I cursed inwardly. "There is no TV in the morning" he said uncertainly. "Oh yes there is" she said. I listened while a set of small feet pattered downstairs and into the living room. Two minutes later he called excitedly up the stairs, "Sue you're right!"

And so began his love affair with *Blue Peter* and particularly Tony Hart's section where each week they showed a selection of paintings children had sent into the programme. Dominic worked for hours to produce an amazing picture called 'Battle on the Starship Enterprise'. Over our dining table was a reprint of Guernica. Dominic must have studied it carefully because many of the figures in his pictures had sideway screams. His picture was Star trek crossed with Picasso.

He wanted me to send it to the programme but I loved it so much I did not want it destroyed (art work was not returned – 7 sack-full's were binned every day). * The Monty Python team must have also watched Blue Peter as they adopted the phrase "*and now for something completely different*" into Python.

---

* I kept Dominic's picture for many years, eventually framing it and presenting it to him on his 40th birthday. He did not appreciate the gesture. He was still annoyed I hadn't sent it to the programme and when I said I thought his son might like it, he said no it would only frighten him. I wish I had retained it, as he has never hung it in his own house.

Kitty and Granville seemed well settled in Grisethorpe Road. They had decorated their living room and held a small housewarming party. Ray Osborne the IS doctor was looking for ice in the fridge when he chanced upon a bottle of Largactil. "Who is taking this medication?" he asked. When told Joanne had been prescribed it by a doctor in Exeter he was horrified. Joanne was seven at the time and this was an exceptionally strong anti-psychotic drug. It had been prescribed for bed-wetting. I remember my mother mentioning it when she worked at Bethlem Hospital as it was used on the (adult) patients. Could this explain Joanne's odd behaviour? Ray told them to stop her taking it immediately.

Their terraced house on Grisethorpe Road was near Anna's nursery and en route to the University, and since Joanne remained at Grendon Road School, we still saw a lot of each other, fetching and collecting children. Bob Merritt came up on a visit to Kitty from Camberley where he was now living. Was he here to petition her for a return? When I dropped into Grisethorpe Road one night to collect some Socialist Workers newspapers Bob was there on his own, baby-sitting. He was in a gloomy mood. He said "I should not have come-it was a mistake. I don't think I can bear to be here when they get back. Can I come back and stay at yours tonight? They are due back in 5 minutes". I said he could and left him to scribble a note and make it back to mine on his motorbike. I thought nothing more of it. He was subdued but pleasant company and we were a comfort for each other. He left in the morning promising to write.

Shortly after he left, I got a phone call from Granville insisting he had to meet me immediately. We met down near Digbeth bus station and he said how upset he would be if he found out I had slept with Bob. I was astounded. Granville, the man I loved, who had left me to return to his wife, who had made me endure months of misery with them both living under my roof, still felt he had some kind of proprietorial rights over me? I refused to satisfy his curiosity about whether I had slept with Bob. Was he really so insensitive to the wreckage he and Kitty had created in both Bob's life and mine?

I found out later that when Granville first saw the note he was thrown into a jealous fit. Kitty had remonstrated with him that he had no right to act like that. She said he was living with her now, and consequently what Bob or I did or didn't do was none of his business. They had apparently rowed about it all night.

Bob wrote to me regularly after this and visited me on several occasions. He was working as a postman in Camberley and I sent him IS contacts in nearby Guildford. He told me he no longer saw a future with Kitty and had various plans for resettling in Plymouth and much later building a cottage in the woods in Cornwall – he was not a city man. I felt a lot of fellow feeling for Bob. We had both endured a great deal at the hands of our previous partners – it gave us a bond.

Catering staff at Birmingham University, were involved with pay disputes around this time. Although I had neither the time or interest to take part in student politics, indeed as a body I didn't particularly like or identify with students, this was different. I have pictures of Sue and I on the picket lines with John Murphy and Bill Carson.

April brought the exciting news of the ending of the fascist military dictatorship in Portugal, which had existed since the 1930s. It started as a revolt by military officers but was soon coupled with an unanticipated and popular campaign of civil resistance. It was a near bloodless coup, called the Carnation Revolution because red carnations were posted into the muzzles of the guns when people went into the street to celebrate the end of the dictatorship. African wars had been consuming 40% of the countries budget so one of the first acts of the new regime was to disengage Portugal from their disastrous colonial wars. IS comrades made fraternal visits, and Cliff was ecstatic. For him this was further proof the revolution was round the corner.

May was bleaker, bringing more violence to Ireland when the UVF placed car bombs in four cars, killing 33 people and wounding 300. May also saw India detonate its first nuclear weapon, another black day for the anti-nuclear movement.

It was a black month for some of us in IS too, heralded by a brief unexpected visit to me from Roger Rosewell and his partner (I think her name was Bridget). 'Have you heard the latest?' he said, and launched into tales of plots and countermoves he had been scheming with Tony Cliff, without, it appeared, the need to share these with the Executive Committee far less the National Committee of the group. Why did he think I would find this admirable? Especially as they involved comrades in the movement for whom I had the highest regard. Did he think I had some kind of special loyalty to him because of our past? If so he misunderstood where my loyalties lay. I told Granville what he had said. He was furious about these manoeuvrings and demanded Rosewell was censored at the next NC. This was also the NC where Roger Protz and Jim Higgins were removed from their posts in Socialist Worker. It was a tipping point for many of us.

I don't think Rosewell ever got over the slight of being censored. Having resigned as the Industrial organiser he was not making a great success of being Liverpool organiser, his own laziness making him avoid the patient and time consuming task of building a rank and file movement, which he clearly had little stomach for. Plotting coups and counter coups was much more to his taste and the fact that Cliff gave him so much credence diminished Cliff in my eyes too. Rosewell was still being paid by IS but started making plans to quit while ahead. He applied for a position as an appointed official of the National Union of Journalists and told the interviewing panel that he had left IS. Since IS policy had always been opposed to the appointment of union officials, the IS NC suspended him for two months. Shortly afterwards at the beginning of 1975 he slipped out of the organisation. His level of treachery post IS was beyond belief.

He went from Ruskin College to Oxford and then worked closely with Frank Chappell, the far right General Secretary of the Electrical Trades Union. He then wrote an exposé of IS in the *Daily Mail* where he was later employed as a journalist. From ultra right wing Labour he moved to the SDP, addressing a conference on the way, for the right wing Aims group on *Managers and Marxism*, about the role of 'extremists' in industry. This was all just a way station to the Tory party, where he became the advisor to the notorious Lady Shirley Porter, heir to the Tesco millions, who Jim Higgins described as *"the eldritch creature who ran Westminster Council like some branch of the Penal system"*.

Lady Porter later left in disgrace, over the scandal of 'homes for votes', owing Westminster council 37 million and stripped of the 'Dame-hood' originally awarded by

John Major. It was discovered she had been systematically moving council voters from marginal wards and replacing them with owner-occupiers, more likely to vote Tory and had been using council funds to rig the vote. Do I see the hand of Rosewell in all this? Indeed I do. Lady P now lives in luxury in Tel Aviv, Israel, with her loot carefully sorted in tax havens in Guernsey, British Virgin Islands and Swiss Bank accounts. So far all that Westminster Council has been able to recoup is £7000 from a gold plated lavatory seat at her old home.

Rosewell, her latter day 'advisor' recently sold his Tudor Manor House in Oxford auctioning off rare antiques worth millions, to move into an 18th Georgian mansion in Rochester. Nowadays he writes books on medieval stained glass church windows. What a wanker. That I ever housed him, let alone gave him bed-room I count as one of the worse mistakes of my life. But then hindsight is a wonderful thing. At the time when he was first building the group (way before the time he later claimed the organisation existed) he seemed like a dedicated comrade albeit one who lived in a fantasy world where he thought he was Eliot Ness. Wrong, he was more Al Capone, though posturing with a toy luger rather than a real firearm and assassinating by slyness. About the same time Glyn Carver another fantasist was earning his keep as a Manchester organiser. Convinced the comrades needed to know how to handle firearms with the revolution just round the corner, he acquired a rifle and while fiddling around with it shot himself in the foot. What princes they were!

In June I had to sit three finals papers in Sociology. I tried to focus on these and pushed work on my English course to one side, but I was worried about the outcome.

I had effectively lost the whole of the previous terms work in both English and Sociology due to stress, and my concentration levels were still well below par. Bob asked me if they would kick me out if I didn't pass the exams. I did not know. I know I performed badly – but enough to scrape through it seemed, though the marks would affect the overall grade in my Finals.

Terry had taken Dominic and Anna to Beverley's for a week at the end of May to give me some revision time – I imagine without Margaret this time. I got a lovely postcard hand written by Dominic from Weston-Super-Mare it said: *We are by a pool and I'm writing a rime – this. 'the fishes are in the pool and they drive me up the wall'. I had a paddle in the water and on the front theres the place were I pabelled and I had a goon the donkeys. Good by from Dominic and Anna. To hasel.*

At least my children seemed to be weathering the enormous storms in our lives pretty well. Dominic's school report for the term he was seven said his reading and comprehension were of a very high standard and his stories and creative work full of originality and imagination. It was mentioned that he was an extremely gifted illustrator. Maths was more problematic – he worked slowly and was easily distracted.

I recalled seeing his maths book on parent's night, which contained a flick cartoon in the corner of his book. Mr Fairfoul had caught up with him and written Dominic this is your maths book, but clearly Dominic thought this was a better use of his time! Quietly subversive my son! He also used to fold his arms and refuse to close his eyes during morning prayers as he said he didn't believe in God. I asked him why. He couldn't give me a reason. I suggested he reserve judgement until he had found out why he did not believe and could argue his corner. Unfortunately a female head with a name, which sounded pure Roald Dahl, Mrs Betty Gaukroger, had replaced the progressive Mr Chew. She had a personality to match the name and we were subjects for her disapproval.

Between April and June Nurses had taken industrial action over their pay with a series of lightening stoppages. In June they shut 50 wards up and down the country. COHSE their union received the support of many trade unions and groups like IS. This led to a story in the *Daily Mail* that outside agitators were behind the strike and lurking behind the nurses. Granville was named as one such agitator. This in turn led Joanne to write a story at school, which included the rather startling information that *'my dad was on the front page of the Daily Mail for looking up nurses skirts'.*

Our revolutionary ways and unorthodox life style were obviously the subject of staff room conversation as Joanne overheard the head mentioning her name and then saying in a confiding aside – 'she's from that family I told you about'. I must have really got up her nose when she sent out a circular some three years later asking parents to send their children to school wearing red white and blue to celebrate the Queens Silver Jubilee in 1977. Most of Anna's clothes seemed to contain one of those three colours, but I left no stone unturned and managed to send her in a green dress instead.

Dave Adshead, who later became a (bad) building worker, had replaced John as my driver for a brief time for paper sales and we ended up in bed together a couple of times. I felt I had to move on and get Granville out of my system, but Dave had a wife and I didn't want to disrupt anyone else's life so I did not pursue this, although he later forced himself on me. Another 'socialist' who thought women were just there for men's convenience.

June brought terrible news. I was in the IS bookshop when Terry came in to tell me Pauline Marks, Marco's wife had been killed outright in a car accident. She had left the LSE, and was doing research with the feminist sociologist Anne Oakley. She was on her way to Anne's house when a car travelling in the opposite direction crossed the central reservation and hit hers, instantly breaking her neck. Anne later commented about the death in her semi-autobiographical book* *There is something especially shocking about unexpected death; and in one so young and full of life. Even now I have difficulty grasping the fact that Pauline is dead. Such a death has to be a salutary lesson in never knowing one's chances, in never really being able to count on anything.* At the time few cars were fitted with neck restraints. If they had been, she might have survived.

Stuart Hall later told me that Marco and Pauline were on the point of splitting up. To Terry, Marco's display of grief was disproportionate in the circumstances, but her memorial celebration was very low key. Just short comments from a few of those who knew and loved her, no flowers, nothing religious and donations to the National Council for Civil Liberties. I understood completely why he felt so bereft, especially if they had been alienated from each other. My father sent him a couple of letters. He had always been close to Marco.

---

* *Taking it like a Woman:* Ann Oakley. P78. See also P2–3 as a rationale for the book which is in many ways the same as mine – *we must claim the right to pain and passion though examining our own history*

The second letter was dated 27th August a month after Pauline's memorial. The 26th August was the fourth anniversary of my mother's death. My father said in the letter how much he missed his own wife and how dearly he had loved her. It is sad that sometimes one has to experience the finality of loss to appreciate its magnitude. I am glad that Marco went on to have many years of happiness with a feminist who had been Pauline's tutor, a lovely woman called Kate.

Roger Griffiths a Lucas Steward who lived near the Pedley's, on a new estate in Erdington, now entered my life. He was good-natured, swore and drank a lot, with a beer gut to show for it. He smoked heavily – Park Drive cigarettes – and was notorious for high volume snoring. Roger was a born romantic. He had bought a new house in anticipation of a marriage that did not happen and had filled it instead with male lodgers. It had all the features you would expect from a hard drinking bachelor household, including an unkempt and greasy kitchen. One day his lodger found a mouse in the toaster. "You should have pushed the handle down and toasted the fucker" Roger told him.

Ours was no grand passion (I was all passion spent) but it was an easy, happy relationship because it was uncomplicated. You did not have to second-guess what he thought and he clearly thought a lot about me. He also took a real interest in Anna now three and a half and Dominic, who benefitted from some very neat haircuts, as Roger had been a barber in a former life. It filtered through to me that Terry did not approve. He thought Roger was a rough diamond. He was, but he was also an immensely caring rough diamond and that was what I needed like salve on a wound. Unlike Terry, he also had a well-developed sense of humour and was generous to a fault.

Sue was also a big help to me. She had her final exam pending too. We would set aside blocks of time for revising and take it in turn to make each other cups of strong coffee and tea and build in breaks. Sue had an LP of the music from the musical *The Assassination of Marat Sade* and we played the songs loudly in the breaks, particularly the one with Judy Collins singing '*We want our rights, and we don't care how, We want a revolution NOW* with the French doors open to irritate Miss Mildenhall next door who had taken to throwing weeds over into our garden because she said they originated in ours. We had a row about this, and I said it was a pity she had nothing else to worry about. I can see her point of view more now. It can't have been easy for Muriel in the autumn of her life to find she had shipped up next to a hotbed of non-gardening communists.

I needed a holiday after the exams and found I could stay free at a flat in Paris through some contacts in the Students Union. I took off for a week taking along John Hope, a hippy who looked like a bit like Cat Stevens and was part of Henry Miller's household. Roger was uneasy about this but I reassured him that John was just a casual friend. The flat in Paris was uninhabited and stripped of furniture – it was the last week of a student lease. The last tenant, a Japanese student stayed on to give us the keys. It was on the 2$^{nd}$ floor of an arrondissement in an old part of Paris. The bath was the size of a butlers sink and the only latrine was at the top of the building and shared by all the flats. We had a mattress on the floor to sleep on. It was the first time I had been abroad since I was eleven.

We ate out all week, surviving on cheap wine, cheese and baguettes. It was hugely enjoyable. I remember John pouring wine down the throat of the giant carp in the Tuilieres Gardens and being stung at the price of a cup of tea in the same gardens though I did try to warn him it was a tourist trap. Summoning the waiter he asked if he could speak English and then said did he know the word 'robbery'.

We were more successful in the bars, having been forewarned that you paid less in the back streets if you stood at the bar and did not occupy a seat. I loved the Impressionist Gallery and the cheap Algerian food we bought on the Left bank. We also got cheap meals in the Cité University canteen by flashing my Students Union card – infinitely better than the canteen food at Birmingham University. On the last night we visited some comrades from Lutte Ouvriere who lived on the outskirts of Paris, and got hammered on their grandmas home made Calvados, jumping the barriers at the metro because we could not afford a final ticket and sprinting for the last train with the guard in pursuit.

I came home with a surfeit of wine tucked into the lining of a large fleece jacket. Duty free was very strictly controlled then. On family holidays I could remember being asked to declare what we were carrying to a customs officer and having our cases marked with a chalk cross if we passed the scrutiny. I was a bit of a risk taker, though never in the same league as Kitty's shoplifting. I had stopped going into shops with her because she was so blatant, I was sure she was going to get us both arrested. But I used the university bookshop as a lending library in protest at being set essays based round one expensive book when there was only one copy in the library. I used to shop lift them using white gloves, extract the information I wanted and then return them unmarked to the bookshop shelves.

On our return John decided to try out life on a kibbutz and took off for Israel. He wrote to me later in the year telling me he was finding the experience interesting but also disturbing. He found the Israelis 'egoistic, slightly paranoid and extreme nationalists'. He called the kibbutz 'Camps of sublimation'. He welcomed letters as it felt a bit like prison, but he was coming back soon. His roommate was a Spanish Trotskyist.

In Argentina, Isabel Peron succeeded to the Presidency in June following the death of her (unlamented) husband. It was to be many years before the odious Lloyd Webber treated her to the lachrymose musical re-enactment of her life.

Another military junta bit the dust in July, this time in Greece. At last! We were ecstatic about that. In August Nixon finally resigned, followed by his deputy Gerald Ford issuing him with a formal pardon for Watergate in September. Ford's chief talent during his brief time in the White House was his tendency to fall over frequently, both literally and politically. September also brought the deposing of Haile Selassie, – the ending of a seven Century dynasty and the beginning of a Civil War in Ethiopia.

In July there was a sugar shortage due to a drop in sugar cane imports from the Caribbean, now supplying to a more lucrative market in the US. For some weeks before the trade crisis was sorted out it was difficult to buy. I had yet to denounce the white poison in my tea, but Roger seemed to be able to unlock a secret supply.

We decided to take the kids (the bread snappers Roger

called them) away for a break in their summer holidays. We drove down to the South West and stayed overnight with my father before travelling on to Cornwall to stay with Jimmy Rule, an IS member in Camborne. My father had decorated his front dinning room with a collage over the fireplace, which consisted of bus, train and theatre tickets, photo's of Victorian ladies in a state of undress, post cards and much else. He said he had been doing a bit of B&B trade and people had said they had never stayed in a place like his before. I could imagine.

Jimmy was kind and welcoming and so was his family. His wife told me that Kitty and Granville has stayed with them the previous year but had omitted to mention Jo's bed wetting – she thought it was very thoughtless. Jim took us all to a beach that he knew, and Roger and I went in for a swim – he had brought no costume so went into the sea in a pair of jeans. A short distance out I turned to swim back in and found I couldn't. There was a tremendous current I could not get through. I was out of my depth and began to panic. I grabbed hold of Roger and then realised I was pushing him down in the water and he was struggling too. We yelled out "Help" but no-one took any notice at first, we were so near the beach – they probably though it was horseplay.

But Jimmy came down to investigate and wading out he nearly entered the current himself. Jimmy was a short stocky man who had spent years in the Merchant Navy but the current was too strong even for him. Retracing his steps he accosted the first man he saw on the beach, "Quick" he said those people out there are in trouble, we need to form a human chain". The man was with his mother. "I shouldn't get involved if I was you" she told him.

Meanwhile I had decided I had to try to rescue myself. I began swimming parallel with the current – I concentrated on putting one arm in front of the other and blocking out everything else. My persistence paid off. The current eventually deposited me on the beach at least half a mile down from where I had started. I was so exhausted I lay on the beach for a few minutes not able to think of anything. When I looked up, Roger was a few yards from me covering his nakedness in the sand and telling me to get him a towel. He had kicked off his jeans because they were dragging him down. Half an hour later they were washed up on the beach ripped to shreds from razor sharp rocks out at sea.

Jimmy was white faced when we rejoined them. He and his wife had been on the beach with all our children and had not relished the prospect of telling Dominic and Anna their mother had drowned. Jimmy said he had visited the beach a number of times with his kids and had not known it was this dangerous. We were all deeply chastened by the experience and relieved at our lucky escape. After that I lost all confidence in swimming out of my depth in the sea.

The summer also saw a final break between Kitty and Granville. The reconciliation had not worked, and Kitty had embarked on an affair with Mike Rice. She also discovered she was pregnant, and there was some question as to whether it was Bob's or Mikes. Both gave her some financial support when she had a termination.

Granville was utterly contrite. He disappeared for a few days and told me on his return he had been to Pembroke where we had our ill-fated holiday, as a kind of penance for the way he had treated me. He told me how he wished he could put the clock back. He said he had written to Kitty to say that he had squandered a rare and beautiful love with me, but that he did not feel he had the right to break up my new relationship with Roger. What I had with Roger was a good, conflict free, supportive relationship, but we had been together a relatively short time and my feelings for him could not compete with what I still felt for Granville, despite all the pain he had caused me.

I had written to Bob early September telling him that I was thinking of getting back with Granville but was very anxious about hurting Roger. I also told him I had been turned down when I had made my first enquiries about the mortgage I would need in order to move the following year. Bob came up for a weekend visit as he could see I needed someone to talk to. It was a fraught time.

Granville gradually edged his way back into my life. At a party at Mary Pearson's when Margaret was still making a play for him, he quietly took off his jacket and put it round my shoulders as we stood outside talking, and in lots of small attentive ways made it clear where his attentions were focused. "Please will you let me woo you all over again?" he asked. We took a day's break to drive up to Cannock with the children, and while they played and explored he laid me down on a blanket and made love to me. I came home and cried tears of happiness. The passion, the love, the longing that had been driven underground for so long, had not been extinguished

But how was I to tell Roger? I did my utmost to spare him any hurt, but he took it incredibly badly. So badly, that after an evening sinking vodka, he came back to my house selected a kitchen knife and threatened to commit hari kauri in front of us. He stood with the knife aimed at his midriff while Sue and I screamed for him to put it down. It took a long, long time before we got him to release it. I was in shock for days. Roger disappeared into a bout of heavy drinking, emerging at meetings wearing dark glasses but studiously avoiding me. I wrote to him and got a brief reply saying he needed to stay unapproachable as he was still in love with me, but while he might not talk to me at meetings 'believe me I'll be thinking'. Roger offered marriage to Lynn Pedley when she was deserted the following year. Later he married someone else. He called his first child Anna.

Bob tried to reassure me. He wrote to say Roger must have known what would happen if Kitty and Granville broke up. He also told me that he had held onto Kitty for too long, had sent her some money for her birthday, but when she neither acknowledged it nor responded he asked for it back and she had sent him an abusive letter. He said he was not a saint and for him this was the end of the line. 'I know I hang onto people long after they have ceased to care for me'. He thought it advisable we did not meet again – he did not think Granville would like it. The last time I got a letter from him was just before I moved to Manchester in 1978. He was in Cornwall and buying a cabin in the woods.

September 1974 was the IS conference. I went with Granville. The warmth and delight in our renewed relationship was in contrast to the gathering storms in the organisation. For several years the main focus in IS had been on the building of a Rank and File movement in which IS could have a modest influence. Granville had been more successful than most in this respect. Although he was re-elected to the National Committee along with John Palmer and Rob Clay of the

IS Opposition, Jim Nichol was now National Secretary, an apolitical hatchet man given the task of setting up an 'organisational commission' to ensure the future under-representation of those who supported the IS Opposition at conference.

The organisation under the influence of Cliff was changing, now seeing our hard won militants as a conservative force in the organisation and insisting the emphasis should be on the recruitment of young workers who they claimed were more revolutionary in orientation. At one point anxious to reinforce Cliff's position Chris Harman rushed to the stairs to take the podium. He slipped and fell back down the stairs. There was a hushed silence broken by Higgins loud voice "Encore!" he roared.

October saw Harold Wilson call the second General Election of the year, which resulted in yet another hung parliament, with Labour achieving a majority of only three. It also brought a group of us from IS together for a weekend in Blackpool, increasingly concerned about the inner cabal that was controlling decisions within the International Socialists and believing they had some divine right to do so. Between 1971 and 72 the number of IS branches had grown from 87 to 113 and Socialist Worker paper sales had shot up – it was estimated our readership then had been in excess of 50,000. But according to Cliff the paper had latterly become 'unreadable'. Roger Protz had been sacked along with Jim Higgins in May. The new editor was Paul Foot. Sales of the four rank and file papers were not impressive – a legacy of Rosewell's time as industrial organiser. IS was on the cusp and beginning to internally implode

The group had a small but significant presence in the

rank and file movement and had recruited time-served militants like Harry Wicks* to join us. Our manual worker membership in factory branches had grown from 613 to 1,155, but we had failed to integrate a further 750 as no one had sufficient experience of running factory branches successfully.

Rather than slowing the growth to reassess how we recruited and to create a better infrastructure to ensure we did not demoralise and lose new members, Cliff was urging further expansion based on the delusional idea that the revolution was imminent and we were ready to declare ourselves as a Party.

We were moving away from a movement with a sense of reality, to one dogged with secrecy and manoeuvrings, and we were angry at the victimization of Protz and Higgins. Jim had given up a 25 year long key post in the Post office, where he was a branch secretary on the Executive Committee, to work full time as the IS National Secretary, at Cliff's behest. Unfortunately he had the fatal flaw of opposing Cliff when he thought he was wrong and having the authority to quote Lenin back to him. Not many of us could do that or had his wonderfully funny acerbic wit, which you opposed at your peril

Either way it was good to be by the sea that October with a group of intelligent comradely people debating real politics and free from the poisonous atmosphere that had started to permeate an organisation which had claimed so many years of our lives. My kids came

---

* A railway man by trade, Harry was a founder member of the Communist Party. He was sent to the Lenin school in Moscow in 1927 for a three-year course in revolution. He later became interested in Trotskyism and was expelled from the CP. He met Trotsky in Copenhagen in 1932 and acted as his bodyguard.

too and had a whale of a time. Harry was particularly impressed with my sons cartoon skills.

November 21st. I was waiting for Granville to come back from a meeting in North Manchester when the news came through that there had been two pub bombings in the city Centre. One was in The Mulberry Bush a pub at the base of the Rotunda building in the city centre and the other at The Talk of the Town a basement pub in New Street. Twenty-one people had been killed and eighty-two injured. It was believed to be the work of the IRA, although at the time the provisional IRA denied this.* One of our members had been in town shortly after it happened and told of seeing a hand in the middle of the road. Just a hand. It was a long time before Granville got back, as the whole of the centre was cordoned off, by which time I had began to worry he was caught up in it.

The aftermath was just as shocking. The atmosphere in the city was electric and Irish people feared to leave their houses. Bricks were hurled through windows of Irish families and violent reprisals looked likely. Larry Connolly a very brave local Convenor at Lucas's went into work and talked the workforce round. But I realised the pressure on the police to make a swift arrest was immense. They would arrest the first likely suspects and beat them into submission till they confessed. And so it was. The Birmingham six were to serve 20 years for a crime they did not commit – one of the grossest miscarriages of justice in the annals of British law and despite the evidence of a *World in Action* programme which

---

* Only in 2014 did the provisional IRA accept some responsibility – saying "it went against everything we claimed to stand for".

cast considerable doubts on the original convictions, all appeals were rejected.

Two days afterwards Roy Jenkins the Home Secretary brought in *The Prevention of Terrorism Act*, which he described as draconian, allowing the police to arrest and detain for seven days anyone suspected of involvement in a terrorist activity (we have gone so much further since). The law allowed for the deportation back to Northern Ireland or the Republic of Ireland of anyone found guilty.

Christmas was coming. To earn extra money I went on Christmas sorting at the post office. Like all the temporary staff I was on the second-class mail until a full-timer got talking to me. She mentioned she had suffered a hand injury at work and had to fight to get compensation. I said I knew someone called Jim Higgins who had been active in the postal workers union and her face lit up. "But that's the man who got me the compensation!" she said. After that I could do no wrong. Transferred immediately onto 1st class mail, I was invited to use the full-timers rest room and plied with tea and biscuits whenever I needed a break. The power of the unions!

# 1975
# FINALS, I MOVE HOUSE, GET A JOB AND GET EXPELLED

Two hung parliaments in one year and the Tories were ready to change leaders. Margaret Thatcher replaced Ted Heath in February 1975, the same month that the miners secured a 35% pay increase. She must have made a vow then to make her mark by breaking the Trade Unions, and the NUM in particular. The same month there was a tube train crash at Moorgate, which killed 43. Moorgate was the stop I used to use when I worked in the city.

This was the year of the first EEC referendum and the Labour Party and much of the left was opposed to staying in Europe (we had the Commonwealth and EFTA as trading partners then). In March there was a National Front rally against European integration, but in June 67% of the public voted to stay in the EEC.

Charlie Chaplin, who had been persecuted and driven out of the United States in the 1950's by the McCarthyite witch-hunt, received a knighthood in March. In April *Monty Python and the Holy Grail* came out at the cinema. Less memorable was the first BBC edition of *Jim will fix it*. Given what we know now, I have to say that the guy gave me the creeps right from day one. I wasn't alone. The choice of Saville to head the programme was very controversial within the BEEB and led to at least one resignation.

I had to start seriously considering where we were going to live after June. I started house hunting. Haunch Lane had been bought for £4000 and we hoped to sell it for £6000 giving us some capital for two deposits. Kitty was staying on at Grisethorpe Road for the time being, though the relationship with Mick Rice was at an end. He was now going out with Henry Miller's daughter Helen.

I started to look for a Victorian terrace, as they seemed the most likely to fit my price range. I knew I would need to move out of the leafy suburbs but this did not bother me much. Moseley was too expensive but there were terraces down near the border with Sparkhill, which might suit us.

I was inundated with work. I had to telescope two years English revision into one. I realised I hadn't a clue about critically evaluating literary texts and poetry, and a lack of grounding in English grammar due to my poor schooling did not help. I was most confident in the paper I would take from the Centre for Contemporary Cultural Studies. I loved the lectures we had with Stuart and Michael Green. For me this was where the two parts of my degree fused.

Eventually I found a house at 50 Springfield Road on the Moseley borders, which looked promising. It had three bedrooms, two living rooms, a breakfast room a tiny kitchen two outhouses and a small but adequate garden. The Irish family were in no rush to move as they had a lodger. He was obviously a chain smoker because his bedroom reeked of nicotine. There would need to be a fair bit of refurbishment. Unfortunately it was on a bus route but I thought we could cope with that. We were right opposite two corner shops, which was also useful and not far from the Stratford Road with its curry houses and sari shops.

Terry and I decided to sell Haunch Lane ourselves and early in the year made a homemade sale board. One day a rather seedy guy called from a firm called Newent Properties. He was quite convincing about the size of the market he could open up for us and his commission rates were way below most high street estate agents so Terry decided to give him the business. He had only signed the contract giving Newent Properties the selling rights and their board had just gone up, when we got a knock on the door and a woman up the road told us it was a scam company that had been exposed in the *News of the World*. Apparently they did nothing to sell their customers houses, their phone was never manned but if you pulled out during the three-month period and used another estate agent, because you had signed giving them exclusive selling rights, they could claim their fee. Terry was incensed and decided they would not get a penny from him – we would just defer the sale till the three months period had passed. That suited me as it gave me longer to find a mortgage.

Women getting their own independent mortgages were rare in 1975. We were pioneers. Till I got work I had no evidence of income, but I did have the advantage of well connected friends who were prepared to employ me at least on paper in order to solve that problem, and the advantage of a decent deposit.

At that time Local Authorities were giving mortgages and prioritising those that might have difficulties going down more conventional routes. I applied with my 'employment letter', details of the house I wanted to buy and praise be, they offered me a mortgage. Now all I had to do was find a 'real' job to cover the costs.

A week before my English finals I realised I had revised on too narrow a syllabus and needed to add Sir Walter Scott to my study list. I had already read Lukas on *The Historical Novel* and ploughed through *The Heart of Midlothian,* but now needed to add in another three of his works. If you have ever tried to read three Walter Scott novels in a week let me tell you, the task is Herculean. I read *Old Mortality*, *Quentin Durward* and *Rob Roy* in a week. I barely slept. I will never read Sir Walter Scott again.

My experiences with the University Health Centre had been mixed. I had received barely contained rage from one doctor treating me for a fallopian tube infection because I mentioned that the original treatment at the Women's Hospital had almost certainly caused the infection in the first place (despite this being the opinion of two other GPs-in those days patients were not expected to have opinions). They came up trumps now however and allowed me to sit my Finals in the Health Centre, which took a lot of stress out of the exams. I knew I managed the CCS paper well, the rest less so. However it was over.

My next hurdle was to find a job. I walked straight out of the Health Centre, drove straight to Hall Green Technical College which was the nearest FE college to where I would be living and asked them if they had any teaching hours to offer me in Sociology or English. I struck gold. The full time sociologist was leaving at the end of the term and the department had done nothing to advertise his replacement. I was offered 28 teaching hours on the spot, half with 'O' level students, half with

'A' level students, two hours English with the NNEB nursery nurses and an hours General Studies with the apprentices. I had an income!

While I would have preferred a full time job, they were clearly saving money employing me as a part-timer. I was doing more than the statutory number of hours for a full timer and part-timers received no holiday or sick pay. Full time jobs were contracting as unemployment rose and Marco wrote congratulating me on getting a job "in this era of near impossibility". At the beginning of September, doctoral students of Stuart Halls like Angela McRobbie applied for some hours at Hall Green. They were significantly better qualified than me but they got few hours – I had mopped up most of them.

I then went and signed on for the summer. Shortly after, the Haunch Lane house was sold, and I was able to complete on 50 Springfield Road. I had my own house now, a job and a degree. I was awarded a 2:2 – Stuart Hall said it should have been a 2:1, which made me a bit tearful. Still a 2:2 while not good enough for research was good enough for employment and I had no desire to stay longer in academia. My father was tremendously proud though and sent me an effusive letter of congratulations. He henceforth addressed all my letters with the appendage BA (Combined Hons). I was the first in my family with a degree.

He also mentioned Kitty had been to visit Bill Groves and was fed up with her dull job and said he would gladly invite her for a short stay or "would she get the wrong idea? "(more like the right one I thought, as it was obvious to me he had taken quite a shine to her – something she was hardly likely to have reciprocated). His natural caution must have kicked in at this point, because he added "of course I couldn't keep her and Joanne for very long at current day prices". I didn't reply.

Terry had prepared a list, dividing our belongings down the middle, which Granville thought was a bit mercenary. "I would never worry about possessions," he said. I did not object, it seemed the easiest way and there were few if any quibbles about who had what. Mike Pedley came with his van and helped us move. It took quite a few journeys because I took carpets too, knowing there would be little enough money spare, after I had done some essential repairs and bought replacement furniture and a new cooker. We also acquired a lodger, John Sturrock the photographer for Socialist Worker. He was hardly ever there but it was useful for him to have a bed available somewhere in the middle of England as he was covering the whole country with his work and it helped towards some of the refurbishment costs.

I remember that summer for reggae clubs – the popular music of dominance in Birmingham, the little curry houses in Sparkhill, where you ate mutton curry with your fingers and a spectacular physical fight between the academic legends of EP Thompson and John Rex at a party at Stuart Hall's – I never found what that was about. I also remember taking Dominic to the Danish Food Restaurant for his birthday. Dominic has always had a love affair with food but even as a small boy he was discerning, He knew that you could eat as much as you like for a set price. When they saw this small boy walk in (Dominic was short for his age) they said they would only charge half price for him. They surely regretted the offer as Dominic worked his way through 11 courses, selecting only the best cuts of smoked salmon, caviar and the best cuts of meat. I almost had to carry him home.

Granville and I took off for Ireland late August with Keith Sturgess who had borrowed a large tent from a scout leader. The weather was wet much of the time and the two men competed terribly, having races, and playing football and we toured round the Dingle peninsula and much of the West coast. I remember the creamy Guinness that tasted like liquorice and the mackerel the fishermen gave away on the beach, and Keith being horribly sick by the tent door when he stayed behind in the pub to chat up the barmaid and came back the worse for wear. I also remember Granville quoting from Yeat's *Innisfree* as we walked down the 'bee-loud glade' in Ventry full of the sounds of bees humming through the huge overhead fuchsia bushes.

That summer also saw the return of John Hutchinson from London. He had got a job with the Telford Development Corporation and had brought an idyllic cottage in Ironbridge, high on a hill overlooking the River Severn. The cottage was in a terrace row called *Paradise*. What an address! I was reminded of the lyrics of Alex Glasgow's song *The Mary Baker city mix* – similar to Pete Seeger's *Little boxes* – the lyrics were about characterless corporation homes with the final line 'meanwhile the architect has saved himself a cottage in the hills.' We all visited in Mike Pedley's van – I remember Mike cropping all the dandelion heads on the hillside to make wine.

Holidays over I concentrated on getting the house decorated, choosing very expensive hand blocked brown William Morris wallpaper for the front room – it had a border down the side, which had to be cut off –

very tricky – and pine panelling the chimney breast in the back room which we turned into a study. Granville wanted it all white like Brecht's study, I wanted it Wm Morris Green – we compromised with green alcoves and the rest white. Kitty on a fleeting visit refused to believe Granville had pine-panelled the chimney breast. She seemed quite distressed that he was displaying DIY skills he had clearly not utilised when they were living together. I bought a cheap chip board sink unit which I couldn't put together and a West Indian carpenter called Peter Appleton came and put it together for me and stayed on to build cupboards and work surfaces in the tiny kitchen and fitted wardrobes in the bedrooms.

One of my worst mistakes was getting the hall painted what I hoped would turn out a soft Italian orangey pink. It looked more like a cheap brothel when the painters had finished. I had made friends with Jenny, an upholsterer who lived two doors up. Trusting her judgement as she had a good eye for colour, I brought her round and sat her on the stairs with me. "Could you live with that colour?" I asked. We sat there contemplating not just the colour but also the cost of bringing the decorators back. The stair well was the only part of the house I could not decorate myself. Jenny reluctantly agreed she couldn't live with it. I had to ask them back to paint the walls a rich yellow instead. My other worst mistakes was getting Mike Shakespeare an IS comrade who claimed to be an electrician to do the re-wiring. He made a total balls-up and I had to get in a competent electrician to finish the job. The lesson learned was never get a friend to do your house repairs. Mary had a similar nightmare with Dave Adshead.

This was the first house I chose and decorated myself

and I wanted it to look good, stripping the plywood and plastic handles off the lovely old Victorian doors and removing the boarding from the stairs which covered over the original spindles. I felt the house was sighing with relief as we restored it gradually to its Victorian glory. Meanwhile Terry had brought a house in Hillcrest Road in Moseley a few doors down from Margaret. He clearly wanted his own space.

Jim Higgins paid us a number of visits – he always came with a mistress – at this stage in his life it was Ruth Nelson, later it would be Jane Allen. He had a soft spot for me and I was the one he turned to when his sister died prematurely. He rang and talked with me for over an hour. Few who had seen him in political mode would imagine that big Jim could cry but he did. "She was such a pretty girl," he kept saying.

Jim was also the first to introduce me to the life enhancing qualities of a gin and tonic. He liked Dominic too – (unlike Donny Gluckstein, who was the most obnoxious brat I ever met, Dominic got a zero nause rating from Jim). Jim was very amused one day when out shopping with Dominic they spotted a Superman T shirt with a huge Zigzag border around the super hero. "Look Jim" said Dominic, "Superman farting". He was less complimentary about the daughters of his first marriage (he had a third daughter by Marion his second wife). "They're poisonous", he said.

Able to consume fast quantities of liquor he once stayed with us when he was writing an article for *The Spectator* and insisted in taking me for an expense account lunch at a restaurant near the college. I was by then in my second year at Hall Green and had an 'A' level class in Sociological Theory at 2pm. After a G&T a bottle of wine (or was it two bottles?) and a large brandy I was not entirely sober and remember thinking I must keep talking for the whole hour and give no one a chance to ask questions. I recall slurring my words and the total silence that descends on the room when a class is caught in fascinated disbelief. I did not repeat a similar tired and emotional performance ever again.

In September I had to go to the Crown Court for my divorce. Terry was doing a DIY divorce to save money, since we had pre-agreed any potentially contentious areas. Adrian Davies my kindly university solicitor came along anyway just to make sure everything went off OK. I asked why he was limping. "Old war wound" he said. I nearly made a quip but was glad I did not. It turned out he had been a fighter pilot in WW11 and there was shrapnel lodged in his leg. So, a war hero and an old school gentleman-they existed! I was so grateful for his consideration.

We had to wait through several cases of unmitigated misery before ours was called. Terry presented our divorce case and rattled off everything we had agreed but was stopped mid-stream by the magistrate. "I cannot give you a divorce", he said. Terry looked startled. "You have not mentioned the grounds you want a divorce," said the magistrate. Maybe it was a Freudian slip, but Terry sorted it out, citing two years separation.

It had all been quite traumatic but the decree nisi was granted. Terry and Peter his witness and I went for a stiff drink afterwards because we needed to reassert our own humanity after hearing all the misery that had led others to the divorce court. Also Terry had something to tell me. "Margaret's pregnant," he said "but I'm not marrying her". I did not know what to say, "do you want me to congratulate you then?" I asked, unable to fathom his feelings. "Well I can't ask her to have a termination" he said "not after the way it affected Beverley, but there is a history of miscarriages in her family so it may come to nothing" I was shocked and rather sorry for Margaret. What a cold fish he was.

I was now preparing hard for my teaching assignments. I had never taught before, had no teaching practice experience and really did not know how to go about it. I could lecture (my acting training came in handy here) but I had no experience of organising lessons. Sociological Theory seemed a particularly fraught area. I prepared book lists and model answers to questions. I had friends at Hall Green, chiefly Paul Mackney, an IS member who had previously lectured at Poole Technical College. He was a great ally.

There were others less so. A huge man called Bill Gibbons, an ex-policeman who taught law, largely on the basis of his work experience, as he had no academic qualifications, eyed me with suspicion. By subject area and friendship with Paul I was clearly marked out in his eyes as another 'pinko', another one to bait. It was to our eternal delight that, sometime later, we discovered he had surreptitiously been taking 'A' Level Law himself at an evening class in a college on the other side of the city. Imagine our even greater delight when we heard he had failed. We had something on him now, but I pitied the Law students exposed to this ignorant mans teaching.

The Head of Dept was Mr Hallsworth. A short man with heavy lensed glasses, he was never able to recognise who I was. He once ordered me out of the office when I was photocopying – I had been there some time by then – with the words "How many times have

I told you students you are not to use the photocopy machine?" When I pointed out I was, de-facto, in charge of the largest department in the college, he just stared myopically at me and walked out without a word. As sociology was, at the time, the most popular subject in the college and I had responsibility for more students than any of the full-timers you would have thought he might have given a little thought to who was running the show, especially since not only was I in charge of book ordering and student references but also because his salary was linked to student ratios.

I had an 'O' level class who were clearly looking for an easy ride. They had been told Sociology was an 'easy' 'O' Level to pass (a curse on whoever told them that). They were rather dismayed when they discovered it actually required a lot of reading and keeping up to date with what was going on in the world. I was quite flummoxed when, giving them conflicting theories about how society functioned I was asked 'Yes miss but which is the right one?' Thinking for themselves had clearly not figured in their previous education. They were impatient to get their 5 obligatory 'O' levels but they did not want to be made to think in the process, and were inclined to disruption.

But their disruption was muted compared to the apprentices. I had really pulled the short straw with this lot. When Tom Sharpe produced his novel *Wilt* about a demoralised FE lecturer in 1976, many of us fell on it with howls of recognition-particularly his description of 'Meat 3" the apprentice butchers. I had day release car mechanics for one hour's General Studies at 5pm on a Friday afternoon. What kind of sadist gave me that kind of time slot for a subject they all thought irrelevant I do not know. My only hold over them was that they had to get my signature of attendance on their day release form or they didn't get paid. I was expected to teach them *The Lord of the Flies*-no way. They made me feel like Piggy already, totally persecuted. They were always trading snide sexual comments and once, one of them tried to touch me up. The margin between control and chaos was a close one.

I had been told in extremis to give out copies of *Sex for Boys* that we had in the book cupboard. Instead I let them chose their own subjects and take turns to introduce them, but also interspersed this with what I hoped were useful topics like *'Your rights under the law'* and guest speakers like community policemen. One particular Dixon of Dock Green was rather thrown when he called for questions, to have one apprentice telling him about his own arrest for loitering with intent and being punched in the stomach in the police van. The DC asked what he did when he came up before the magistrate. "Pleaded guilty," he said. "Why did you do that," asked Dixon. "Because I was guilty" said the lad "it was being punched in the stomach I objected to"

The same lad later went on to conduct a spirited lecture on *The Grateful Dead* telling the class to 'shut the fuck up'. It worked. My most attentive lecture was "*Cooking in a bedsit*" – they were keen to impress their girl friends with their pre-seduction culinary skills and asked lots of questions. But one hour with them took more out of me than all the other classes put together. Still I won a few round. They would sidle up to me and ask if I wanted a radio for my car and I would ask where they got it from, but they did wire one in for me in the end. I also got cheap MOTs in the college workshop.

The classes I always enjoyed, (though it was a headache finding babysitters twice every week,) were my Tuesday and Thursday evening 'A' level Sociology classes. Teaching adults who wanted to be there was such a joy by contrast with the younger full time students.

As there was little room in Paul's staff room I was given a desk in with the Executive Secretarial staff. Being something of a fish out of water, they treated me as if I was not there, but would always ask me if I had a nice weekend every Monday morning and before I could reply they would say "that's nice dear". Testing my theory that they never listened to anything, I told them one Monday, "not really, I was burgled, the house caught fire, my husband left me and I was bitten by a rabid dog." Sure enough back came the reply "that's nice dear". The phrase became a family joke.

By the end of the first term I had amassed enough loot to purchase a colour TV, our first, and a little mobile black and white TV for the kids room. The Hitachi was to last for 25 years. The following year we bought a video player too.

The job gave me some measure of financial security. Having lived on next to nothing for years I was good at economising and saving for the holidays.

I still needed to run the car though it was on its last legs, because all the children (including Jo) were still at Grendon Road School. After a few months, when the children were used to the route, we got them bus passes and they went to school on the bus. I was a bit troubled about this initially and questioned them closely to make sure there were no problems. One day Anna told me that a man had looked at them funnily on the bus. I asked what they had done. Jo and Dominic said they had found seats away from him. I asked Anna what she had done. "I went and sat next to him," she said. That was my first indication that my daughter had no sense of self-preservation or potential danger. I enjoined Dominic to keep a close watch over her and not let her sit separately from them again.

The noise of the buses, which rattled the sash windows in the front bedroom, gradually became less noticeable and the corner shops were much utilised for quick purchases. One was a cramped over crowded shop that sold crisps, sweets, papers and cigarettes, with a hardworking Asian family in charge, it was open all hours, the other a real old fashioned grocer that sold wonderful bacon. Our only supermarket was a Mac Fisheries*, which was between the college and the house. Dominic would meet me there once a week with a shopping trolley and we would do the bulky shopping together.

We also found we were a short walk from Sarehole Mill. This was set in a unexpected rural backwater on the banks of the River Cole in Hall Green. A mill had been on the site for centuries but the current building was over 200 years old. The mill was used mainly to grind wheat but between 1756–61 when it was leased to Mathew Boulton†, it was used it as a flatting mill producing sheet metal for button manufacture. More interesting to me was the connection with J L Tolkein, who used to live across the road from the mill and who found in the mill and its rural surroundings the inspiration for his

---

* A supermarket chain developed from merger between the original chain of fish shops and express dairies supermarkets. They ceased trading in 1979

† Mathew Boulton, with James Watt introduced Boulton and Watt steam engines to hundreds of factories, leading to the development of industrial mechanisation.

Middle Earth stories. To find this rural retreat so near us, in marked contrast to the noise and chaos of Stratford Road was a great bonus.

Our garden backed onto Moseley Secondary school and I realised I would need to grow some shrubbery to offer some privacy from the school kids. My next-door neighbours on one side were an elderly couple Kath and Jeff, obsessed with entering competitions. They had won quite a few. We shared a ginnel through to the garden gates. Two doors up were Jenny and Bob Billingham, living in the end terrace with their handsome young son Rueben, who was a year younger than Anna. She was quick to make friends with him. Bob was a builder and had renovated their house dramatically. He laid a new floor of linoleum tiles for me in the breakfast room too. Jenny was tiny of frame and part Portuguese. She was a feisty and talented interior designer and I admired her talents and her calm disposition. I was a bit suspicious of Bob – he was just too good looking. There was a beer advert at the time for Ansell's Bitter men. He looked like one of those. I guessed he was a bit of a ladies man. I was right on that score, but there were more disturbing things about him I was to later discover.

Meantime the 1975 IS conference was being rigged by Nichol and Cliff. Delegacies were to be decreased from 1in 15 to 1 in 30 members and voting was to take place in districts rather than branches where there was more sympathy with our IS opposition position. They also changed the leadership structure from an Executive committee, which carried on the everyday work between monthly National Committees to a Central committee with a National Committee with only advisory status, which was entirely unconstitutional.

Largely as a result of Granville's efforts there were over twenty AUEW members in Birmingham IS, organised in two factory branches and an industrial branch, these included 10 shop stewards, two convenors, six members of the AUEW district Committee and several Trades Council delegates. All had been in the group for between two and eight years. Birmingham engineers worked through the Broad Left committee and had agreed the Broad left candidate Phil Higgs a communist party member for the role of National Organiser. This went contrary to a later national IS decision to run their own candidate.

One of our leading industrial recruits was Arthur Harper, convenor of Tractors and Transmissions and district president of the AUEW. A short stocky man he had the bearing of a pugilist and proudly wore his paratrooper wings on his jacket lapel outside work. Arthur had gained the district presidency because he had the full support of the whole Broad Left. For the AUEW comrades to declare independence from such a body would have been political suicide. As Mike Rice, now a leading Birmingham engineer put it in a letter to the Central Committee, it would be "five years work down the drain". Ironically it was less than 18 months since IS had been enthusiastically supporting work in the Broad Left. Now the engineers and those of us who supported them were branded 'Conservatives'. We were hauled before a Control commission in November as the ISO document had got into the hands of *The Morning Star*. Steve Jeffreys told us to disband. He was told instead to "shape up or ship out, you cunt" by Vic Tambling a very angry engineering worker.

This added weight to the December 1975 party

council edict to dissolve or face the consequences. We declined. I was then phoned as faction secretary and told that all ISO members were suspended and our expulsion would be moved that day. Sue Baytell an office worker at the centre was sacked and then expelled.

I still have my expulsion letter from Jim Nichol. It reads:

> *17th December 1975*
>
> *Dear Hazel*
>
> *The Central Committee has today expelled you from the organisation for refusing to accept the discipline of the organisation by refusing to disassociate yourself from the IS Opposition Faction.*
>
> *Yours fraternally*
>
> *Jim Nichol*
>
> *National Secretary.*

I particularly liked the fraternal ending – the man was all heart. Granville had already ditched the IS organiser job and got a job at Telford College as a senior lecturer. It saved them sacking him. His expulsion, after all the years of work he had put into the organisation was a source of great bitterness to him. No less mine, the organisation had claimed sixteen years of my life.

# 1976
# THE WORKERS LEAGUE, A LONG HOT SUMMER, THINGS FALL APART

With such an array of revolutionary talent suddenly ejected from the IS Group, the mood was for a political re-grouping and it was not long in coming. We need a name for the new organisation. I groaned inwardly when *The Workers League* was proposed by Roger Protz and accepted by the others. Even worse, *Workers News* was to be the name of our new paper. I thought it was so last century.

I could not summon much energy and enthusiasm for this new organisation despite the presence of many talented and capable people prepared to give it a go. It still meant going back to the beginning. I thought of all the years it had taken us to get as far as we had with IS and I really hadn't the stomach for more. Nonetheless I waded in to help Sue Baytell with the administration and organisation of meetings, but it brought back a memory of a conference, years back when operating a pooled fare system we were asked to put down our transport costs and one of our members wrote down "One sunny day".

How many sunny days had we already wasted in dark pub rooms planning revolutions that didn't happen? I was still angry about all the same things and knew I would be so till my dying day, but I wanted other things in my life as well as politics – I was just not sure what they were or how I could get them. Certainly at my best I found I could teach confidently and well, but much of the time I busked, as there just was not enough hours in the day for the amount of preparation needed. I called it teaching by the doorknob method. As you turned the doorknob you hoped for divine inspiration – and the confidence to sound convincing.

With Granville travelling up to Telford daily, all the pressure of renovating the house fell on me. Together with childcare, and my own teaching job it gave me little time to do much more. Gradually I experienced a sense of things winding down. Granville troubled me hugely. He had started drinking very heavily. He could down a bottle of whiskey in a night. Sometimes he would take a bottle to bed with him. We had a narrow hallway and sometimes when he came back he would ricochet from wall to wall all down the corridor.

The job at Telford involved him in 3 hours driving daily and he had soon acquired College drinking buddies in Derek Anderton and Dave Wallace. Anderton was an older man and a friend of Adrian Henri the Liverpool poet, and Dave a talented cartoonist. Through one of the cartoons he drew of Granville, I saw how he portrayed himself to his drinking pals, flared trousers, kipper tie akimbo, copy of Workers News in his back pocket and a few words of dialogue which include "I'm in my prime, fighting the good fight – evaded responsibility" So, he had no responsibilities? No wonder women thought he was available, dealing as he did in endless half-truths.

The three Musketeers drank in a pub called The Market Tavern in Telford, which was a stopover pub.

Granville started staying overnight when he had a late evening class, ostensibly with John Hutchinson. John lived locally enough, but his home was as cheerless as his hospitality and it was clear to me that Granville was not always stopping there. One day he brought back a bunch of limp daffodils, which had spent some hours in the pub with him. I knew what that denoted-he was having another affair. This time with a mature student, a single mother called Anne O'Shea.

On top of so many other things falling apart this was not easy to bear. I think I must have mentioned that Granville was playing the scene to Sue Baytell and was surprised when she urged me very vehemently to just accept it because "you wouldn't want to lose such an amazing man". My God I thought, are you enamoured of him too? It was apparent that much of his behaviour stemmed from his expulsion from IS, but it still hurt that I was the one to have to cope with all the fall-out at a time when I also felt unhappy and uncertain myself.

Anne did not know about me, or if she did the issue was fudged – as ever. We did eventually talk and in the end she decided she was being sucked into something to fraught with problems and bowed out, but there were months of distress I tried to suppress. Unfortunately without much success and I am ashamed to say the kids got the brunt of it, being bawled out for the smallest thing. I look back on some of those memories now of how I treated them and I shudder at the recollection. I wanted so much to love and nurture them, instead I sometimes made their lives miserable and I cannot forgive myself for that.

Early in the year, Margaret (who had not succumbed to a miscarriage), gave birth to a daughter. Terry named her Eleanor after Eleanor Marx – there had recently been a TV series about her. I offered Anna's wicker crib to Margaret as a peace offering and token of friendship and asked if I could come and see the baby. Terry accepted the crib but was very coy about arranging a visit. Having asked several times I got exasperated. "What's the matter?" I said, "does she think I am going to turn the evil eye on the baby?" "As a matter of fact that's exactly what she does think" said Terry. I was gobsmacked. I stopped trying after that. It was evident Margaret saw herself as my opponent. Not a good situation for my kids.

Early in the year Mike Rice married Helen Miller. The house next door to ours had come up for sale and they had put in an offer to buy it. They moved in part way through the year, and Bernard Berrow, another ex IS member came with them as a lodger. They got very friendly with Bob and Jenny and suddenly we had a little colony of friends in Springfield Road and suddenly I did not feel so isolated. We pooled resources, so between us we had a Black and Decker drill, a lawnmower, and various tools. The only frustration was when you wanted to use one of them and found it was locked up in someone else's house.

We arranged garden gates between the three properties and that gave us a bit of flexibility, because if Jenny or I were late home the kids would just check out who was at home in one of the three houses. I would often find my two eating baked beans with Rueben and we would return the favour. Terry also got to dropping in when I was not home, ostensibly to see the kids but actually on raids. I had thought that having agreed to so equable a division of everything he would be satisfied but I found him walking off with records and books and I had to ask for things to be returned.

Teaching also got easier with the arrival of another IS member Dave Evans to Hall Green to teach Sociology. We studiously avoided getting involved in factional politics-it was more useful to share resources. Dave had done a Cert Ed and produced some useful teaching plans and recorded useful radio programmes. Given my link with Marco who was now the Chief Examiner in Sociology for the Associated Examining Board I also had useful material to trade.

This year I had a whole class full of Black Zimbabwean students. They found it hilarious when I tried to pronounce their surnames. They were a challenge to teach though, as our subject area was based on British society and whereas students who had grown up in the UK already had first hand experience of the education system, the class structure, and much else, suddenly I had 18 young people with no knowledge of the structure and culture of British society and rather colourful and grammatically inaccurate English to boot.

That year we were all into wine making. One early afternoon Jenny brought round a bottle for me to try. When Helen and Mike came home they brought round some of theirs. I contributed one of my bottles and by the time Granville and Bob got back we were one happy and very sloshed bunch. Somewhere in the middle of all this, we fed the kids. It was like a scene out of Steinbeck's *Tortilla Flat*. We started about 2pm and we were still sitting round our table at 10pm.

In the wider world there had been a breakaway from the Labour party in January by some Scottish Labour MPs disaffected with the Labour Party's failure to secure a devolved Scottish Assembly. The SLP was soon experiencing entryism by the IMG (the International Marxist group) who were expelled at the first Congress at the end of the year. The IMG then formed the Scottish Democratic Labour Party. Neither organisation survived, those that didn't rejoin the UK Labour Party joined the SNP or disappeared into the political wilderness, a fate I feared for us.

In March, Harold Wilson resigned. We now know he was experiencing the onset of Alzheimer's. Jim Callaghan replaced him. The Labour Government's position was precarious though, and when John Stonehouse resigned later in August they lost their majority. The fact that they were relying on an MP just out of Brixton Prison on remand and about to be sentenced for fraud and faking his own death in 1974 was itself bizarre. There were some parallels with the Lord Lucan case, though Stonehouse never murdered anyone as far as we know. He was also revealed as a spy for the Czech Socialist Republic by MI5, though not charged at the time due to insufficient evidence. Truth is often stranger than fiction.

In China, expressions of grief for President Zhou Enlai during the traditional day of mourning – the Quinming Festival in April were brutally put down by the gang of four, one of whom was MaoTse Tung's wife. Sixty people were dragged from Tianamen Square, summarily beheaded and buried in secret graves. The gang were to hold onto power till Mao's death in 1978. In 1977 a post punk band also took the name, later it was to be associated with the SDP – who said history repeats itself first by tragedy and then by farce?

Other things passed us by that seemed insignificant at the time, like the formation of the Apple computer company and the Body Shop, and the rise of an anarchic punk group called *The Sex Pistols*, just as in the previous year the decision of a Glastonbury farmer Michael Edis to start an annual music festival didn't appear of much interest. Concord, the supersonic jet of the Anglo/French aircraft industry made its first commercial flight to a fanfare of trumpets. A plane so excessively expensive we would never travel on it, was to last only thirty years.

Then came the legendary long hot summer – the hottest for 350 years. In June July and August the average temperature was 30C every day, and with rainfall virtually absent, the rivers and reservoirs started to dry up. In the worst affected areas, water supplies were turned off and replaced by public standpipes. We were urged to recycle grey water from washing onto plants, hose pipes were banned and slogans like 'save water-bath with a friend' became commonplace, though people were encouraged to shower rather than bath. For kids it was wonderful – long days outside and no-one fussing over cleanliness.

Tourism to Ireland had taken a nosedive since the Troubles so it was cheap to arrange a car ferry to Eire. We decided to spend a month camping on the West Coast, travelling with Leni Solinger and Tony Clarke, two ex-IS teachers in their estate car. The children were to stay with Terry. We had only a small tent but Tony had all the camping equipment necessary and was up for the award of worlds leading Boy Scout. Certainly his knowledge of flora fauna and fishing was exceptional and we all benefitted from his initiatives, but gradually his need to always be right about everything began to rankle. The only time I took him on though was when he started propounding on ballet. He was talking arrant rubbish, but even on a subject where I clearly had far more knowledge than him, he would not accept that he was wrong and I was right. Leni his American girl friend was much more easy-going. In some ways at least, the holiday was idyllic.

We had miles of pristine white beaches all to ourselves, spotted basking sharks, boiled whelks and crab claws on the beach and visited favourite spots on the Dingle Peninsula. We also got as far as Galway to visit Yeats tower, Thor Ballylee, a legendary place for lovers of poetry and literature and to Dogs Bay one of the most spectacular beaches in Ireland, separated from Gurteen Bay by a sandspit – two stunning white, mile long horseshoe shape shell beaches.

We mainly camped on farmer's fields. I had brought a Polaroid Instant Camera that took lousy pictures but had the advantage that we were able to present one farmer with an instant picture of himself with his prize heifer. He looked at it with disbelief for some time "Sure isn't science wonderful" he whispered in awe. Trouble is no-one had told the cows we had been given permission to camp in their field and we came back from the beach one day to find they had tried to use their bulk to collapse our tents and then crapped all over them. There was cow-pats in all our cooking pots too.

This was an Ireland that hadn't changed in centuries and a million miles from the troubles. Farmers road down to the pub on rickety 'sit up and beg' bikes for their evening Guinness and for the craic, local singers and musicians playing the tin whistle, the Bodhrán and the spoons, entertained with traditional songs and there was a lot of spontaneous joining in. As visitors viewed curiously in many isolated places off the beaten track, we were often asked to contribute a song. Unfortunately the only one we could remember all the words for was *The Wild Rover* – I was sick of singing it by the end of the holiday. We were already big fans of the music of *The Chieftains* and loved this aspect of our holiday.

One day when we were driving in Kerry, we stopped at a farmhouse that felt like walking into an Edna O'Brien novel. There was a black cast iron 'skilly' pot hanging from a chain over a peat fire, on the mantelpiece above was a picture of the Pope and President Kennedy and several empty Guinness bottles. A chicken clucked in and out of the door while we asked if we might fill our water containers. "Sure" said the farmer's wife, a small wiry woman with two front teeth missing, and she pulled on a pair of white wellingtons and picked up a jug. What was she doing? "Follow me" she said and walked us across a field before flattening herself on the ground with the jug and collecting water from a concealed spring to pour it into our containers. There was no running water in the farm "It's why the kids are a little mucky missus" she explained. She did all her cooking in the skilly pot – even making cakes and soda bread in it, as there was no cooker. They had no car – just one rusty old bicycle. She was amazed that Leni at 30 had no children and that I had only two. What amused us though was when she asked if we wanted to buy some lamb and opened the back room door to reveal a large chest freezer and her old fella watching a colour TV!

The most important event in the region was Puck Fair – farmers save all year for this annual three-day drinking festival in Killorglin. The fair dates back to the early 17$^{th}$ Century and has pagan roots. We went to watch the opening ceremony in the jammed main street, where a wild goat, wreathed in garlands is crowned King Puck, before being hauled up onto a platform above the crowd, where he stays for the duration of the festival. The pubs were all open till 3am and doing lively business throughout, but since every second shop seemed to have Guinness on draught this was no problem (I remember buying a handmade leather belt, a packet of cornflakes and a pint of Guinness all from Dick Macs in Dingle). While we were at the fair we also saw a huge gathering of red haired gypsies who had come to trade horses.

The locals we talked to told us there was a prejudice in Ireland against Kerry folk who were seen as unsophisticated yokels. Joke – how can you spot the Kerry bride? Answer – she's the one in the white wellies. Railway announcement, the train for Dublin will leave platform one at 19.18 and the train for Kerry will leave when the big hand is on the 7 and the little hand is on the 6!

Despite all these rich experiences, there was an underlying sadness to the holiday. Granville was detached from me, impatient and clearly with thoughts elsewhere. Etched on my memory is an image of him standing silently on a rock, naked, his back to me looking out to sea. He had a dancers body, beautifully proportioned and I wanted to record it somehow – capture the moment. It was a study in isolation. He was good company with Tony and Leni, particularly Leni but he cut me out. Leni must have noticed I was withdrawn because she asked me if I missed my kids. I did. It was the longest I had been away from them and part of me yearned to be home. One day I will return to those beautiful places and repeat the experience now my heart and mind are at peace.

We returned to hear of the appointment of Dennis

Howell as Minister for Drought, and as if to mock the appointment, Mother Nature opened the heavens a few days later and gave us a very wet September and October, though water restrictions were not lifted for several months. The long hot summer also culminated in a riot at the Notting Hill Carnival on 30th August when 100 police and 66 members of the public had to be taken to hospital. The trouble was triggered by the arrest of a black youth, apparently for pick pocketing. Various other black youth had come to his aid using dustbin lids and milk crates as weapons against the police. One police van was turned over and gutted by fire. Notting Hill, which had been a slum area of bedsits in the 50s and 60s, had a history of racial violence – the teddy boys had made frequent attacks against the black community in the late 1950s now the tables were turning. The festival, which began in 1964, was to see further disturbances in future years.

One of the people who helped me out sometimes with the kids was Sarah Cummings, a feisty single mum in the Communist party, who lived, when I first knew her, in an upstairs flat on Brighton Road in Balsall Heath, a predominantly Afro-Caribbean and Asian area of Birmingham. Her twins wanted to have a cat and call him Blackie, but she said "If you think I'm going out shouting Blackie round here you can think again".

She had a large family, an older girl who did not live with her, Michael her son and twin girls. When she moved to Moseley with a new partner, Dominic and Anna would often go for an overnighter. I felt a real affinity with her. I remember collecting Dominic and being told she would rather keep him for a week than a fortnight. She said she had made all the kids supper and then later when she and her partner had got a Chinese takeaway he polished that off too. She was to go on to have a fifth child and also bring her up largely on her own while working as an FE lecturer. I think she ended up as a college principal. Whenever I thought the going was tough I always remembered Sarah and how she just got on with life.

Granville's unerring record for writing off cars was legendary. He had enthused years earlier over a wonderful old Wolseley 14–6, the type used by the police force in the 1950s, which an elderly acquaintance in the South West offered him for next to nothing. The car had a tiny mileage and been loved nurtured garaged and maintained for over twenty years without a scratch on it. Granville burnt it out in a week. I remember having to rescue him from the hard shoulder of a motorway. Now once more without a car and needing one for his Telford job, our elderly neighbour offered him his beautiful old dark green Singer Gazelle.

He had been driving it a couple of weeks into the September term when I got a phone call from the Royal Shrewsbury Hospital asking if I knew Mr Granville Williams. I was asked if I could come and get him, as he had been involved in a car accident. Terribly anxious, and car-less I went next door and Helen lent me her mini to make the journey. It turned out Granville, reckless as ever had tried to overtake a lorry on the brow of a hill only to meet a car coming at speed in the opposite direction. Swinging the wheel sharply he had crashed into a field and straight into a very large tree. He was showered with glass – had cuts to his face and there was glass embedded in his arm, some of which is, as far as I know, still there, but he came out of the wreckage with no worse injuries. The car however was a write off. I was so cross with his continuously suicidal driving I did not speak to him all the way home.

November brought news that Jimmy Carter a relatively unknown peanut farmer from Georgia had won the US presidency for the Democratic Party against Gerald Ford, the apologist for Nixon. No loss there then. We had seen little cinema that year – why waste so many summer days? But one film released that month was so striking it stayed in your memory for all times and that was Martin Scorsese's *Taxi Driver.* Robert de Niro's, portrait of an insomniac ex Vietnam vet turned taxi driver who gave us the catch phrase *"You looking at me?"* was hailed as a classic. Travis, the edgy anti-hero – a complex mix of violence and heroism, kind of summed up the times.

Inflation, industrial action and political instability continued to dog the government. Politically the Workers League was beginning to unravel. Roger Protz had joined CAMRA and was about to embark on a post political career producing Good Beer Guides, and Jim was working as a free-lance journalist with Jane Allen who was to become his third wife. We were still producing the paper, but the spark was not there – people were looking for alternative paths to take, some back to the Labour Party others immersing themselves in trade union work or campaign work – Granville for example would help form the Campaign for Press and Broadcasting Freedom three years hence. My life and focus would also change too, in ways I could not then foresee.

However there was one very significant strike for trade union recognition, which began in August 1976 and was to run for the next two years, mobilising support throughout the Labour Movement and that was at Grunwicks, a photo processing plant in Brent London, especially significant because it centred around Asian women who became known as the 'sari militants'. During a decade of industrial disputes, Grunwick's became the cause célèbre of trade unionism and industrial relations law. At its height it involved thousands of Trade Unionists, and numerous police confrontations. All together there were 550 arrests on picket lines – more than any other dispute since the 1926 General Strike.

Grunwicks employed 80% Asian women mainly from East Africa. Some of them were highly educated, but barred from professional jobs in the UK they took what they could. Owner George Ward took advantage of what he saw as a malleable labour force, paying slave wages of £28 per week for a 40hour week with compulsory overtime (when the average wage was £70 for a man and £45.30 for women). The women worked in a climate of fear – having to ask permission even to use the toilet. Those that complained were sacked instantly, joining APEX – a right wing white-collar union to demand their jobs back. Ward, backed by NAFF, (The National Association of Freedom), a far right anti-union organisation composed of businessmen, Tories, aristocrats and military figures saw this as a head on fight with the unions. NAFF were to pay all Ward's legal bills during the dispute.

Christmas we spent with my father, dining out in a Torquay restaurant for a change. Anna wanted a Barbie. I bought her a more normal looking small doll. In contradiction and against all the urgings of sanity, I bought a pair of killer heels. I wore them just once. My feet were not cut out for such shoes. I don't know if I was trying to inject a bit of a frisson into my relationship with Granville. If so the dampness of Fred's spare double bed was no help. After spending a night between sheets that felt as is they had been dipped in a bucket of cold water, we smuggled them out to the launderette and put them through the dryer. Fred might live in a beautiful part of old St Marychurch, but he did not believe in too much comfort. The year ahead was to offer me little either.

# 1977
# HOPE DESPAIR AND THE END OF AN ERA

Another IRA bomb in the West End got the New Year off with a bang, though this time no one was hurt. Another year of pay restraint under Callaghan's Labour government, relying increasingly on a Lib-Lab pact to stay in office, was to bring more industrial conflict with the Grunwick strike rolling on. Meanwhile the Sex Pistols following their sacking by EMI, celebrated Silver Jubilee year with "*God save the Queen – a fascist regim*e," which resonated with an alienated punk youth culture with no sense of hope in the future. Meanwhile her Majesty embarked on an expensive Commonwealth tour....

I was well established in Hall Green now, and having some success, even accolades from my evening A level students, principally Harry Nichols a 50-year-old plasterer who embraced his 'A' level Sociology course with such zeal and enthusiasm I could barely keep up with him. Casually mentioning Daniel Bell's *End of Ideology* he had read the book from cover to cover by the following week and wanted to discuss an interesting point on page 59! He called me a 'haughty talker" and we stayed correspondents and friends for a number of years. Another evening class student, Andrew Whitehead, who was not notably successful in his first A level attempt, later wrote to say I had inspired him so much he had given up his job, gone full time, improved his 'A' level grade and gone to University where he had Terry as his tutor. Now embarking on a Masters degree at the Centre for Contemporary Cultural Studies, he told me it was all down to me!

Despite those successes I did not see myself as a natural teacher, though in the course of the year I was pleased to assist Paul Mackney construct a pioneer course called *Wider Opportunities for Women*, which was to be instrumental in securing our boss-eyed Head of Dept a post as Vice Principal of Exeter College (a bad case of the OBE's – other buggers efforts). Meanwhile the college couldn't even offer a Part Burnham to Dave and I – though it was rumoured they might offer one, if not two. Obviously waiting for one of us to throw in the towel. Only my mortgage and the need to provide a home for two children restrained me.

I felt a huge responsibility for my Zimbabwean students, as it was clear to me that they were struggling with the concepts and theories of sociology, and in addition had real problems with essay construction. I was aware that many had also struggled to find the finance to come here to get an education. Irene Jokonya in my 'O' Level Group, was the daughter of a teacher and her whole village had clubbed together to fund her education.

After each class I would tell the students that if there was anything they were unclear about they could come and see me for additional help. Within ten minutes of the class ending, Irene would be at my staff room door and I would spend a further hour giving her private tuition because she found everything so hard. Of all the staff only the geography teacher and I offered this extensive help. When Irene took her 'O' levels we were really concerned as to how she would do. I met the geography teacher in the corridor when the results came out. "Do you want the good news or the bad news?" she said. "Good" I replied. "Irene has passed in just two subjects, Sociology and Geography" she said. "And the bad news?" I asked. "She has signed up for both subjects at 'A' Level" she said.

Dominic was due to go to Secondary School in September. Joanne had now moved with her mother down to live with the Holden's in Bedford, and was attending middle school there. I spent hours talking to various people trying to weigh up which was the best secondary school for my son – none of them were that outstanding but of them all, Moseley school a couple of houses down from us seemed the best choice – at least he wouldn't have to travel. I duly applied and secured him a place.

This left the dilemma of Anna, as Grendon Road was too far away and she was too young to travel on her own. I tried very hard to get her into a good Hall Green Primary near the college but with no success and had to settle for a September transfer to the Primary at the bottom of our road, which was suspiciously undersubscribed and seemed to lack all the imagination and creativity of Grendon Road. I began buying all the kit and uniform Dominic would need in September.

We took a short camping holiday in the Yorkshire Dales during the summer. The weather was not good. We had all three kids with us and it was a hard work. I vowed I was going to have a holiday abroad soon – the dubious pleasures of the wet English summer time were minimal as far as I was concerned. At one site we met two young lads boasting of joining the Territorial Army. They had their big Army boots with them and attached themselves to us on a day trip to the coast. The others had gone in the sea and I was watching the lads sparring around on a cliff when one of them accidentally pushed the other and he disappeared over the cliff. I approached the edge with trepidation as it was about a twenty foot drop and was amazed to see that the lad had landed on his feet, his boots were so heavy they had weighed him down. A doctor who had witnessed the fall had rushed over to see if he was OK. The lad starting boasting about his army training and the doctor looked up at me "Thank God we've got a Navy" he said.

During the rest of the summer, I launched myself into a final phase of decoration, tackling the middle bedroom, which after all this time still smelt of nicotine. I stripped the walls back to the plaster and brought a builder in to remove the boxed in fireplace and re-plaster the chimney breast. When I got home I found he had removed an exquisite little cast iron fireplace, which had been concealed behind the plywood and dumped it in the yard. I had to ask him to come and put it back in again.

Those of us who appreciated the craftsmanship in Victorian houses and furniture were in the minority then, but this did mean we were able to snap up some bargains. I got an iron and brass double bed frame in a junk shop on Stratford Road for £10 and a rosewood chest of drawers for the same amount. I had decided to give the much larger front bedroom to the kids, that I could later subdivide into two to give them both private spaces, and was in the process of decorating the middle bedroom for us to move into. I could now wallpaper efficiently and was making a matching blind.

Holidays over, I was walking back from college one day when I had the most oppressive premonition that something was wrong. I could not shake it off. Walking into the house, Anna rushed to meet me. "You mustn't go upstairs" she said. "Granville is working very hard up there and must not be disturbed". I was taken aback – why had he issued such an emphatic edict to my children, both playing quietly in the breakfast room. I was not going to be told where to go in my own house, but I mounted the stairs in trepidation. As I reached the top of the stairs someone rushed out of the back bedroom and locked themselves in the bathroom. I noticed the curtains were drawn in the back bedroom and I went and looked inside. On the narrow single bed was a naked Asian girl. "Who are you?" I asked in disbelief. "Nasreen" she said. I went and hammered on the bathroom door. Granville opened it with a towel around his waist to hide his nakedness. "What the fuck is going on?" I yelled. "He laughed nervously. He actually laughed! " Get yourself out of this house and take her with you" I shouted "and if you come back, you had better not be in my bed tonight".

I went downstairs. I noticed the study door, which led out into the ginnel was open. He had sneaked this woman in round the back of the house so the kids would not see her and then intimidated them into staying downstairs. Within a few minutes there was a flurry on the stairs. I edged back and watched from the front room. The woman was in stilettos with a cheap leopard-skin coat on and gaudily made up, it looked as if she might be on the game – who else would have travelled all the way back from the Barley Mow in Telford (which was where they had come from after a drinking bout) to be here in these circumstances? Then again no self-respecting prostitute would, although Granville's ability to bend the truth was now unparalleled.

I went next door and rang the bell. Bernard answered the door. "Bernard", I said "I want you to take me out and make me very drunk tonight – don't ask why". He agreed – it was more an order than a request. Returning home that night after midnight I climbed the stairs to find Granville sleeping peacefully in the back bedroom, the hint of a smile on his face. I was so angry. He had inflicted the worst possible humiliation on me and now he was sleeping like a baby when I knew I would not get a moment's sleep all night. I was not going to allow that to happen. I went downstairs into the kitchen and got a bucket. I filled it with the coldest water I could run and then added two trays of ice cubes for good measure. I carried it back upstairs, crept into the bedroom and chucked it all over him. He sat bolt up in bed, water dripping down his face and an ice cube perched on his head. "You're mad!" he said. "Bloody right!" I said, "I'm livid."

The war was maintained for a week. It was the nearest I had come to throwing him out. I was outraged by his behaviour. I finally confided in Mary Pearson. It was a mistake. She said he was great as a lover, but she wouldn't want to live with him. I was gutted – so he had even had sex with her? I was utterly shocked and wondered why I went on caring so much.

I made a kind of tally in my head of all the ways Granville had made me feel loved as opposed to all the times he had acted with unthinking callousness. And that was the problem, because it was so unthinking. He didn't deliberately go out of his way to cause me pain. He was always genuine in his contrition. But it was if he had a factor missing in his personality, an inability to understand the impact of his behaviour on others. Here was an apparently sensitive and aware individual very taken with romantic poetry, the kind of man it was easy to fall for, a committed socialist fighting for a better world, yet so wrapped up in his own needs he treated, not just me, but many other women as if we were his play things. Thank goodness I had great neighbours and there were other distractions or I would not have survived. Granville was more in Telford than he was in Birmingham so that helped, while I tried to make sense of my life and decide what to do. What was happening in the wider world made my domestic problems seem relatively unimportant but I was not prepared to accept this as an excuse for insensitive and callous behaviour.

One distraction was the news that Roger Griffiths had bought a house four doors down from us. Our friends were beginning to take over Springfield Road! He had been with Lynn Pedley briefly as she struggled to come to terms with single parenthood, abandoned by Mike when her baby was just months old. He had run off to France with his language teacher and was to build a new life in a tiny village in Provence. I remember buying her a new pushchair for the baby as she had been left without a penny.

Roger moved into his house and started a vigorous programme of renovations, knocking the wall down between the breakfast room and the kitchen and before they went further, throwing a house warming party. It was the usual boozy do. He had installed a lodger called Martin who kept a grass snake in a tank in his bedroom and had various other lodgers, taking the small back bedroom for himself. He was back to his hard drinking bachelor days.

The morning after the party, I was woken early by the doorbell ringing insistently. It was Martin. "Come at once", he said, "you must see this". I followed him down to their house. As I came into the house I heard the deep sonorous tones of Rogers snoring but could not work our where they were coming from. "In here", said Martin leading me into the breakfast room. There hanging from the ceiling were a pair of legs encased in blue jeans, ending in a pair of cowboy boots. But where was the rest of him? We climbed the stairs to the first floor and there he was. Lurching to bed in the small hours Roger had dropped down the cavity where they had taken up some floor board, fallen through the hole, and being trapped between floors by his beer belly had promptly fallen asleep vertically, his head slumped on his chest and snoring fit to wake the dead. It was one of the funniest things I had ever seen and I wished I had brought a camera to record the scene.

On the political front the Grunwick strike was entering its second year and becoming increasingly violent. Jayaben Desai the strike leader, had her foot run over by the manager's car and two days later another woman was hospitalised when she was knocked over by a car on the picket line. The postal workers had joined the action refusing to handle mail from Grunwicks and for a company that relied on the postal services that was a major blow. But it is clear the strike was no longer just about the right of a couple of hundred Asian women to join a union and be reinstated, it was a major confrontation between the far right and the left. Thatcher described George Ward as a "champion for freedom".

Yes, the freedom to exploit, intimidate and sack. Lord Scarman had been called in to conduct an enquiry as the strike lengthened, but attempts to negotiate through ACAS were stonewalled by Ward who refused to give contact information on the strikers saying their opinions were irrelevant, as they had all been sacked.

More and more trade unionists including Arthur Scargill and a contingent of miners came to lend support on the picket line, but official action from the TUC was inadequate. Jayaben Desai described it as 'like honey on your elbow, you can smell it, you can see it, but you can never taste it'. Certainly APEX who had made the strike official, were now looking for a way out. Thatcher the new leader of the Tories, interviewed by David Dimbelby made it clear she was pledged to limit the power of the unions if she got into power.

Even more disturbing was the role of the police. There were nightly scenes on the television of clashes between the strikers and the police. Women on the picket line on the first day of a mass picket in June were punched kicked and dragged across road by their hair, Jonny Patel of the strike committee who went to their aid, was repeatedly hit by a policeman yelling in rage "You Paki bastard". In response, by Friday that week, there were 1,500 on the mass picket line, engineers, dockers, seamen and builders; a contingent also went from Birmingham. This put the police in their place, but not for long.

The Metropolitan Police Special Patrol Group were an armed, specially organised section of the police force, supposedly set up to deal with "terrorism" – this was the first time they were used in a trade dispute, brought in to help with the bussing of scabs into the plant. The

Squad operated independently from police divisions, had their own radio channel and fleet of vans and were to earn a reputation for violence and the use of lead bars and other unofficial weaponry. Two years later the same unit was to murder Blair Peach a young teacher on an anti-racist demonstration, when he was hit on the head with a lead bar. The murderer has still to be formally identified and convicted decades later.

With the scabs being paid 25% more than the original workers, and with the usual media coverage of 'trouble makers', coupled with the spinelessness of the UPW leadership, the blacking of mail from Grunwicks was called off. On November 7th there was a call for a final day of reckoning and 8,000 turned up. The police were savage, meting out indiscriminate violence – a striker had his face smashed through the glass of a police van and heavily protected policemen used truncheons against lightly clad protesters. Picketers were kicked senseless on the ground by police, who walked away laughing. 243 pickets were treated for injuries, 12 had broken bones, and 113 were arrested. It was an augur of things to come.

When further pleas for the blacking of essential services, was met with only excuses by the TUC, Mrs Desai and three other strikers began a hunger strike outside Congress House. They were suspended from the union without strike pay for four months. The TUC had decided its priority was to bolster a minority Labour government, rather than focusing on winning a strike against a vicious employer who had the backing of the far right and the National Front.

The strike finally ended 14 July 1978, tragically without reinstatements or union recognition. But it had achieved two things. Firstly it had destroyed two myths, that black workers and women were hard to unionise and it destroyed the notion that women worked for 'pin money'. The strike also came after lull in political and strike action, and put industrial disputes back on the agenda. These were to culminate in the winter of discontent in 78/9 and the fall of the Labour government. By then I would no longer be living in the Midlands and my story would be taking a different turn.

Granville had performed yet another act of contrition and was back in my life. He had pulled himself back from the brink, realising he was going right off the rails and heading for alcoholism and vowed to turn a corner (again). He had a phrase he frequently used. "I have learned the price of experience" I was to hear it once too often. I charitably attributed some of his behaviour to the expulsion (just some of it), but I vowed I would never excuse him doing anything like this to me ever again. But the experience brought on a deep depression and I had to ask the doctor for some anti-depressants to get me through.

What the doctor failed to do was warn me these should not be taken with alcohol. One night Dave Lovell came to babysit for me. He brought his own tipple with him – Black velvet, a mix of Guinness and cider. He offered me a glass. Later that night I started to hallucinate. I was convinced I was being hurled into the corner of the room although in reality I was in bed and clutching the bedclothes. It was terrifying. The feeling of being totally out of control and not knowing what my brain would conjure next was not an experience I would ever want to repeat.

I was not prepared for Granville's next announcement a few weeks later that he had applied for a job as Senior Lecturer in Communications at Salford College of Technology and been shortlisted for interview. (I would have liked to have been consulted). I realise now, he felt he had to make a break from the heavy drinking culture of the Barley Mow and all the consequences of this.

I was just at the end of a major refurbishment of the kid's room and had painted a huge life size Dennis the Menace and Minnie the Minx on their cupboard doors, when I got a phone call to say he had got the job and accepted it. This faced me with a real dilemma. Did I want to move and did he want me to move? Had he taken this job just to create a split? He assured me he had done this because he needed a change and because this was a really good job prospect. I had just spent two years refurbishing our house, my son was just settling into a new secondary school and I had a job.

On the flip side, I hated the job and it offered me no security or permanence. I could not face the prospect of another year at Hall Green. Birmingham had been a good place to live but it had never been my choice and with the disintegration of our political life here I was finding the mood demoralising and I was desperate for a change in my life too. There would be no loss in moving Anna to another Primary school. On the flip side was the fact that if I did move I would be taking the kids 80 miles away from their father and I didn't know how he would take that.

Manchester was not unknown to me. Mark Abrahams and his wife lived there and the kids and I had stayed with them not so long ago. They had taken us for a trip into the Peak District, which I loved. Bob and Hazel

Wright old IS mates also lived there and were good friends with Granville. I recalled Manchester as a soot blackened city, but one with a fascinating history and a thriving cultural scene. True Birmingham had the Rep and the Midland Arts Centre but the City Council had hardly shown much commitment to the aesthetic and cultural life of the city – I recalled that when I first came to Birmingham they had invited bids for a mosaic for the underpass and then accepted the cheapest.

My life had been wrapped up in politics, family, getting an education and earning a living over the last few years so this had hardly seemed much of a drawback but things were unravelling now and I was not opposed to the idea of moving. But it would take some time and a lot of planning if I committed to the idea. I needed to sell the house, get another mortgage, find new schools for the children, and find another job. It could not be done before the end of the next summer term realistically. And to try and get a clear view as to whether Granville wanted this was impossible. His attitude was, come if you want to and if you don't that's OK too. It frustrated me so much I hurled a cup across the room one day in an act of fury at his attitude. Either way, we would have some months of separation as they wanted him to start at the beginning of the year and that would give me a few months to decide if I really wanted to make the move.

Bob and Hazel offered to put him up at their home in Eccles, and he bought a fancy touring bicycle to travel to and from the college. He was taking his physical fitness seriously – it even had a water bottle fitment – something Bob found quite hilarious because I don't think he rated Granville as a cyclist.

I decided to defer telling Terry but he got wind of the possibility anyway. Margaret got on her moral high horse and began asking people didn't they think it terrible that I was proposing to sever Terry from his children, though this was far from my intention. It looked as if she was keen to swell her own part of the Mandrell dynasty too anyway. I was sure that it would not be long before Terry found himself well and truly locked into fatherhood again.

# 1978
# LAST FEW MONTHS IN BRUM

I had decided to throw my towel in with Granville despite all my reservations. Warts and all I still loved him but apart from that was the lure of something new. I phone Mark and Ruth in Manchester and they were delighted with the prospect of us coming to settle in the city and arranged to send us regular copies of Manchester Evening News so I could check on available properties. I also sent off for information about schools.

I decided to sell the Birmingham house myself. I put up my own For Sale board and low and behold, who should appear on my doorstep but that old crook from Newent Properties. I took great satisfaction giving him a flea in his ear and literally pushed him off my doorstep telling him if he ever showed his face in my road again he would regret it.

Granville was home every Friday night and stayed till the Sunday. Occasionally I would go and stay with him at Bob and Hazel's to get the feel of the city and to do some house hunting. Ironically they lived on Granville Street in Monton. I loved their little local pub that had a meat raffle every Saturday – if you won, you got a Sunday roast for the price of a raffle ticket. It was a tradition that had gone back many years, and had its roots in poverty. Sociologists had been talking for years of the embourgeouisement of the working class, but with growing unemployment, it felt like the good times were nearly over. The auction was an echo of an earlier austere time, which we could be re-entering.

During January and February we heard of more deaths attributed to the 'Yorkshire Ripper'. Ominously the last two had taken place in Manchester.

January the European Court of Human rights found the UK guilty of mistreating if not torturing prisoners in the notorious Long Kesh prison, and Margaret Thatcher no doubt endeared herself to the blue rinse brigade in Eastbourne by commenting that she thought many Britons feared being swamped by people from different cultures.

Since she regarded Nelson Mandela as a 'terrorist', was friendly with Pinochet in Chile and approved of Apartheid South Africa, this came as no surprise. Nor did the Tory parties decision in March to employ Saatchi and Saatchi at enormous cost to sex up their image, in anticipation of an autumn election. Callaghan was to (fatally for him) ignore this and wait till the following year. He was already skating on ice as David Steele the new Liberal leader announced in May that the Lib/Lab pact would be dissolved at the end of the current parliamentary session. Coupled with the coming 'Winter of Discontent' and the famous Saatchi poster '*Britain isn't working*", the Labour Government would not survive beyond 1978. Firemen settled a pay dispute early in the year which had rumbled on for three months, accepting a 10% increase and reduced hours, and the Green Goddess army fire engines which had been on standby during the previous winter months went back into mothballs.

So much for national politics, but I still had work to do in Birmingham apart from planning a move. My

Zimbabwean students were due to take their 'A' Levels in June and I was worried about how they would cope. I was not over-optimistic.

I also had other things at home to worry about. One day in late Spring Rueben, Jenny's little son came round to our house accompanied by Anna with lots of sweets and small toys. They had bought them at the corner shop Anna told me, because it was Rueben's birthday and he had birthday money to spend. Later on they disappeared off to Jenny's house with their loot telling her it was Anna's birthday. About then Bernard came out in the garden asking if someone had picked up £1.50 of his from the table in their house and Jenny and I put two and two together. Anna had masterminded the whole thing.

This shocked me deeply, not just the theft but the sophisticated level of the deception. I told her she had to repay the money to Bernard. Peter Appleton had opened a second hand shop, so we sorted out some of her toys and sold them to him and I made her take the money round to Bernard. Why had she done it? I figured she was worried about the impending big changes in her life. I also examined where I had failed and resolved I had to try harder with her. I was aware she received little or no affection from Granville. He teased her a lot but showed no special interest in her. And now I was taking her away from the familiar and from her father. This was a big responsibility. I had already worked out a plan to send the children down to Brum on alternate weekends and also during school holidays and I was determined that I would keep to that arrangement however unapproachable Terry became.

With Granville away, during the week, various other

males hove into site. I began to feel really targeted. Terry Daley a swarthy, good-looking car worker of gypsy origin, made a play for me. I was reluctant to go down that route, even though after all his disloyalty I hardly felt Granville deserved any particular loyalty from me, but Terry was married and I liked Teresa his wife. They lived in a strange little cottage in Stirchley with mock Tudor beams. I rarely visited as it stank of deep ingrained dirt and cigarettes. They had two little girls, so although Terry tried it on several times I was distressed to be considered fair game.

My West Indian carpenter Peter Appleton also showed some interest in extending our relationship beyond house improvements, though as a Jehovah's Witness we had less than zero in common, even though he was quite malleable in his attitudes on a number of things. He was also married and had six children. After visiting me for purely ulterior reasons he disappeared suddenly. Two months later I was amazed to receive a phone call from Florida. He said he was living it up by a pool and wished I could join him. When I asked what he was doing there he said "just a bit of business".

The business turned out to be a spot of drug running. The next communication I got was on prison notepaper. He had been sent down for five years. He asked me to send him some books by Barbara Cartland. He had found her in the prison library 'Boy that woman understands men' he wrote.' I told him that Barbara Cartland was a half mad old fantasist and sent him books by James Baldwin and Maya Angelou instead. He loved *The fire next time* and said he had been thinking over what I said and reading a lot more. On reflection, he thought I was right about Barbara Cartland.

The only male I could have been interested in was Ray Osborne the doctor. We had a brief fling but nothing more. His interests lay elsewhere. One night I woke to hear my bed-clothes rustling. Someone was pulling the duvet off my bed. I sat up in bed and shouted, "who is that". I heard the door scrape on the sisal carpet and then the sound of heavy feet thudding down the stairs. I stayed stock still for a moment in the dark wondering if I had dreamed the whole thing and then I thought about the sound of those feet on the stairs and I decided I had to investigate – I was alone in the house with the children. I put on the light, pulled on my dressing gown and then putting lights on as I went, I made my way downstairs. I travelled from room to room, flinging open doors, turning on lights but nothing. I checked the front door and the back door and found they were both secure with no sign of being tampered with. I sat down and wondered if my brain was playing tricks with me or whether I was going mad.

I told Ray in the morning and he told me I should have reported it to the police. "But what could I prove" I said? "The place was locked up and I saw nothing. They will put me down as a neurotic woman with an over active imagination". "Maybe," said Ray "but have you thought that reporting this could stop another woman being raped or assaulted?" A week later I noticed the French door from the study that led to the outside ginnel was unlocked. I always kept it locked. I suddenly felt quite weak and a bit sick. After that I got a phone wired into the bedroom and kept one or two emergency numbers on the table by my bed. I also got into the habit of tipping a chair under the doorknob so the door would jam if anyone forced it.

In May I had another of my strange premonitions but this one was very unusual. I have never bet on a horse in my life but just casually overhearing the list of horses for the Epsom Derby I was convinced, with a conviction I could not fathom, that a horse called *Shirley Heights* was going to win. So strong was the conviction that I nearly took out all the building society savings I had accumulated and bet them on the horse. It wasn't a favourite – the odds were 8/1. However I had never been inside a bookies in my life, didn't know what to do and suppressed what seemed like a foolhardy compulsion. But I listened to the race. Right to the end *Shirley Heights* was not in the lead but in the last few minutes he rallied, shot forward and won. I was amazed and then annoyed with myself for not acting on the premonition. If I had put all my savings on this horse I would have been able to pay off my mortgage!

Getting a new mortgage was again a problem as I currently had a local Authority mortgage, which I would lose when I left Birmingham. Granville could not get a mortgage-he was already a mortgagee on a bungalow in Ollerton bought as a retirement home for his parents. I phoned the friend who had helped with my previous mortgage offer and explained that I wanted to get a mortgage for a house in Manchester but I did not have a job there yet. Would he employ me on paper again? "Sure" he said – just let me know what the salary level needs to be" Later he phoned me back. "I was thinking" he said "we could do with someone working for us at least part time in the North of England – not on the paper salary we are quoting of course but maybe you would you be interested?" I was, and that was how for a short time at least, I became a publisher's rep for Pluto Press.

Realising I would need a car to do this job as they expected me to cover the whole of the North of England (the Isle of Man included) I went looking for something suitable with Chris George. He gave the once over to a red Renault 4 that was pretty cheap and apparently roadworthy (this belief proved to be mistaken). In the Whitsun holidays we loaded camping equipment into the back, and Granville and I took off for a short holiday in Northumberland. It was a beautiful healing week. We were on the same wavelength, happy in each other's company as we travelled up through Craster (where we bought the famous Kippers) to Alnwick, visited Lindisfarne and Holy Island and up to the borders at Berwick on Tweed before heading home. Suddenly the prospect of going to Manchester with him did not seem so daunting.

With Granville back in Salford I dropped round to Jenny and Bobs for them to sample some of the mead I had brought back from Lindisfarne. Jenny was pregnant again and rather tired so she went to bed early. Bob started telling me a yarn about the first year in their current house. They had bought the house from a widower whose wife had died from a heart attack at a prematurely young age – she had been found dead in the house by one of their children.

When Jenny and Bob moved in they started making changes to the house, but Bob was convinced someone was watching him and the feeling was particularly intense when he was making structural alterations. "It felt like someone wanted to stop me. Sometimes I would hear sounds but when I turned round there was nothing and then things kept going missing. "I'm not superstitious" he said. "I believe when your dead you're dead, but when Rueben came down one night and said he could not sleep because he didn't like the lady who was staring at him in the corner of the room I freaked out". 'What did you do" I said. "I told Jenny to take him back upstairs".

Just as he said this there was a sudden sound behind us. I jumped out of my skin and grabbed his hand involuntarily. He took this as a cue, swung me round and kissed me and pressing me back on the couch pushed up my Tee shirt with his hand to feel my breast. On top of the ghost story this was too much. I disentangled myself and fled. "Wait for me" he said, "I will be round". No you won't I thought and sure enough he did not come, though he waylaid me on a few other occasions before I left. For me, leaving could not come too soon.

On the way back from college one day I walked into the first building society I passed. It was the National Provincial. I told the manager I was leaving the city to take up a job with a publishing company in Manchester and needed a mortgage. I expected the third degree. Instead he just said "OK fine. Just contact me when you have a property". I had by then secured a buyer for my Springfield Road house. The only problem was she was separating from an abusive husband and until they sold their house (which was in a poor state of repair) she would not have the capital to purchase mine.

In between looking for houses together, Granville had been touring round on his bike. He called me one day to say he had found a pretty special Edwardian house in Whalley Range at a surprisingly low price and asked me to come up and look at it. The asking price was £10,500 because it needed serious upgrading, but that also meant it had all the original doors and fittings. It was huge – two great living rooms downstairs, cellars, four bedrooms and a huge attic with a second kitchen. It had been a home for wayward girls (we later found evidence of heavy secret drinking in the loft). We decided to give it a go. We did not fully appreciate we were buying into the middle of the red light district – it was why these beautiful Edwardian Houses were so cheap relative to other areas. On the surface we were in an area of mature trees and elegant houses, though we were aware it was a stones throw from Hulme and Moss Side which were inner city pockets of serious deprivation and slum housing.

I took some time out during the week to travel up and check out schools. I was delighted to find a beautiful Primary school that could accommodate Anna. The head was a musician who loved sharing his skills with the kids and the Manley Park Big Band was legendary. Secondary Schools were more problematic. I wrote to the city centre High School of Art because I was sure it was the right school for Dominic, but they said they were full and could not accommodate him. I got the same answer from the other school I was recommended, Parrs Wood. It was considered the best comprehensive in Manchester and this was reflected in the house prices in nearby Didsbury. Predictably they were also over subscribed. I checked out the three secondary schools near the Whalley Road house.

Chorlton High school did not inspire, and Mark who had been teaching Maths at Wilbraham had lots of reservations about that school. This left Birley High School, which was in the middle of the Hulme Estate.

The building was an ugly squat concrete shell but it was comfortable inside – they even had their own swimming pool. The teaching staff were an absolute delight though, enthusiastic, dedicated and keen for Dominic to join them. I took a chance and accepted the place. We put in an offer for the house at 21 Whalley Road.

The problem of my buyer remained. Her husband was holding out for an unrealistic price for their house and it was still not sold. She was desperate to move and asked if she could move in before we exchanged contracts and pay the mortgage till we were able to complete. My house was on the market for £7,500 and I needed the capital for all the repairs that were needed and also to take up the other mortgage, as we were getting gentle pressure to complete the Manchester House. I explained the dilemma to the National Provincial manager. "Well if you can cover both mortgages" he said, "you can take up the one in Manchester". I could not believe he was being so reasonable. It certainly meant that if we had the new mortgage we could move, but what would happen if my buyer pulled out? We took a chance. There was only a small deposit needed.

I left Hall Green Tech with few regrets, though working with Paul and Dave had been fun. Paul presented me with an Alex Glasgow LP. The Zimbabwean students turned up in their finest clothes to sit their final exams. If marks had been awarded on the basis of sartorial elegance they would have all scored straight As. Unfortunately the syllabus at that time discriminated against overseas candidates by being too ethno-centric. It has been adapted since as a result of feedback from teachers like me. I only hope that those who failed to pass went on to do well in other fields. Several of them wrote to me after the exam and one or two secured places to do a degree. Harry Nichols got a Grade B and promised to come and visit me in Manchester very soon.

Just before we moved I paid a short visit to the South West to see my dad – I would be even further away from him in Manchester. He had been concerned to read about an outbreak of salmonella which had been traced back to John West tinned salmon. My dad had his utility sideboard full of old cans of food – some so old they still had 2/6d on the lid. Among them were a few cans of John West. He wrote to the company saying he was 'only an old age pensioner' and had these cans with the following serial numbers and wanted to know if they were safe to eat. In due course he got a reply. John West said they were surprised that cans of that age were still in circulation and while they were not aware that there had been any health problems with that batch when they were first produced, they did not consider they were in prime condition now. They sent him a voucher for £2 to buy some replacements.

"Did you throw them out?" I asked. "What! and waste food?" he said. Instead he gingerly opened a can, fed a small quantity to next door's cat and watched it like a hawk for several hours to ensure there were no ill effects to observe. After that he ate the rest for his tea.

He also told me someone had been stealing his milk so he had prised off the milk bottle lid and filled an empty bottle with water, made milky with soap, Dettol and bleach. He had got up early to whip in his milk when it was first delivered and replace it with the bottle of bleach. "Let the buggers try and drink that" he said. Old rogue – he would never change.

I returned to Birmingham ready to move. Anna says she still remember riding up to Manchester in the back of a Salford Van Hire vehicle with Dominic. I was saying goodbye to my old life, my childhood and youth in London, my 20s and early 30s in Birmingham. What would Manchester offer? I was apprehensive for myself and for us all.

Lemn Sissay, the Manchester poet who had no settled life as a child but lived in care, said in a lecture recently "*We are all time machines. We take everywhere we have ever been with us*". I was taking lots of experience and memories with me and I had half a lifetime ahead of me too. Lots more experiences for the time machine.

# INDEX

Hazel Roy lives in Manchester and is currently writing the sequel to this book, which promises to be a marathon as it represents a more fulfilling phase of her life. Since this book was written, she has worked as a university lecturer, an arts development officer, the general manager of two repertory theatres, as an arts and disability consultant, an actor, a theatre director in the UK, Nepal, India and Thailand and has trained with the Theatre of the Oppressed in Brazil and India. She has an MA in Applied Theatre, and her initial theatre work in Nepal is contained in her first book *Three Months in Nepal: A story of travel teaching and child labour*. She is a founding trustee of the UK Charity *New Futures Nepal* and assists other Nepal based charities. For the last 10 years she has taught dance to older people. She remains a peace and political activist, has written several plays and related performance pieces for CND, Feelgood Theatre and a collective called *Artists for Peace*. She has four grown up children, two grandsons and a great granddaughter